MW01130648

CLOTHING FROM THE HANDS THAT WEAVE

Anita Luvera Mayer

illustrations by Rebecca K. Hyland
photography by Matt Brown

ECHO POINT BOOKS & MEDIA, LLC

For my mother-in law, Marcelle Mayer, who introduced me to weaving by giving me a floor loom as a wedding gift. She also wisely raised a son to believe that a loom belonged in the living room.

Published by Echo Point Books & Media
Brattleboro, Vermont
www.EchoPointBooks.com

Clothing from the Hands That Weave
ISBN: 978-1-62654-335-5 (paperback)
978-1-62654-336-2 (casebound)
978-1-62654-337-9 (spiralbound)

Cover design by Adrienne Núñez
Editorial and proofreading assistance by Ian Straus, Echo Point Books & Media

Printed and bound in the United States of America

Acknowledgements

A hand reaches out to give assistance . . . point a direction . . . or extend warmth. My appreciation to all of you for your caring and your support. A very special thank you, from the heart, to:

Jack: a husband who always says "why not?"
Kathleen, Ross and Peter: our three children who keep this household functioning.
Paul and Mary Luvera; parents who never faltered in their love or words of praise.
Phyllis: a super sister, who is an even better friend.
T. Joy and Orville Chatt: "patrons" whose words and deeds at "the beginning" encouraged me to continue at the loom.
Jean Wilson: my mentor and my friend who encouraged me at every hesitant step.
Linda Ligon: an editor who believed in my fantasy.
Matt Brown, photographer; Rebecca K. Hyland, illustrator; and Loa D. Haley, fashion and makeup consultant.

And to those weavers in other times and places who created clothing that had spirit and beauty . . . may that tradition continue.

In addition, I would like to recognize the following sources which served as inspiration for illustrations within the text: Dorothy K. Burnham, *Cut My Cote*; Ida Hamre and Hanne Meedom, *Making Simple Clothes*; R. Broby-Johansen, *An Illustrated History of Costume*; Max Tilke, *Costume Patterns and Design*; Jean Scorgie, workshop notes; and Peter Collingwood, *The Techniques of Rug Weaving*.

Contents

Weaving is part of my being—
something I have to do—
that comes from somewhere within.

I weave garments—loom
shaped garments—based on
and inspired by ethnic originals
that are constructed of
rectangles and squares.

The weaving of garments and the
wearing of them have allowed me
to evolve into an individual, for as
I wear my fiber pieces on the
outside I have gained strength and
confidence within. They are my tie
to a heritage and to people before . . .
a way of touching other cultures
and times.

Having something magical about
what is draped upon the sculptural
human form is an important part
of my weaving . . . embellishments,
fetishes and always a hidden surprise.

Hopefully each creation will affect
both wearer and viewer by its
design, statement and craftsmanship.
It is how I communicate.

Anita Luvera Mayer

Introduction

I am still staggered by how much the weaving and wearing of handwoven clothes has affected who I am, how I live and the priorities in my life. Little did I know that the loom my mother-in-law gave me as a wedding gift would change my life.

I grew up in Anacortes, Washington, a small town of 8500 people in the San Juan Island area. Dad immigrated here from Italy and Mom's parents came from Yugoslavia. Dad's great pride in the opportunities in this country has had lasting impact . . . he has always maintained that "you can accomplish anything with the right attitude and willingness to work for your goal." He not only believed that but practiced it . . . he established a successful grocery business, served as a State Senator, and at 82, self-published a book on carving totem poles, a hobby he developed upon retirement. At our house, you worked; attended high school, then college and graduated with an employable skill . . . I didn't know for years that there were even other choices! Mom's creativeness was part of our growing up, and though I was fascinated with the arts, it never occured to me to take courses in those fields. After graduating I worked in personnel in San Francisco, Jack and I were married, and I was once again in Anacortes. I had lots of time but little money and that wedding gift loom was waiting for me. My mother-in-law, a superb weaver and teacher from Seattle, introduced me to the craft. I have to admit I was not impressed with weaving . . . in fact, I was bored by the second placemat and did not have the faintest idea what that loom was doing. Being a good daughter-in-law, I played at weaving, but really spent my time as a Girl Scout volunteer and talking unsuspecting friends into taking classes with me on everything from pottery to silk-screening. I would hire an instructor from Seattle and finance the course with a group of local people!

Seven years after we were married, Kathleen arrived followed by Ross and then Peter, and I found myself at home caring for small children, with little time and still no money, but needing some challenge besides diapers. I decided, one dreary fall day, to find out what that loom did . . . unfolded it . . . and took odd amounts of jute and opened *Davidson* to page one. I put on a warp, wove a purse, and then put on a second warp. Twelve warps later, I began to understand the basics of the loom. My bridge group (yes, I was playing bridge then), bought all twelve. I was in shock, for people had paid real money for something I had made. I dashed to Seattle and bought more yarn and turned to page two (of the same book). With great trepidation, I even submitted a few items to the local gallery for jurying. They were accepted and when these items sold, I could buy more materials and weave additional pieces.

This went on for some three years . . . I would weave at nap time and late at night . . . I taught myself and unwove more than I ever wove. I made every conceivable mistake, but I was learning and eventually I was selling in some ten different locations in the state. One of the first things I did when I sold those first purses was to open my own savings account —#3365! That had nothing to do with household finances or Jack's attitude, but it was very important to me to establish monetary independence even for buying yarn. That need has not changed and as with other women in my generation, I still have trouble with the "guilts" in spending money on myself . . . intellectually I know that is ridiculous, but emotionally it is one of those attitudes that has been difficult to discard. I don't want to feel accountable to anyone when I buy that silk chenille or antique kimono. However, "earning money with weaving" was not related to my attitude about what I was doing. I considered weaving my profession, never my hobby, right from the moment it became important in my life. I also learned that as I considered myself a professional, my family and friends began to view what I was doing from the same perspective. For years I have written in those spaces on forms that ask, occupation . . . "weaver"!

The first national weavers' meeting, Convergence, was held in 1972 in Detroit, and I had saved enough money to attend. I had not been away from Jack or the children in over 12 years and had somehow lost so much self-confidence that I was uncertain I could handle getting from the airport to the hotel by myself. I was so nervous I couldn't eat for days before departure, but that event was another turning point. First of all, I did manage to find the hotel and then I discovered I could carry on a conversation without being known as Jack's wife, Kathleen's mother or Paul Luvera's daughter. I found me again, buried underneath all those labels. I also, by chance, took Roz Berlin's seminar on double-woven clothes and knew that I had found my focus in weaving. I was so excited I couldn't sleep that night and wrote in my notebook . . . "June, 1972 . . . from this day forward, any major piece of clothing I wear, I will weave." I returned broke but in love with a loom I had seen at the conference. I applied for a booth at the local art festival, somehow wove night and day while tending three small children and earned enough to purchase the loom. People saw my work and wanted classes. I made up a course based on all the disasters that had befallen me trying to teach myself, talked those same friends into taking more courses, and thus began my adult education classes for the community college. I soon found that there was not time to teach, weave to sell and take care of my family, so I eliminated selling and focused my weaving time on developing clothing for my wardrobe. I made skirts that made me look ten months pregnant, coats that weighed 20 pounds, fabric that self-destructed when touched with scissors . . . I even have a dress that has glued seams which feel like coarse sandpaper. I knew there had to be a better way to create clothing and discovered that if I wove rectangles and squares, assembled them selvedge to selvedge, I didn't have to deal with the emotion and trauma of cutting into fabric. I had no idea then that I was traveling a well-worn historic route.

"Wear life
like a loose garment"
Margaret Fisher

I was also trying to do all the things I had done earlier in our marriage . . . super Mom, super housekeeper, super teacher, super volunteer, super everything. I began to feel like a juggler adding another ball to the act but who wouldn't drop any others. I was forced into evaluating how I was spending my time and how I wanted to spend my time. I sat down one fateful night, and wrote down my six priorities and found that family and weaving topped the list. Then I listed how I was basically spending my time. It was cleaning the house, running to the store, worrying about what to cook that night and running to the store again, being a volunteer for everything I was asked to do, and chatting on the telephone. Change began to take place . . . it was gradual, but it was a shift of use of time. I made some choices. I told people when they called "to visit" that I couldn't talk because I was working in the studio (the loom in the kitchen). It took about six months for that message to get across, but I still maintained contact with these friends by scheduling luncheon get-togethers. I found that by planning a week's menu, posting same and shopping once a week, I only had to look at the list each morning to see what to take out of the freezer that day. I also began to do double-cooking . . . freezing one portion and thus having one "free" day a week. That was also when I began my collection of nutritious meals that could be prepared in less than an hour. I also decided that I would give volunteer time to one organization a year and would then call the president of the group and offer my services, sometimes for a specific job. I thus was in control of scheduling my use of time. Being room-mother was always on the list, for I enjoyed that involvement in my children's world away from home; plus each of the three could volunteer me for two field trips a year *if* they cleared the dates ahead. The children always had household responsibilities (set of jobs that rotated each Sunday morning), but as age increased so did the scope of what was expected. My attitude was that if everyone shared in the work, then everyone could have time to play . . . be it flying kites or going to the beach. I still preach this sermon (they are now 21, 17 and 15) and with my eternal faith I keep believing that one day this wisdom will be accepted as a great family truth.

Jack was part of all this internal change too. We began marriage with the age-old belief that man earns, woman tends. I was now also earning and also trying to do all the tending. I played martyr for several years with considerable skill, and then decided that I was really tired of that role and finally said so . . . out loud. It is amazing how communication can relieve a situation. Roles, I must say, did not automatically shift, but the first step was certainly talking about how over-burdened I was feeling. Compromises, arguments, new approaches, change of attitudes . . . all were part of the gradual change of life-style. It wasn't easy, but then no one had ever promised me it would be. I also realized that I was keeping my house clean according to my mother's standards, not mine. And I discovered that my standards were much higher than my family's. I redefined my tolerance level and kept things to that degree.

I was still working diligently at the loom, weaving clothes and wearing them. At a regional conference, because I was wearing my creations, someone asked if I taught people how to make "clothes like that." I confessed that I hadn't, but I was certainly willing to try to put a workshop together. That was in 1977, and the first course led to others the next year in Canada, then Washington, Oregon, and now New York to California. I teach some 12 workshops a year in addition to sessions at national meetings and regional conferences.

Those first times away from the family were traumatic for us all. Jack chose at an early age not to know how to cook, so I taught the children instead. Peter, at seven, could do a mean bowl of tomato soup and grilled cheese sandwiches, and Kathleen at 12 was a pro with meatloaf. They had to learn to do laundry, clean bathrooms, and get up in time to fix lunches for school. Probably the greatest benefit in going away to teach was that I allowed my children to become self-sufficient. They all have basic life-skills that came with experience . . . some humorous and some difficult, but they did learn to cope and gained such self-confidence with each accomplishment. I am able to do what I love best and to be paid for it . . . travel to new places, meet fantastic people who share my love of weaving . . . this in turn has made me a more whole person and I believe a more balanced mother and wife.

My family is still my first priority, but I have learned that I have to center who I am before I can adequately give to others.

The weaving has also given the bonus of traveling to other cultures. Having had 28 penpals while in high school, I have always been intrigued with the world beyond. I began to realize that the clothing shapes I was designing had been worn in other countries for hundreds of years and I wanted to research additional information. My first trip was to Greece in 1975 . . . but what a difficult decision it was for me to go. I had saved enough money, Jack was totally supportive of my leaving, I had my niece to stay with the children, but my own guilts were overwhelming. "A good wife and mother does not go traipsing off to some foreign place by herself" according to local standards. I finally decided that my children would survive four weeks without me and that the experience could change my focus. I was so right and since then, without one pang, I have traveled to Finland, Thailand, Mexico and China!

If I were to summarize the "great truths" realized through the past years of finding myself and defining my work, the following would be included:

1. Make some choices about yourself and your time. It is fearful and difficult, but do it anyway, for you also have the right to change those choices. What are your priorities? One question that certainly helped me to focus my goals: "If you had one year to live how would you spend your time?"

2. Be open to new experiences. There is no guarantee all these will be satisfying or rewarding, but if you want to move off the square you are on, you will have to open that door, go out and take your chances.
3. Recognize your own capabilities. Study, practice, be stubborn and be patient, but attempt to excel in whatever your choice may be. Set realistic goals and try to achieve them one step at a time. A positive attitude is still the magic ingredient.
4. Realize that you cannot be fulfilled through someone else. Your family and friends add richness to your life, but you must find your own inner happiness.
5. Life is a series of phases. You will not be where you are today in a few weeks or a few months. Accept and enjoy what is in your world now . . . be it children or weaving. Do not use up your energy and emotions looking backward or waiting for tomorrow . . . enjoy the now of your life . . . this very day and moment. Agnes DeMille said, "Life is what happens when you're making other plans."

All of this because of a loom, weaving, and the creation of clothing that said who and what I am. There are new crises and challenges ahead, but I know now I can cope and grow from the experiences. You can, too. May my book start you on your way; and remember . . . "if you aren't failing at 50% of what you do, you are not realizing your full potential".

Cheers and enjoy.

"It takes a lot of courage
for a man to declare,
with clarity and simplicity,
that the purpose of life
is to enjoy it."

Lin Yutang
The Pleasures of a Non-Conformist

"The faces of the past are like leaves
That settle to the ground . . .
They make the earth rich and thick
So that new fruit will come forth
Each summer."

Chief Dan George

"Fashion is influenced by history . . . visually touching primitive cultures."

Mary McFadden
New York Fashion Designer

Chapter 1
The History of Rectangular Garments

We enter this world naked. No animal is more defenseless at birth and none is so long in becoming able to care for itself. One of the reasons for this slow development is that we are born without any protective clothing. This need for protection, along with some form of modesty and a desire for self-adornment, led to man's development and use of clothing. It is interesting to note that some anthropologists believe that personal ornamentation was the strongest of these influences. The reason for using clothing does not explain, however, why certain shapes and forms of clothes evolved. Historically we can see that the simple, traditional garments of many cultures have changed very little over long periods of time, yet there is amazing variation in dress from culture to culture. If we compare the sari of India, the oldest known form of women's dress in that country, to the centuries-old kimono of Japan, we can see great differences. Each has been worn in its respective culture for hundreds of years, yet each has changed very little during that time. Why have certain garment shapes evolved and why are there such differences from culture to culture?

A number of influences have determined the shape and form of clothing throughout history and include such factors as the body and its need for movement, the climate, the terrain, attitudes about covering the body, and levels of social status. Although all of these have affected the shape of clothing, it is the shape and size of the material from which the garment is made that has had the most impact. When garments were made from animal skins, the size and form of the skin dictated the final shape of the garment. When woven fabric began to be used for clothing, it was the length and width of the material that dictated the shape and form of the costume. Burnham notes that the proverb "I shall cut my coat after my cloth" essentially means that the size of the cloth dictated the shape of the garment.

Since the size of woven cloth is determined by the width and type of loom, it is possible to look at looms of various cultures and correlate loom type to garment shape. As Burnham says, "If, as in the ancient Mediterranean world, the loom was wide and capable of making great lengths of fabric, the resulting garments were wide and draped. In thc East, the looms were narrow with the resulting garments seamed and comparatively tight." There are exceptions to this theory, but in essence it does explain clothing shapes. It is important to also remember that in early times, those close to the production process would not waste any fabric, and a weaver's skill far exceeded his cutting and sewing abilities. It was therefore practical and logical to use the length and widths directly from the loom in the creation of clothes.

This has been the basis of my approach to handwoven clothes; to create wearable contemporary clothing using rectangles, squares and loom shaping with no cutting into fabric. There are a number of advantages to this method of clothing construction:

a. simplified sewing with no intricate closures or zippers,
b. no complicated patterns,
c. limitless variety using even one garment shape,
d. no fraying problem when cutting coarsely woven fabric,
e. no bulky seams,
f. no emotional trauma of cutting into fabric you have created,
g. unique and individual garments, and
h. space saving since rectangular garments fold flat.

A brief survey of the development of clothes related to loom type will provide a basis for understanding this concept of loom-shaped garments.

Dress of every kind must be made to fit the human frame in some way. Clothes can be fitted at the waist, the shoulder and the neck or envelop the whole body in a type of cloak. As Burnham says,

"The simplest garments are those with no cutting or sewing at all. These include all sizes of woven cloth which may be folded around, draped on or tied to the human body: shawls, mantles, wrap-around dresses and skirts."

Wrapped Garments

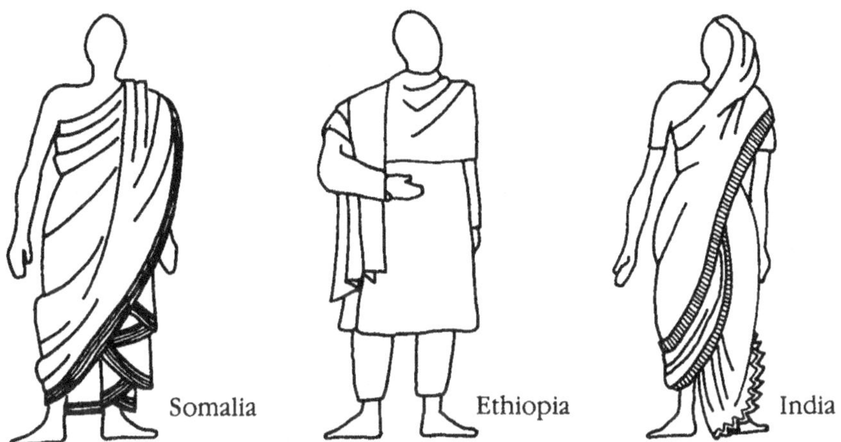

Draped garments made from wide widths of cloth have most often been found in those areas with wide looms. The warp-weighted looms of Greece could produce long lengths of wide cloth that affected Greek and Roman costume. The ancient Greek costume of cloaks, mantles and tunics were all dependent on large, wide pieces of material. These garments were loosely draped with shape derived from the human figure. The Greek men and women also wore a kind of light blanket known as the *himation*. This hung over the shoulder and was fastened by a buckle. The *chlaina* was worn by men, and was just long enough to reach the knee. The *peplo* was the women's garment which was wide enough to be doubled over at the shoulder line.

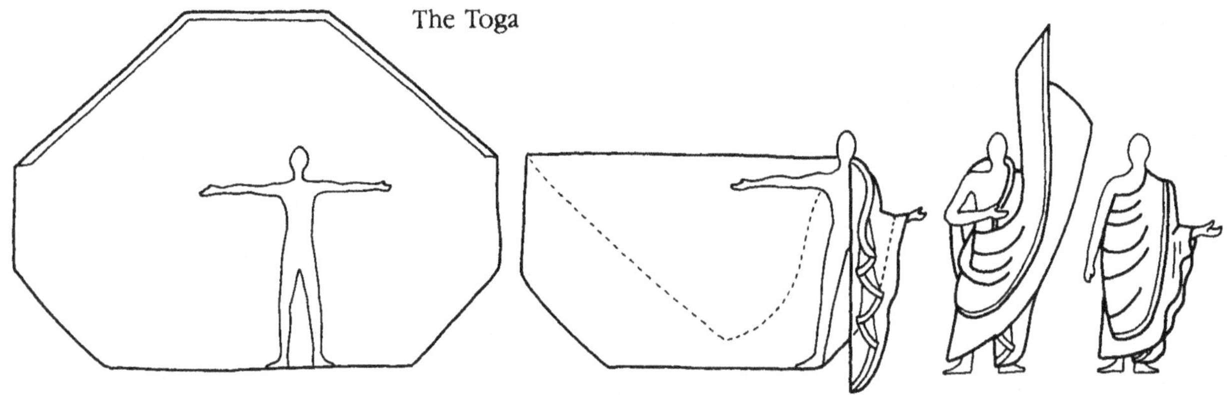

The Roman *toga* developed from the Greek cloak, and though the Greek garment was rectangular, the Roman version had the lower corners shaped to make draping easier. The Indian *sari* is a wrapped garment of a single length of material between five and eight yards long and one yard wide.

Four Different Ways of Wearing the Sari

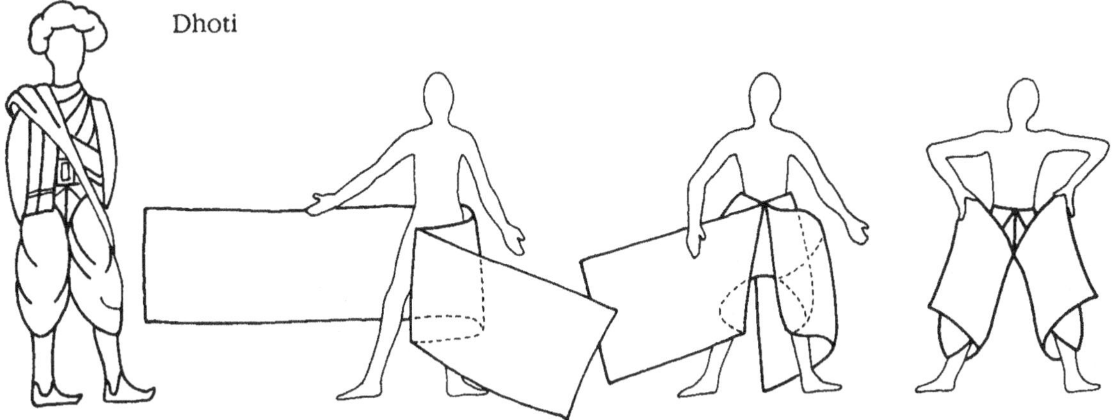

The *dhoti* of India is a long piece of cloth draped from the back, round the lower part of the body and drawn between the legs so the folds are in front. It has been worn this way some 2000 years. The great belted plaid of Scotland was made from a single length of cloth four to six yards long and about two yards wide. The man would lie down on it with one selvedge at knee level and fasten the entire piece with a belt. When he stood up, the lower part was like a kilt and the upper part could be draped around the body. Later it became two garments with the pleats of the kilt permanently stitched.

Some form of wrap-around skirt or sarong is common throughout the world with a long, wide piece of cloth wrapped around the waist one of the most basic forms of clothing.

Skirt Types

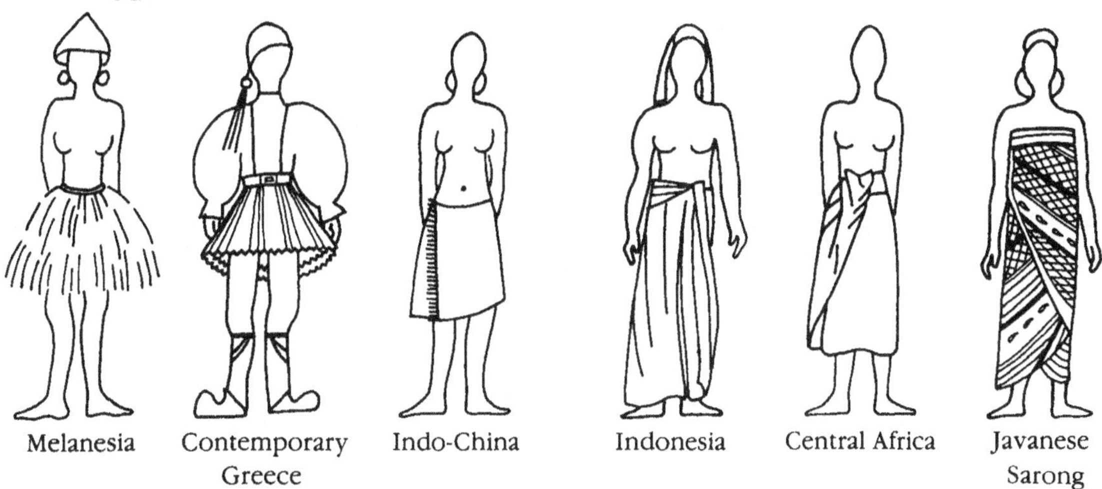

In the areas south and southeast of the Mediterranean, the draped form of dress has been retained to the present. The *haik* is made from a large rectangular piece of material which covers the whole body in a most graceful and artistic manner. Women also wear the *haik*, but rather than drape it around their bodies, they wear it hanging from the shoulders.

North African Woman's Haik

Garments from wide looms are also made to fit through seaming rather than draping. The *jibba* is a simple Arabian top garment made of one piece of wide fabric that wraps around the body with selvedge at the shoulder line and hem. Slits are made for the arms and the *jibba* is sewn together at the shoulder and down the front. The *jellaba* is a North African man's garment which has features of the *jibba*. The wide garment with partially sewn sleeves provides the ventiliation needed in a hot climate, and the loose hood protects from the sun.

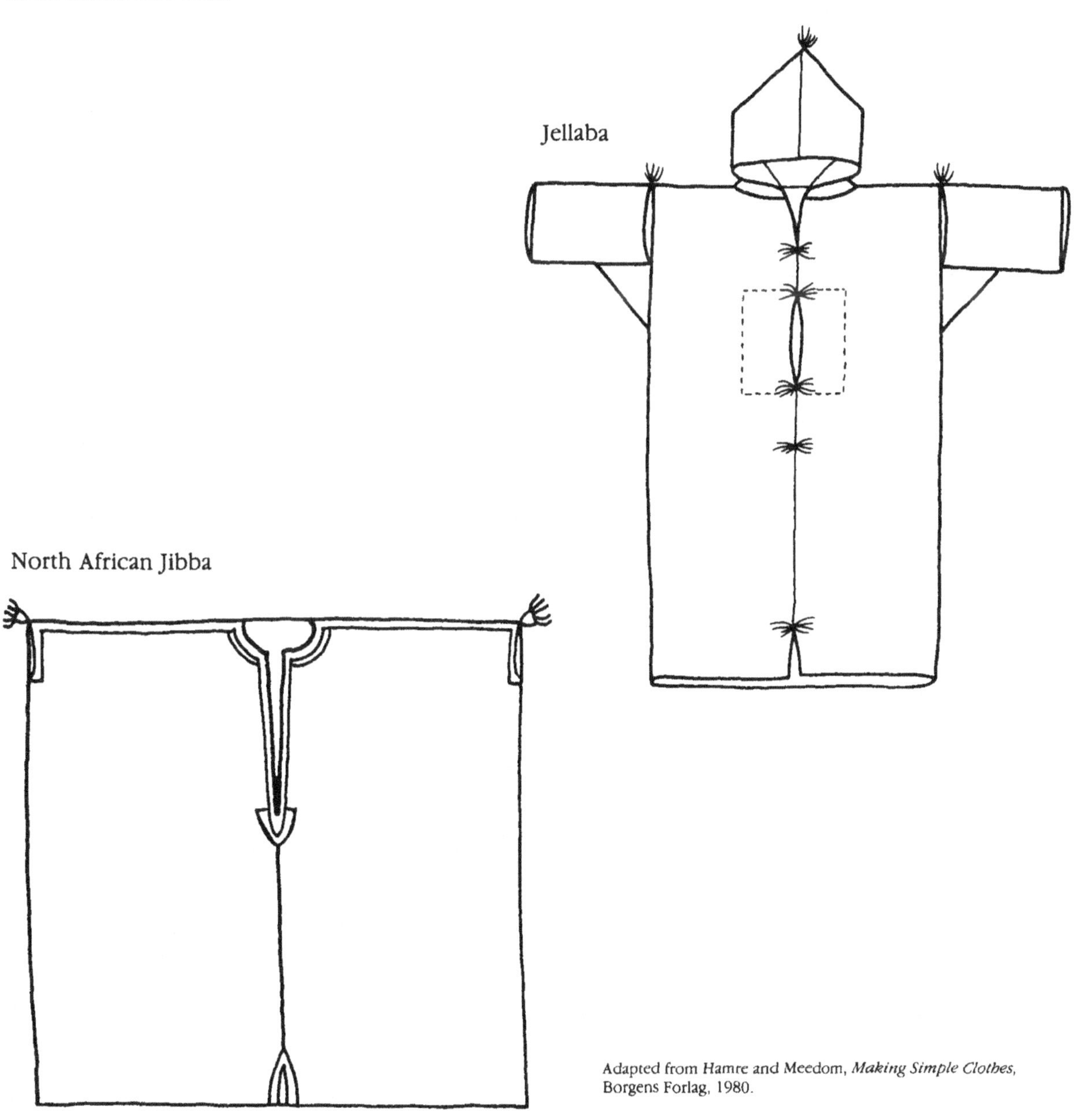

Adapted from Hamre and Meedom, *Making Simple Clothes*, Borgens Forlag, 1980.

Ponchos

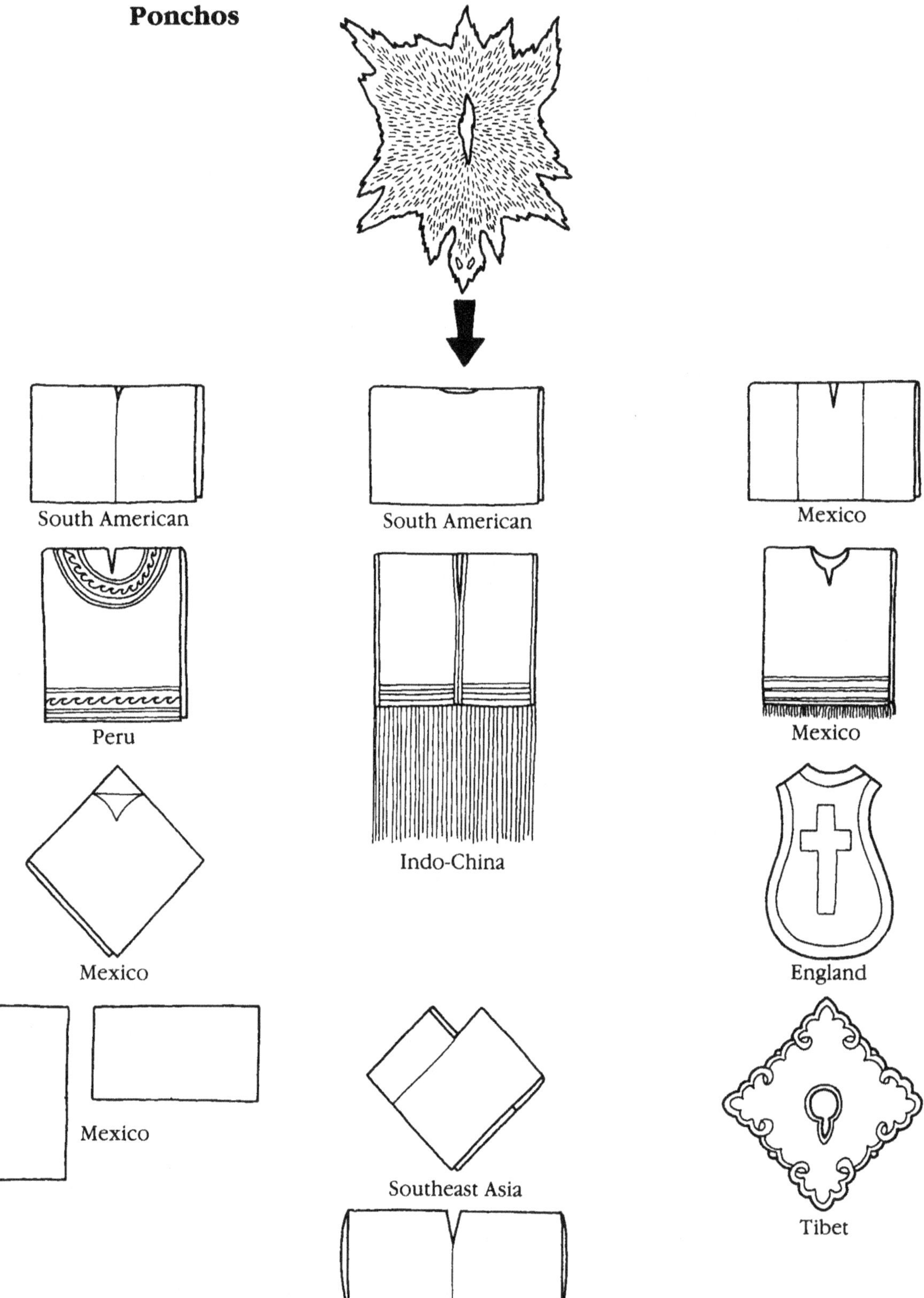

Adapted from Hamre and Meedom, *Making Simple Clothes,* Borgens Forlag, 1980.

Huipils

In those cultures that had narrow looms, backstrap or horizontal, it was frequently necessary to sew widths together to create wearable clothing. The poncho type garment undoubtedly evolved from a hole cut in a piece of hide so the head could be inserted and the hide would hang from the shoulders. With narrow woven cloth, it was logical to sew two narrow pieces together, leaving a head opening. This type of garment is found in various forms in Central and South America, Tibet, Indo-China, Lappland and Northern Siberia.

A sleeveless shirt evolves when the sides of a poncho are sewn, as exemplified by the *huipil*. This style of garment appears under other names in parts of the world from Africa to India. Rectangular lengths of cloth are taken from the loom, the sides sewn and a hole left for the head. The garment can be long or short, narrow or wide, and composed of one, two or three widths.

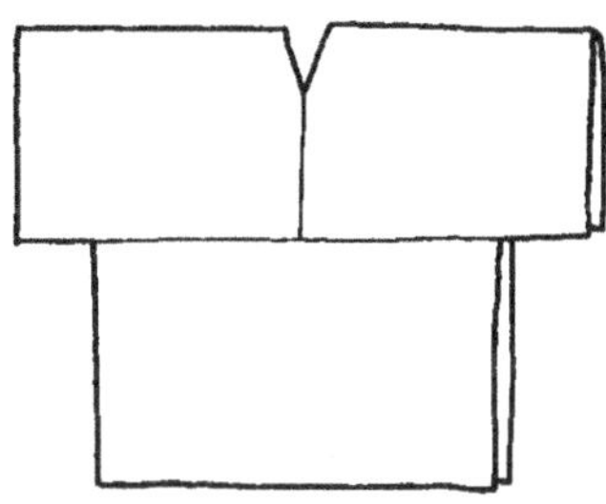

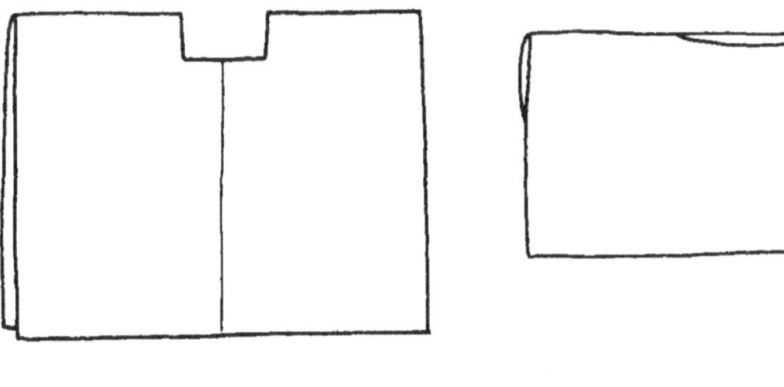

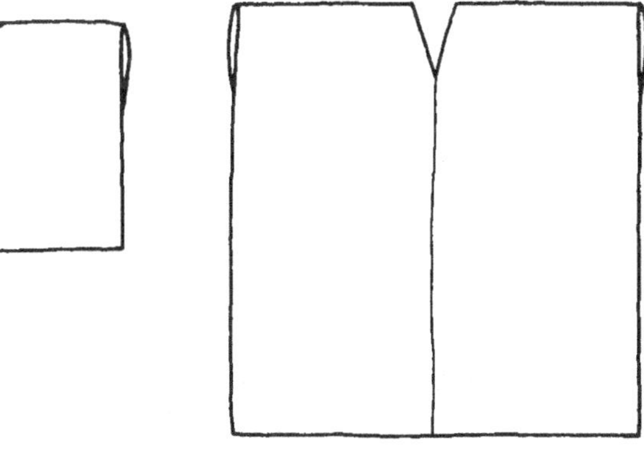

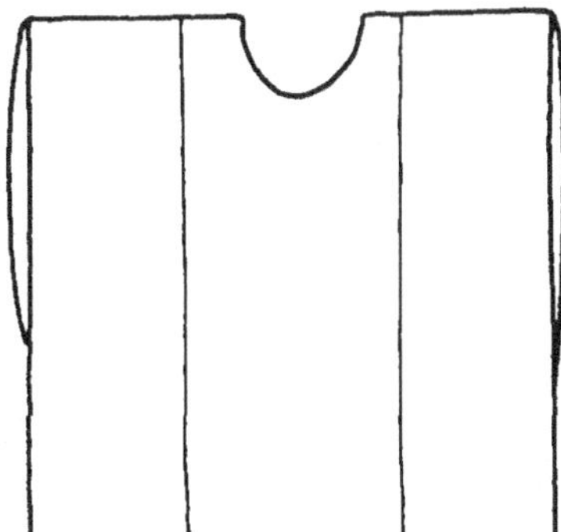

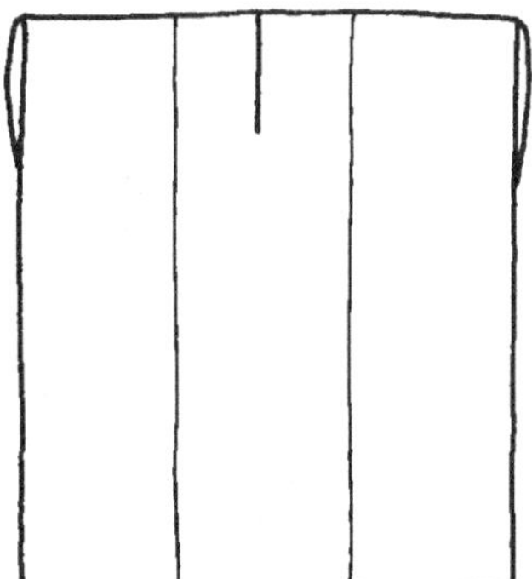

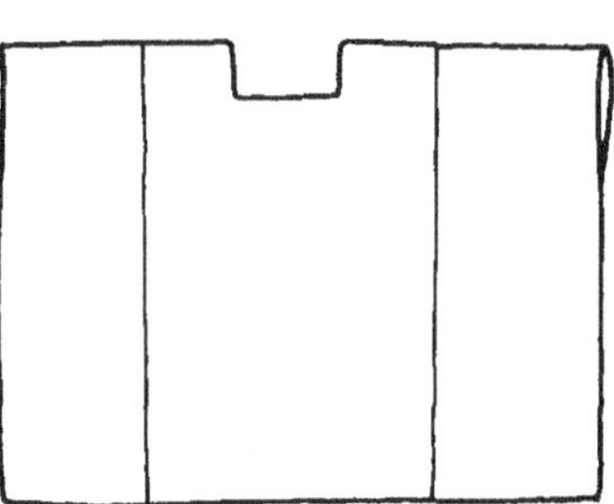

The poncho develops into another type of body covering when there is a neck opening and side seams and sleeves are added. In this form it has many names: shirt, shift, tunic, robe, dress, smock, chemise, *tobe*. It has been a basic shape for both men and women throughout the world since very early time.

The European width of cloth was based on the reach of the weaver sitting at a horizontal loom, throwing the shuttle with one hand and catching it with the other. This width could be as much as 50″ but was usually less, with many materials woven one ell wide (37.5″). This provided sufficient width for a shirt. Burnham notes that the study of the shape of the shirt bears out the importance of loom width in the shaping of garments. One of the early shirts, from the Middle East (shown on next page), is made from one rectangle for the front and back, gussets for ease of movement, and additional rectangles for sleeves.

Evolution of Garment Shapes

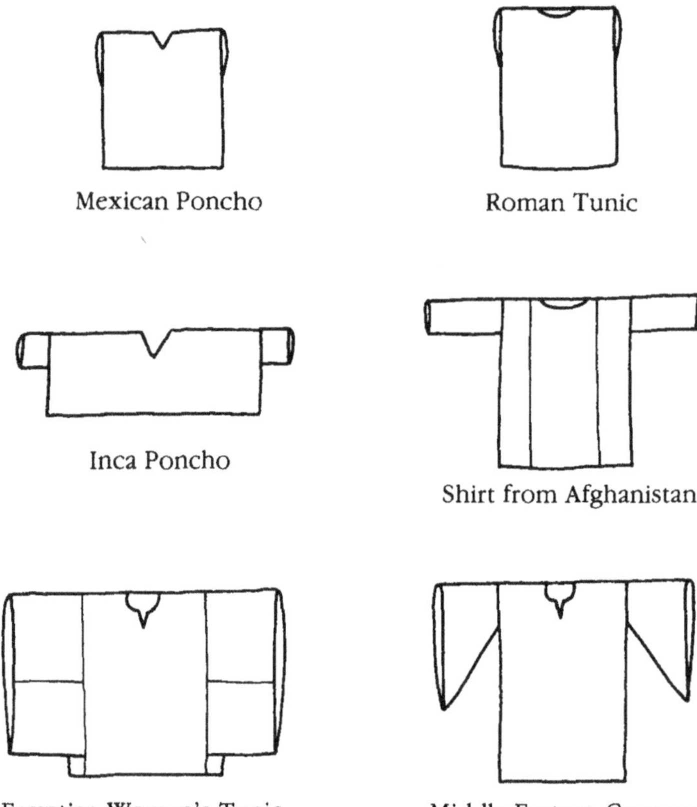

Adapted from Hamre and Meedom, *Making Simple Clothes,* Borgens Forlag, 1980.

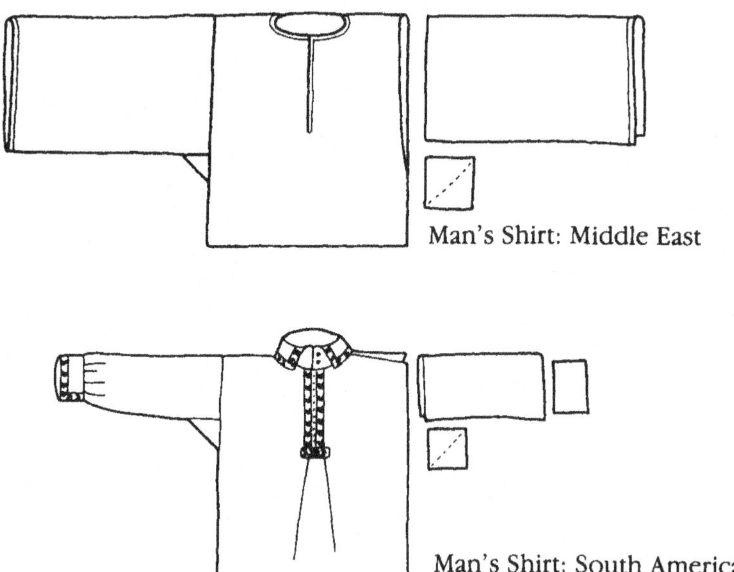

Man's Shirt: Middle East

Man's Shirt: South America

A further development of the shirt comes from South America, although Spanish influence is likely. A back yoke has been added for a smooth fit across the shoulders, and fullness placed lower where it is needed. The front fullness is secured in a box pleat. The smock-frock was worn by farmers and country people during the 18th and 19th centuries in England and is constructed entirely of rectangles and squares. The fit is created by decorative smocking at the neck and on the sleeves. In Eastern Europe and Western Asia, loom widths were narrow (around 18″), so additions had to be made to the basic width of the cloth before the garment would fit comfortably.

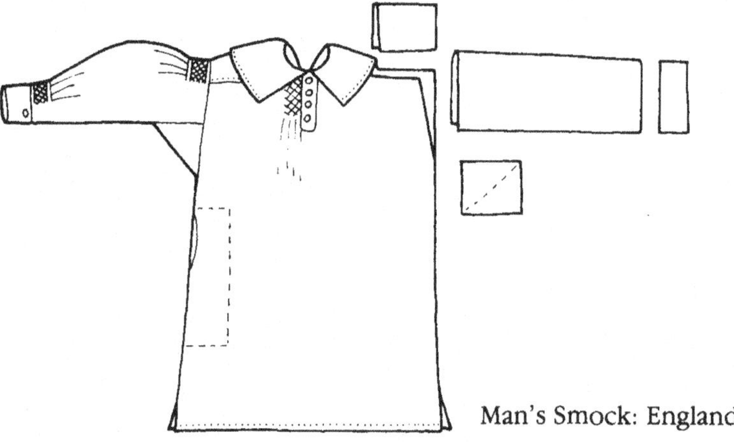

Man's Smock: England

Drawings adapted from Dorothy K. Burnham, *Cut My Cote,* ©The Royal Ontario Museum, 1973.

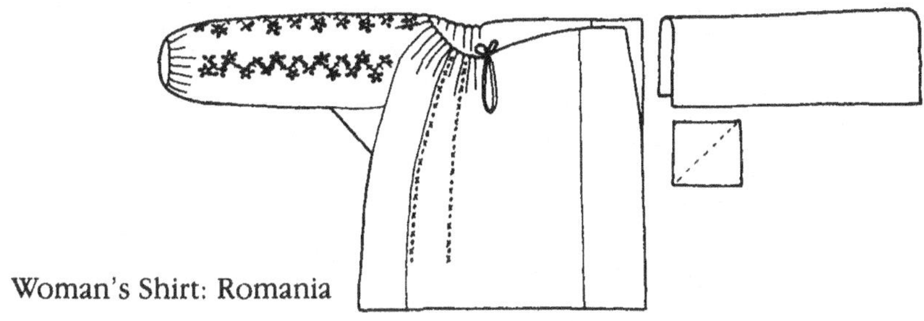

Woman's Shirt: Romania

The shirts of Romania and the Ukraine were made of three widths of fabric, (front, back and the third split for the sides with slits for the sleeves), gussets and gathers at the neck.

Shirts with sleeve and side pieces in one were found in Turkey and Greece, although fabric type and weight were important in this style of garment with a heavily creped weave of silk and/or cotton generally used.

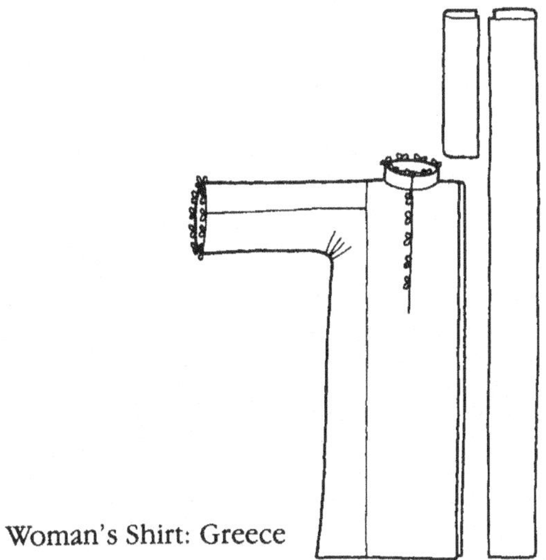

Woman's Shirt: Greece

Drawings adapted from Dorothy K. Burnham, *Cut My Cote,* ©The Royal Ontario Museum, 1973.

Shirts and dresses with width below the sleeves were widespread throughout the area of Turkish influence. The basic form was a single width of cloth without shoulder seams for the body of the garment. Sleeves were attached to it. The width of the garment was increased by the addition of material at the sides below the sleeves. Most often, a full width of cloth was used. Flare was added by slashing full widths on an angle, reversing one of the pieces, seaming these together, and using that unit as the side addition.

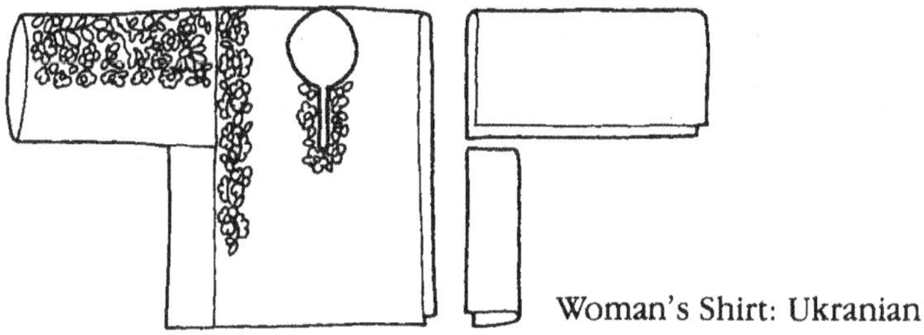

Woman's Shirt: Ukranian

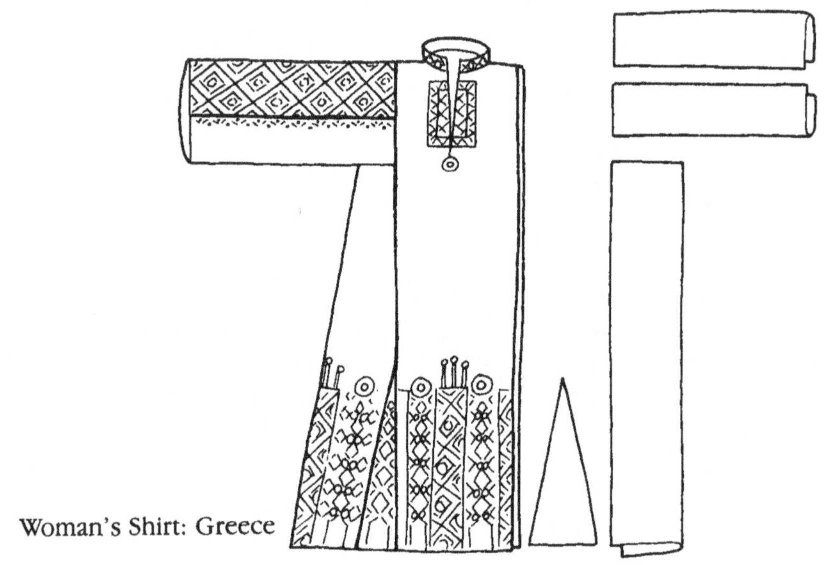

Woman's Shirt: Greece

Drawings adapted from Dorothy K. Burnham, *Cut My Cote,* ©The Royal Ontario Museum, 1973.

Width below the sleeves was a basic approach that carried over into other garments such as the *Szur* mantles of the Hungarian plains as well as many related garments in the Balkans, Asia Minor, Western and Central Asia.

In West Africa, men wove strip cloth 4″ to 6″ wide and these narrow widths were sewn together to create such garments as underwear, women's skirts, voluminous pants, tunics and robes.

Draped clothing becomes possible in this manner also. The Ashanti sews together 20 to 25 strips of narrow cloth each 3½ to 4 yards long. The garment is worn wrapped about the body and draped over the left shoulder like a Roman toga.

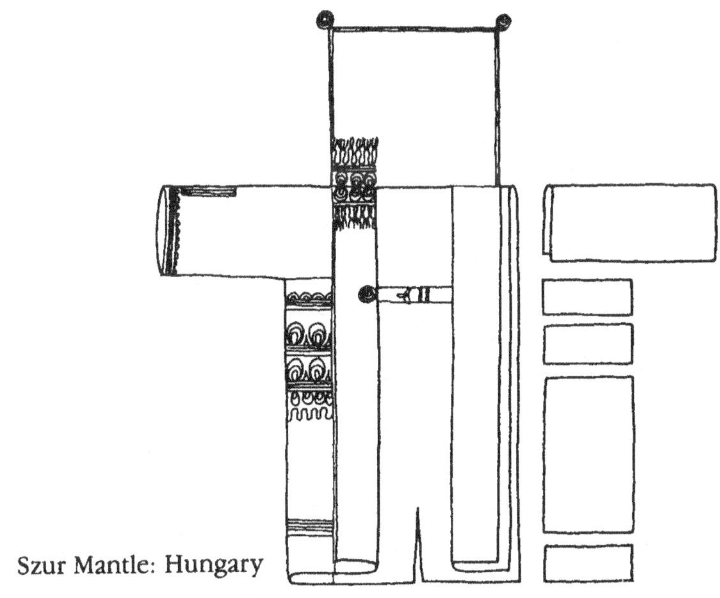

Szur Mantle: Hungary

Adapted from *The Hungarian Szur* by Veronika Gerves-Molnar, ©The Royal Ontario Museum, 1973.

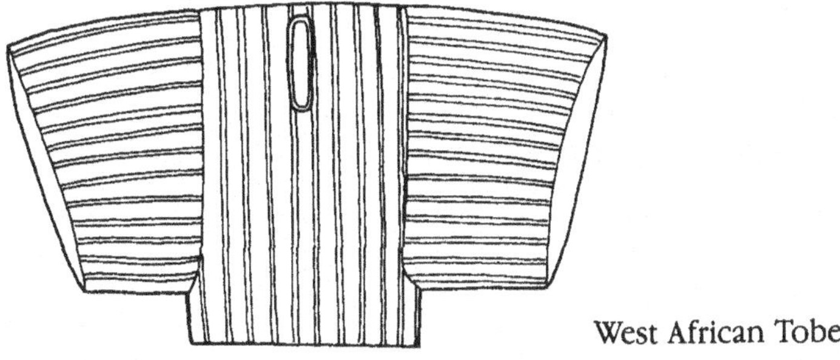

West African Tobe

Caftan Types

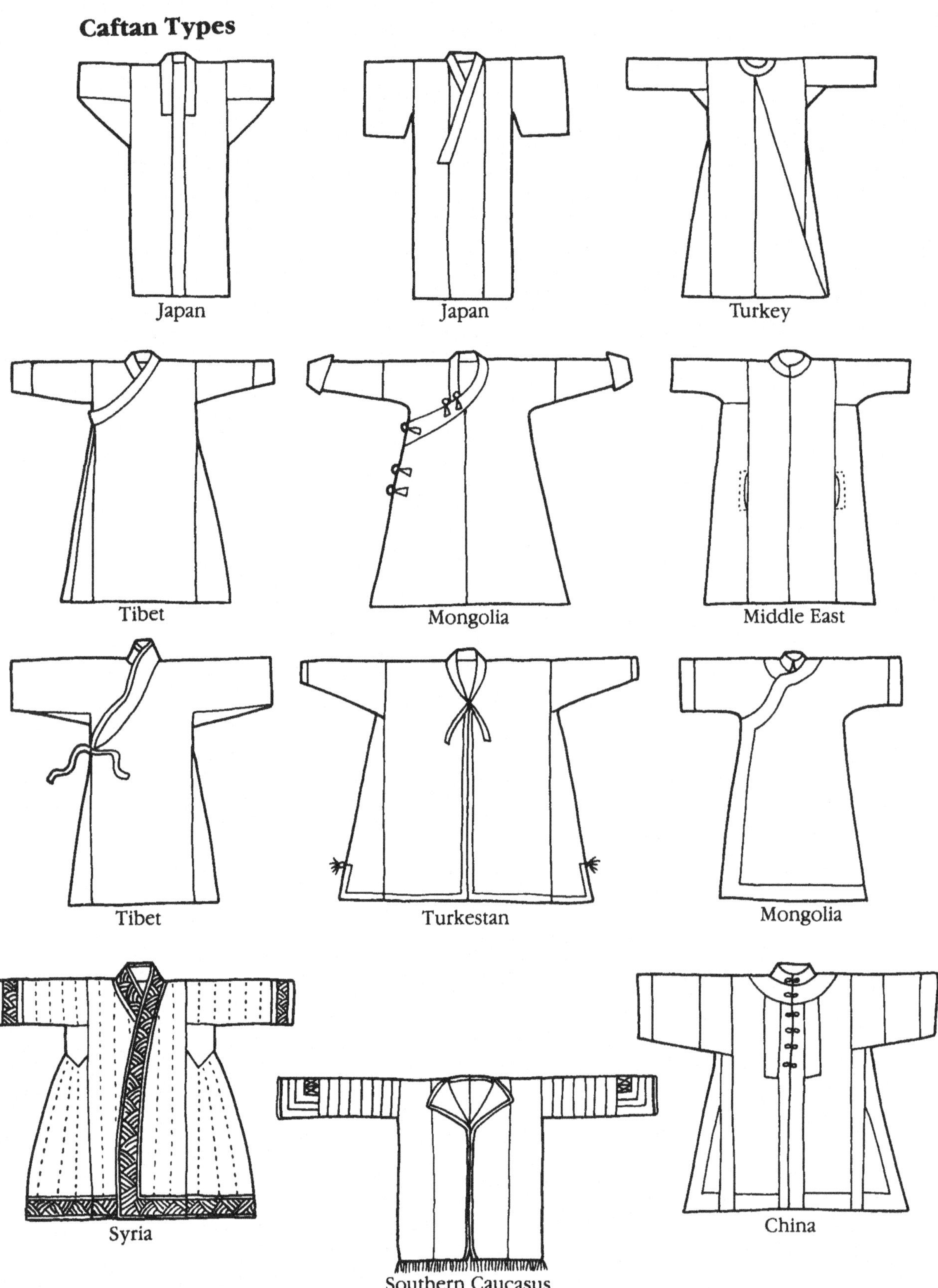

Adapted from Hamre and Meedom, *Making Simple Clothes,* Borgens Forlag, 1980.

Man also discovered that rather than cutting a hole for the head, the garment could be placed over the shoulder and fastened in front like a mantle or cloak. Eventually sleeves were added and this form of dress became known as the caftan. When narrow widths of cloth were used, two widths had to be put together to fit the body, and it was natural to use a back seam, sew the side seams and leave the front open. This made the garment easier to put on and it could be wrapped around the body.

A short jacket from Taiwan (19th century) is an example of this concept in its simplest form. With refinement it became the ancient Chinese robe and the kimono of Japan.

Buttons and buttonholes were added to this basic shape and it became the overcoat, jacket and waistcoat.

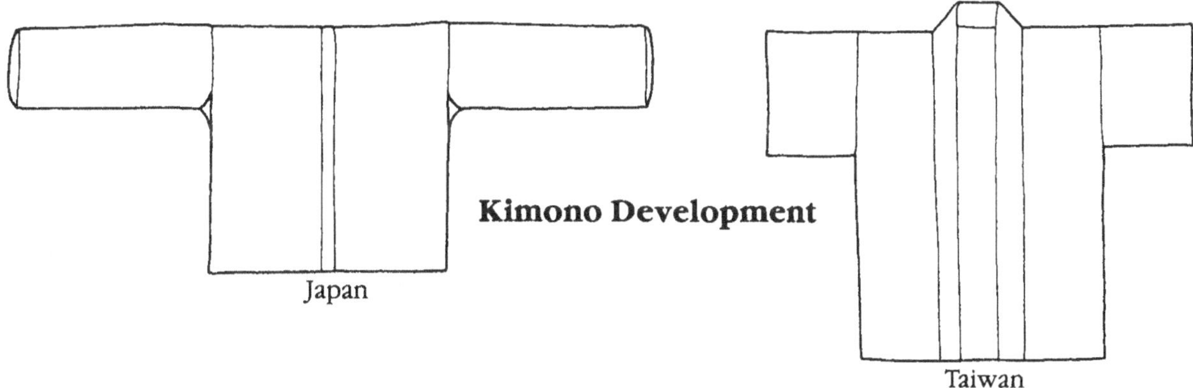

Kimono Development

Waistcoats and Jackets

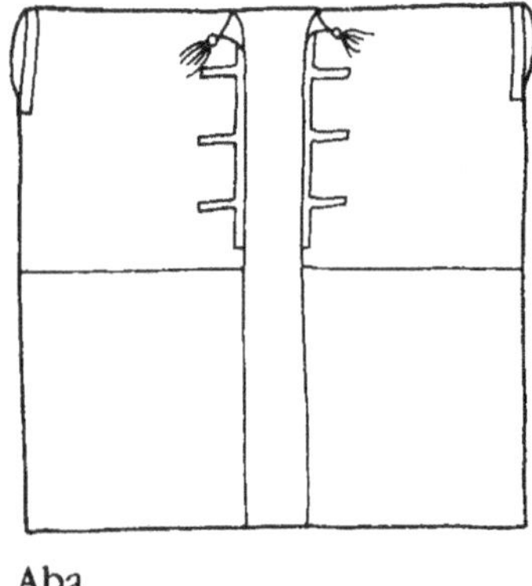
Aba

The aba is a similar garment from the Near East in that it is open down the front, but it wraps around the body with two widths of cloth sewn together at the waist and shoulder.

The vest was comparatively late in origin but is now found in nearly every culture. It was introduced as a part of a man's wardrobe about 1665. As Erickson notes, "This type of sleeveless tunic was derived from a doublet and it linked the garments of the past with those of the present." The vest has no sleeves and is open in the front and sometimes at the side. It is worn both to keep the body warm and for decorative purposes.

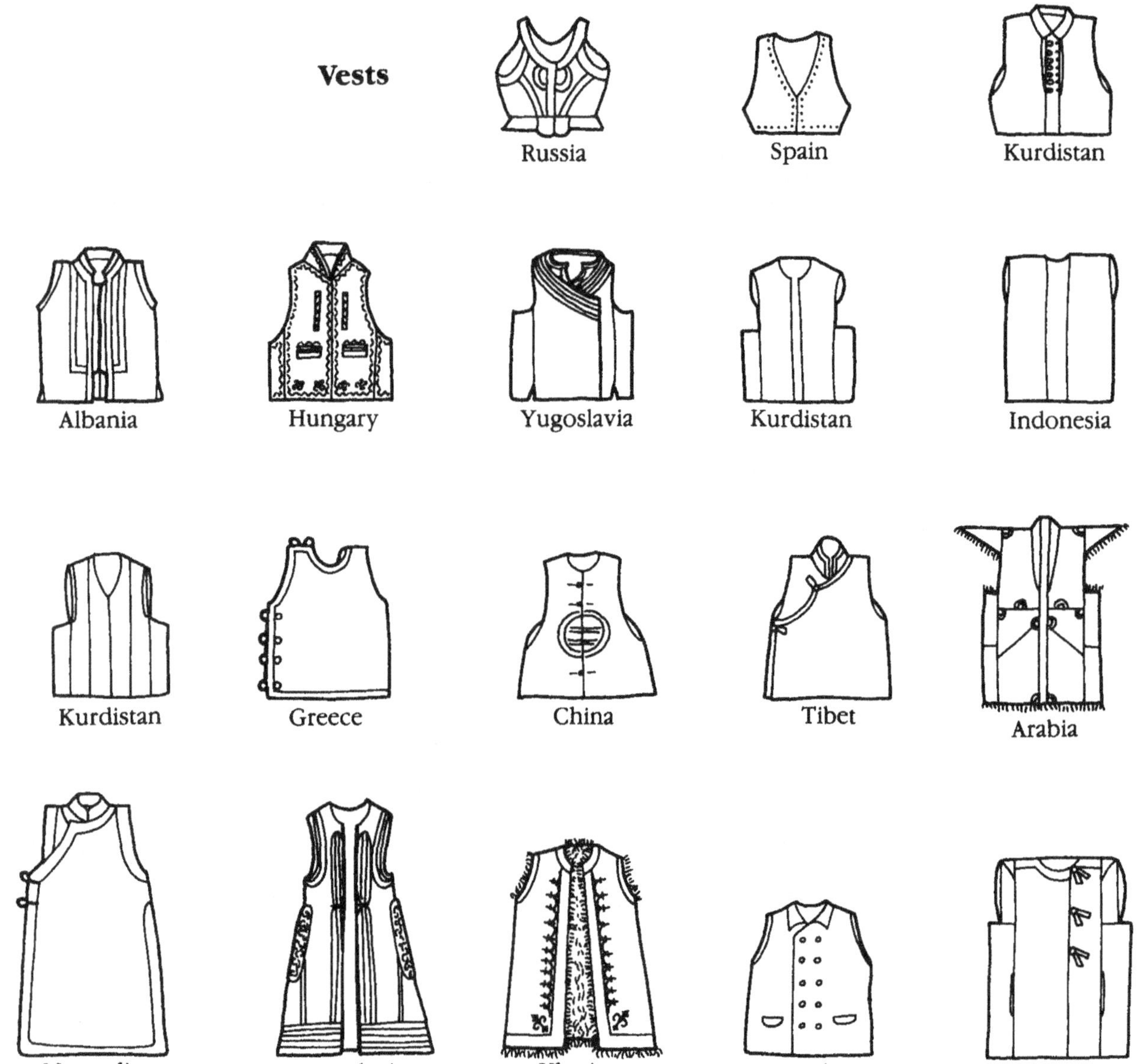

Vests

Russia Spain Kurdistan

Albania Hungary Yugoslavia Kurdistan Indonesia

Kurdistan Greece China Tibet Arabia

Mongolia Yugoslavia Ukraine Sweden Contemporary

Adapted from Hamre and Meedom, *Making Simple Clothes,* Borgens Forlag, 1980.

Trousers were introduced in Persia and China by people from Central Asia before 500 B.C., and were originally made of leather fitted tightly around the legs. As woven material replaced leather, it became possible to make trouser legs wider by utilizing the widths of fabric from the loom. Then it was discovered that two trouser legs could be joined by a drawstring which passed along the top and made still greater width possible and allowed the wearer to sit cross-legged with comfort. The evolution of the tapered legs derived from the frugality of the cut. The leg gusset was cut from the leg in a simple triangle, leaving a tapered leg.

Trousers

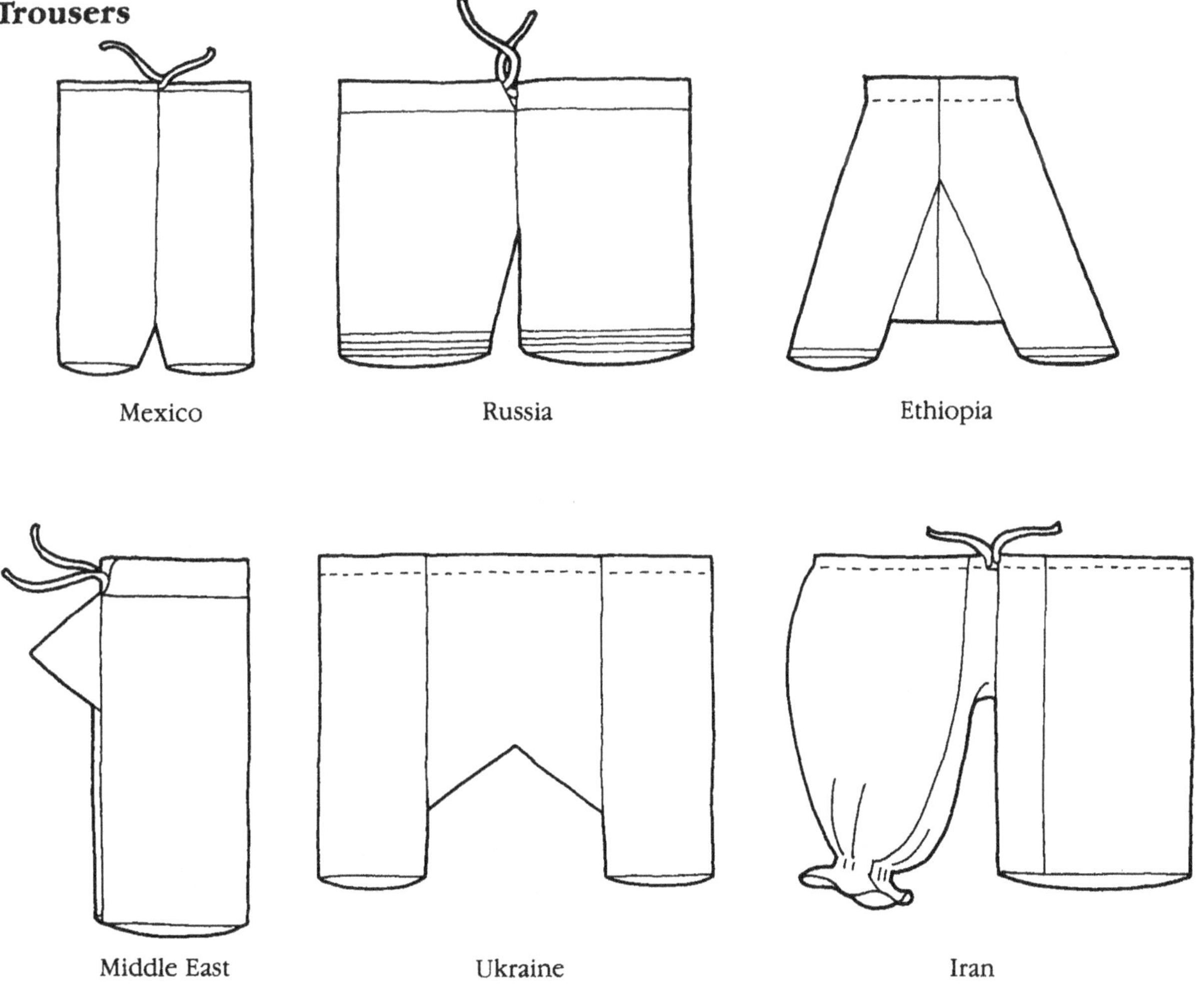

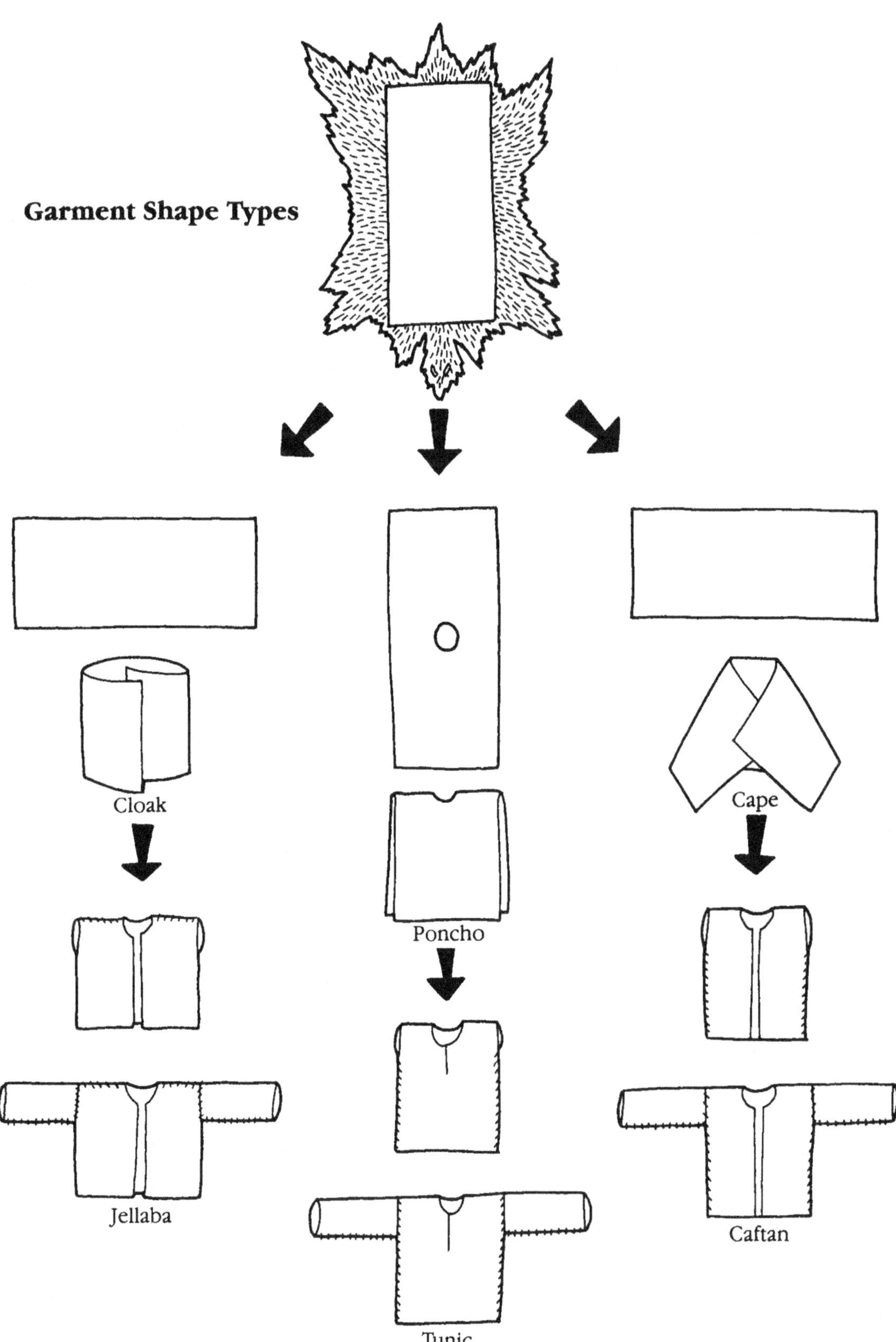

Adapted from Hamre and Meedom, *Making Simple Clothes*, Borgens Forlag, 1980.

We have reviewed a variety of garment shapes. It is possible to categorize these into three prototypes according to a theory developed by Max Tilke and other authorities. They believe that a length of cloth that wrapped around the body evolved into a garment with shoulder seams (*jellaba* type), while cloth that hung from the shoulders with a hole for the head developed into a closed garment (tunic type) and cloth that went over the shoulders like a cape developed into the garment open down the front (caftan type).

Some of the ways you can use loom widths in the design of contemporary clothing is shown in these garments constructed from one, two or multiple rectangles.

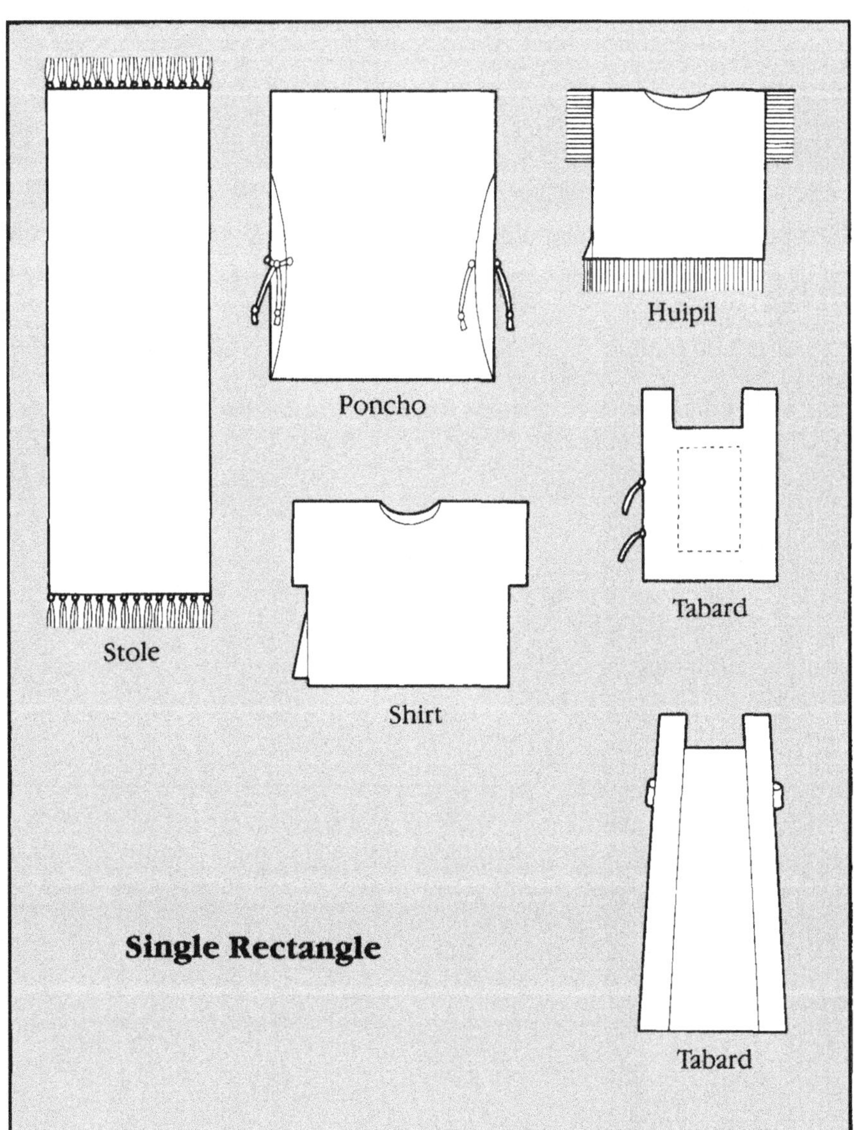

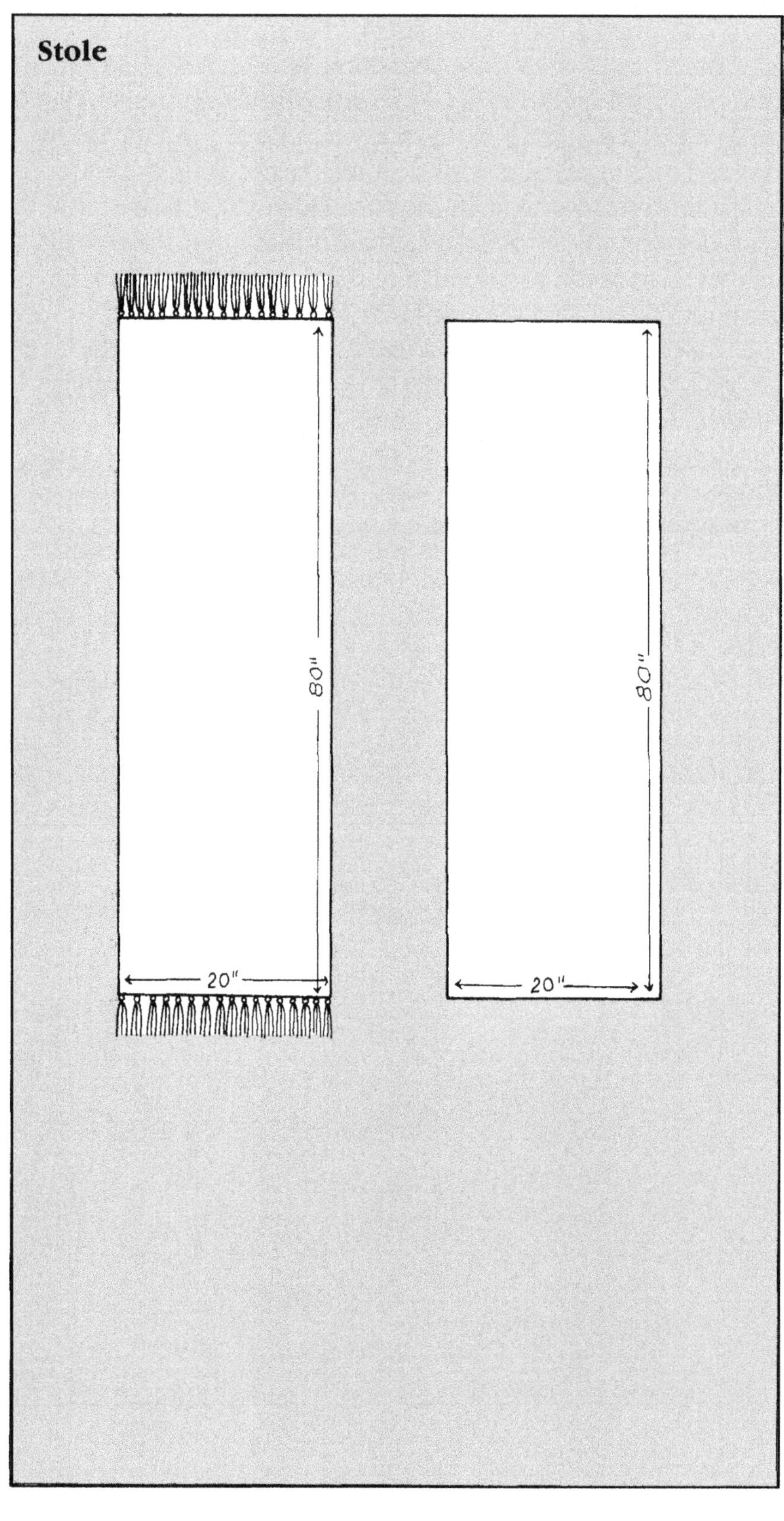
Stole
80"
20"
80"
20"

Poncho

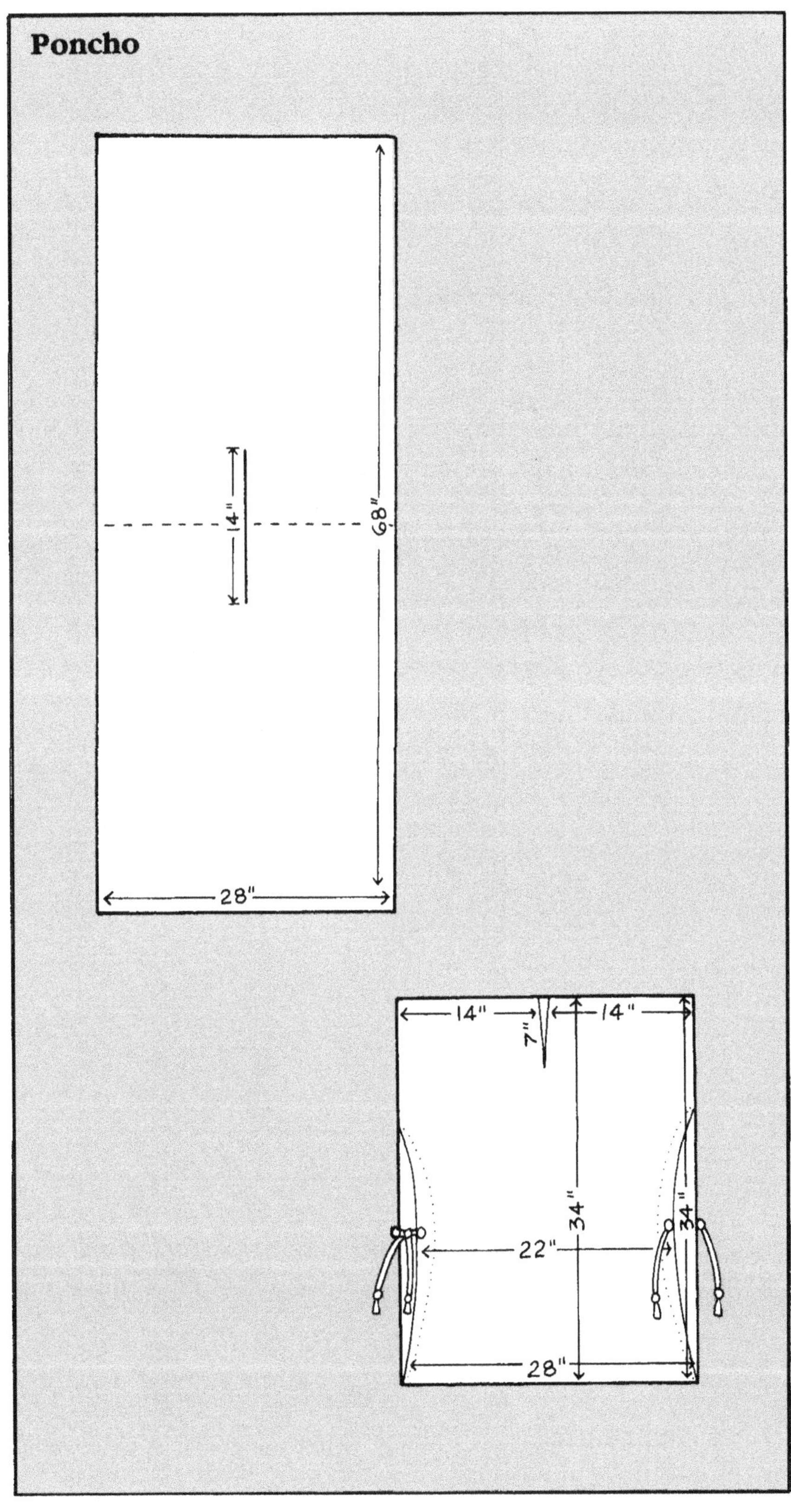

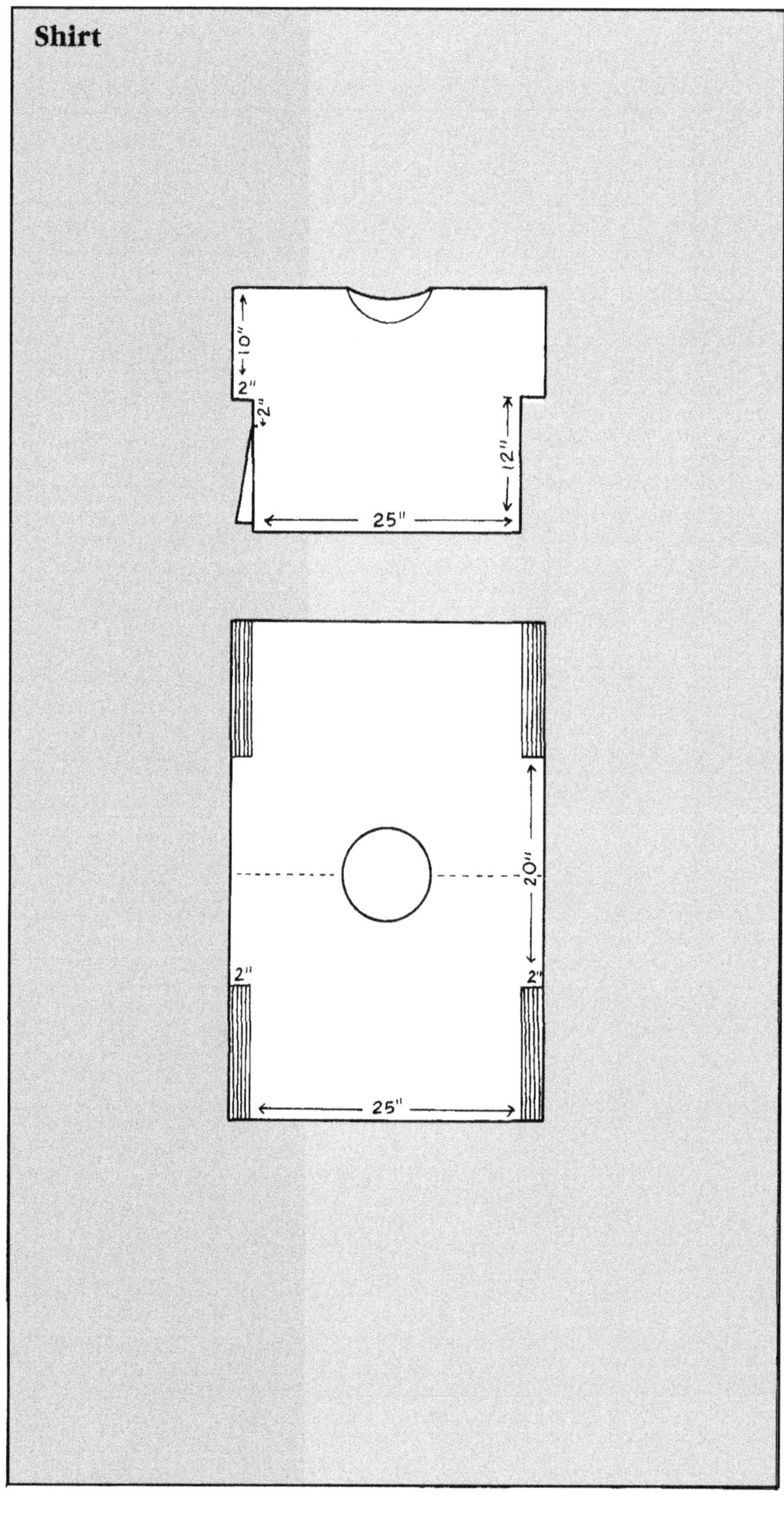
Shirt
10"
2"
2"
12"
25"
20"
2"
2"
25"

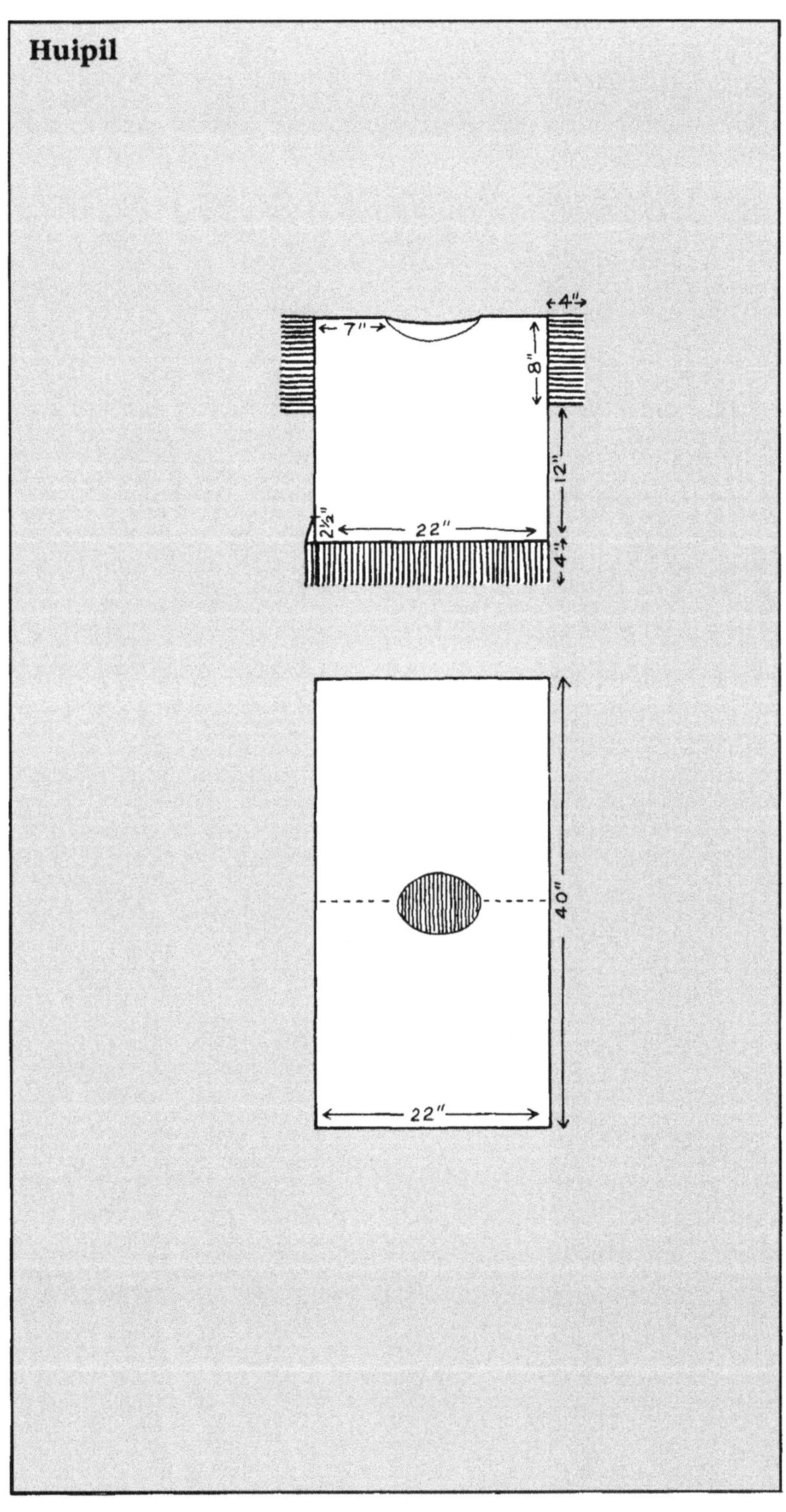
Huipil
4"
7"
8"
12"
2½"
22"
4"
40"
22"

Tabard

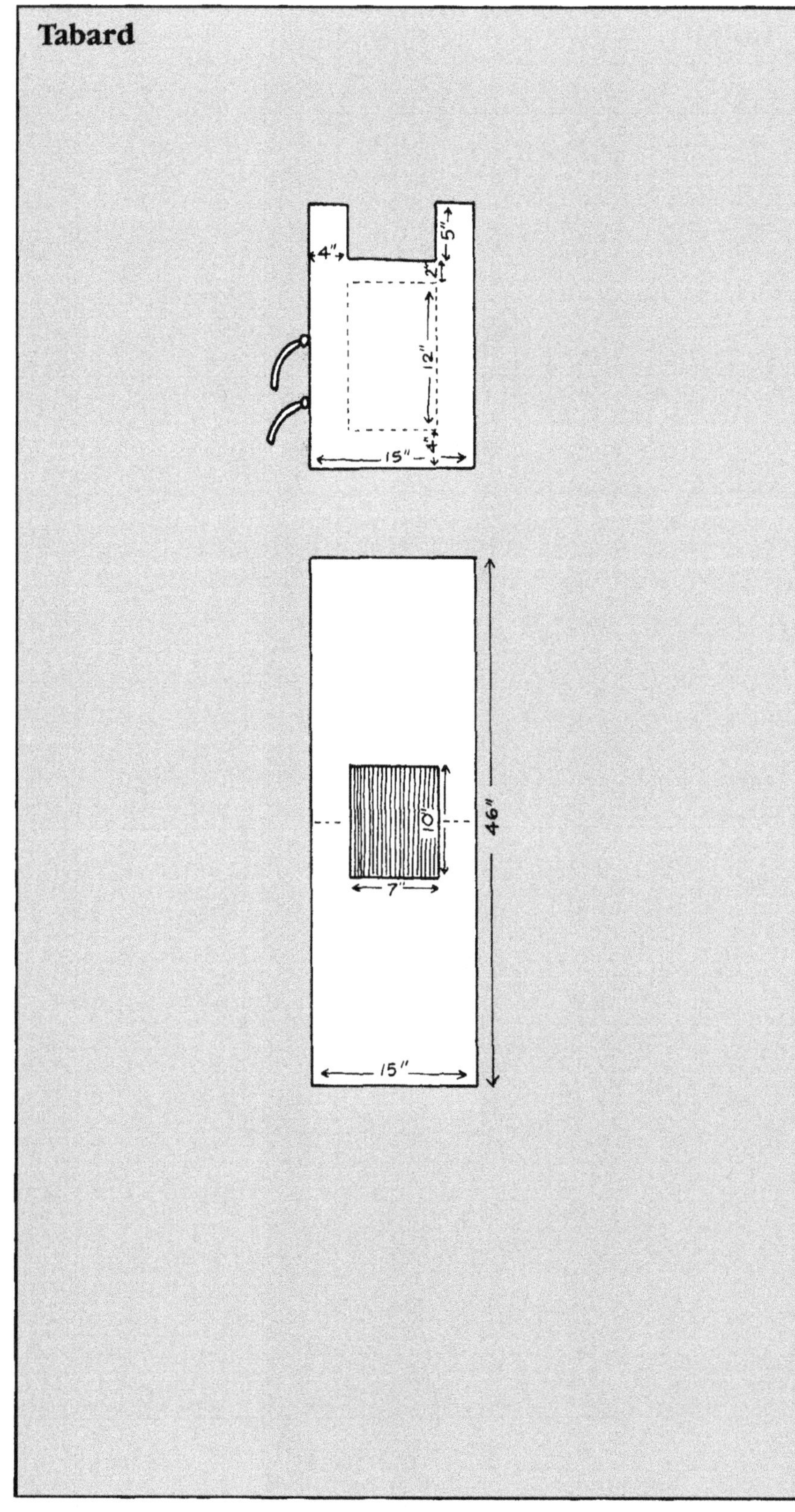

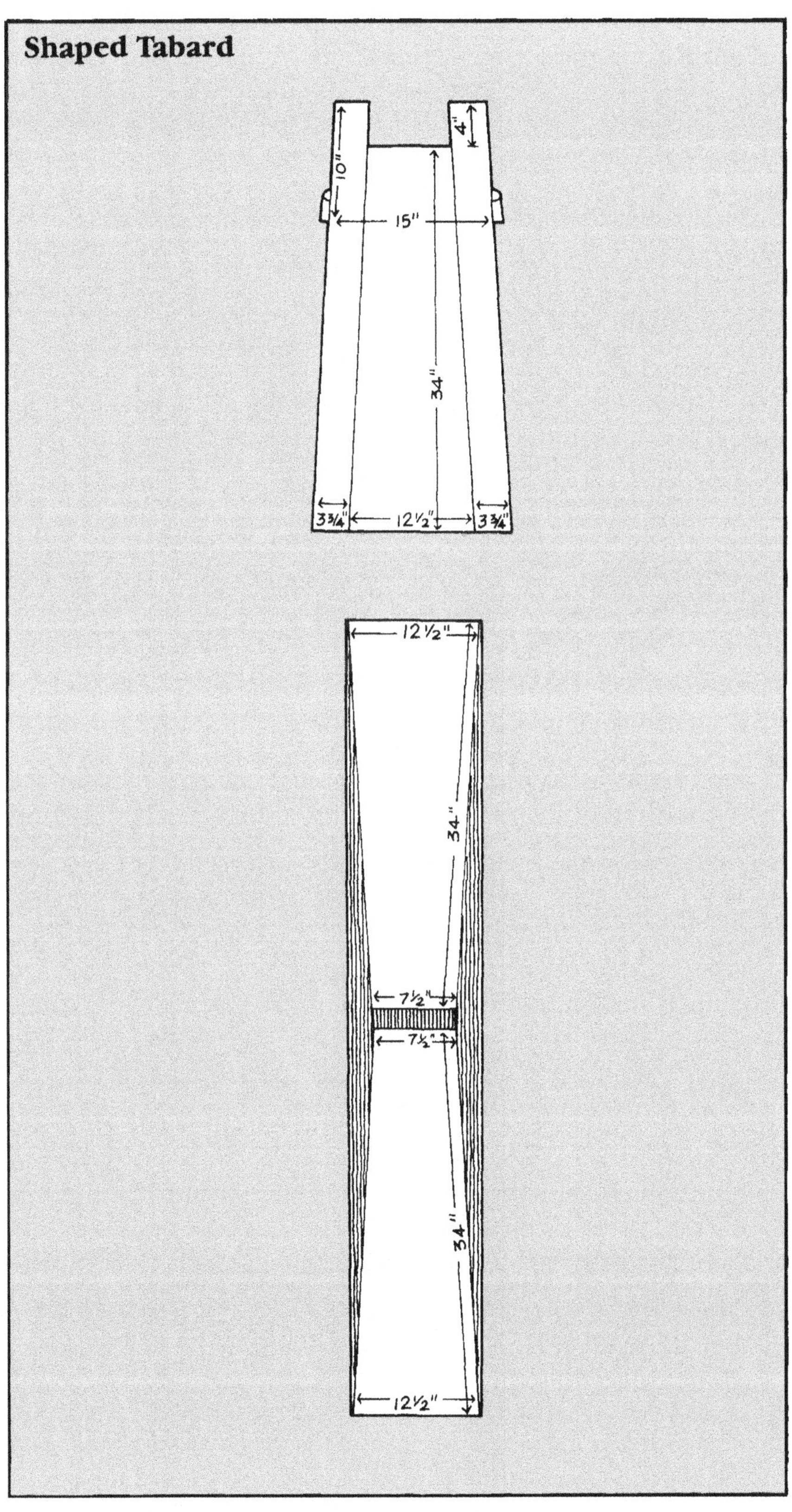
Shaped Tabard
10"
4"
15"
34"
3¾"
12½"
3¾"
12½"
34"
7½"
7½"
34"
12½"

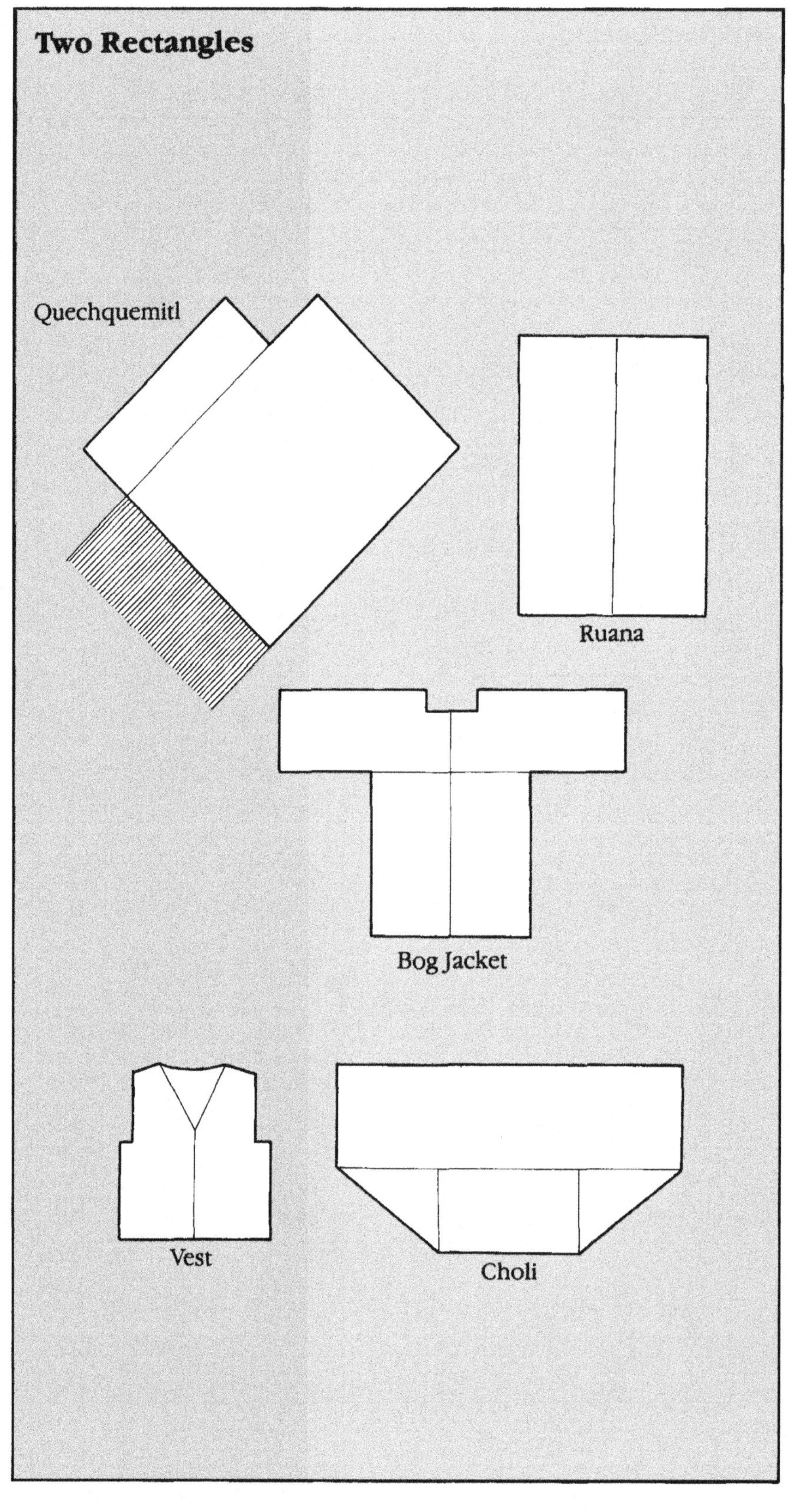
Two Rectangles
Quechquemitl
Ruana
Bog Jacket
Vest
Choli

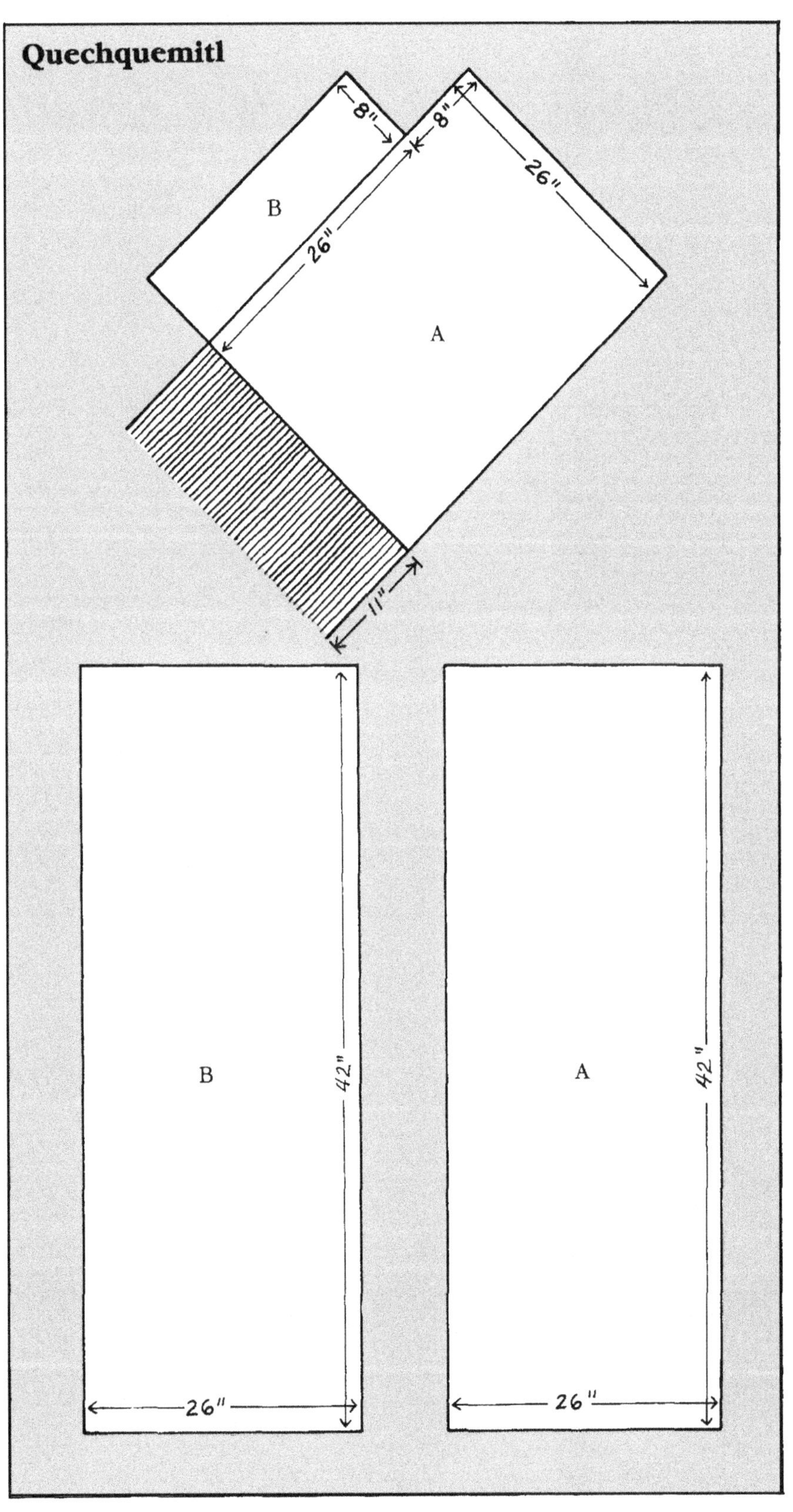
Quechquemitl
8"
8"
26"
B
26"
A
11"
B
42"
26"
A
42"
26"

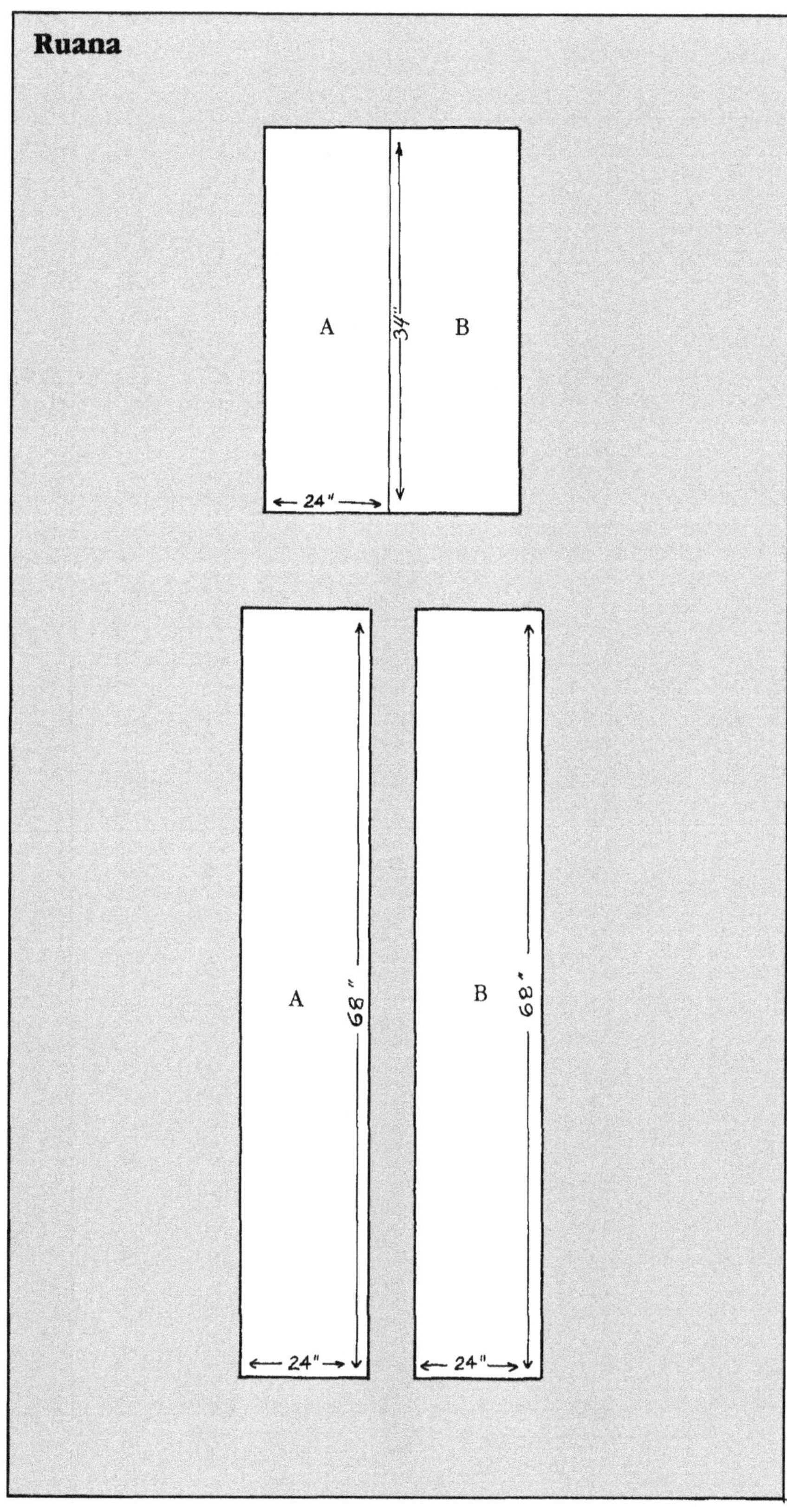
Ruana
A
34"
B
24"
A
68"
B
68"
24"
24"

Bog Jacket

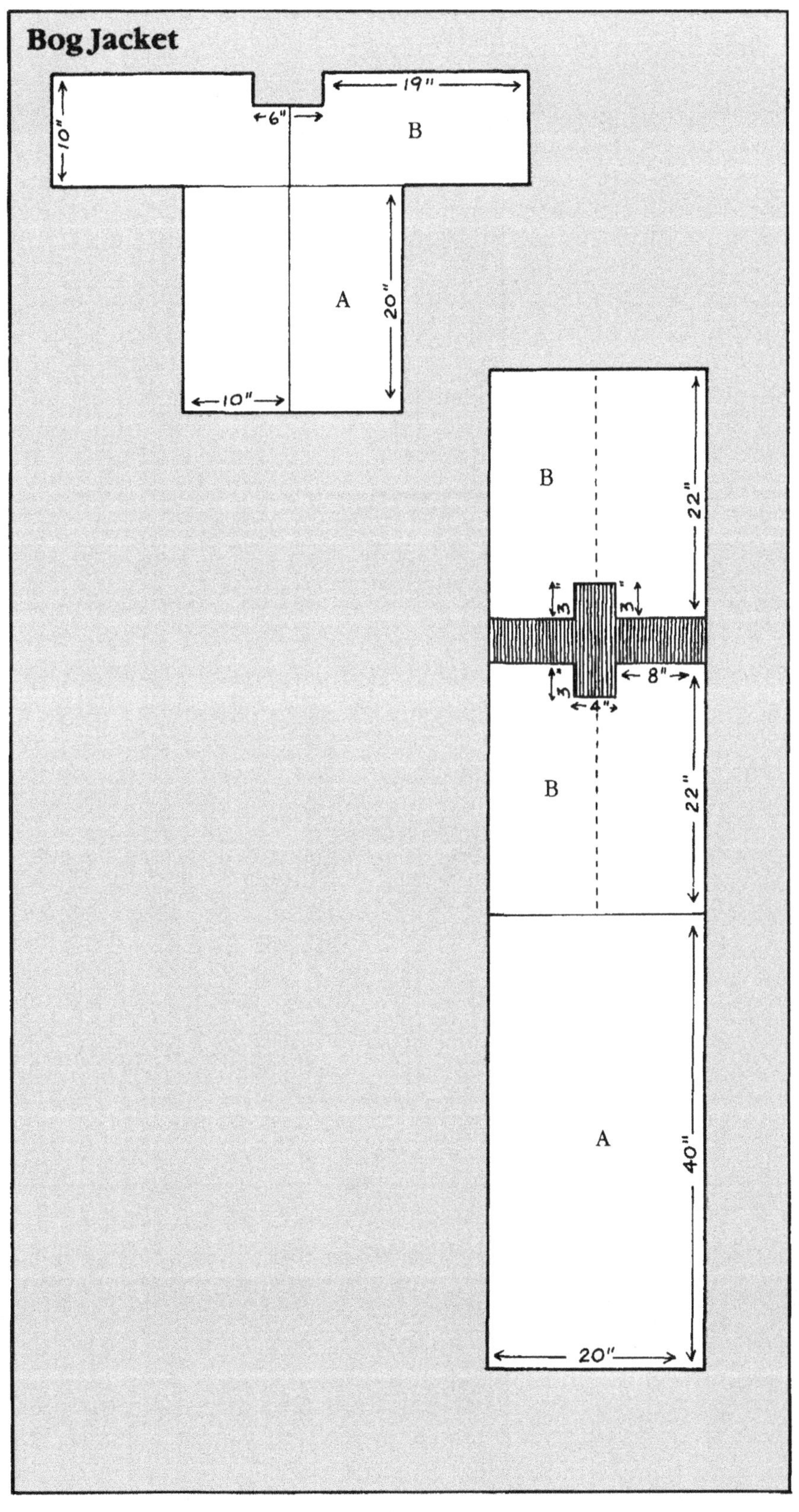

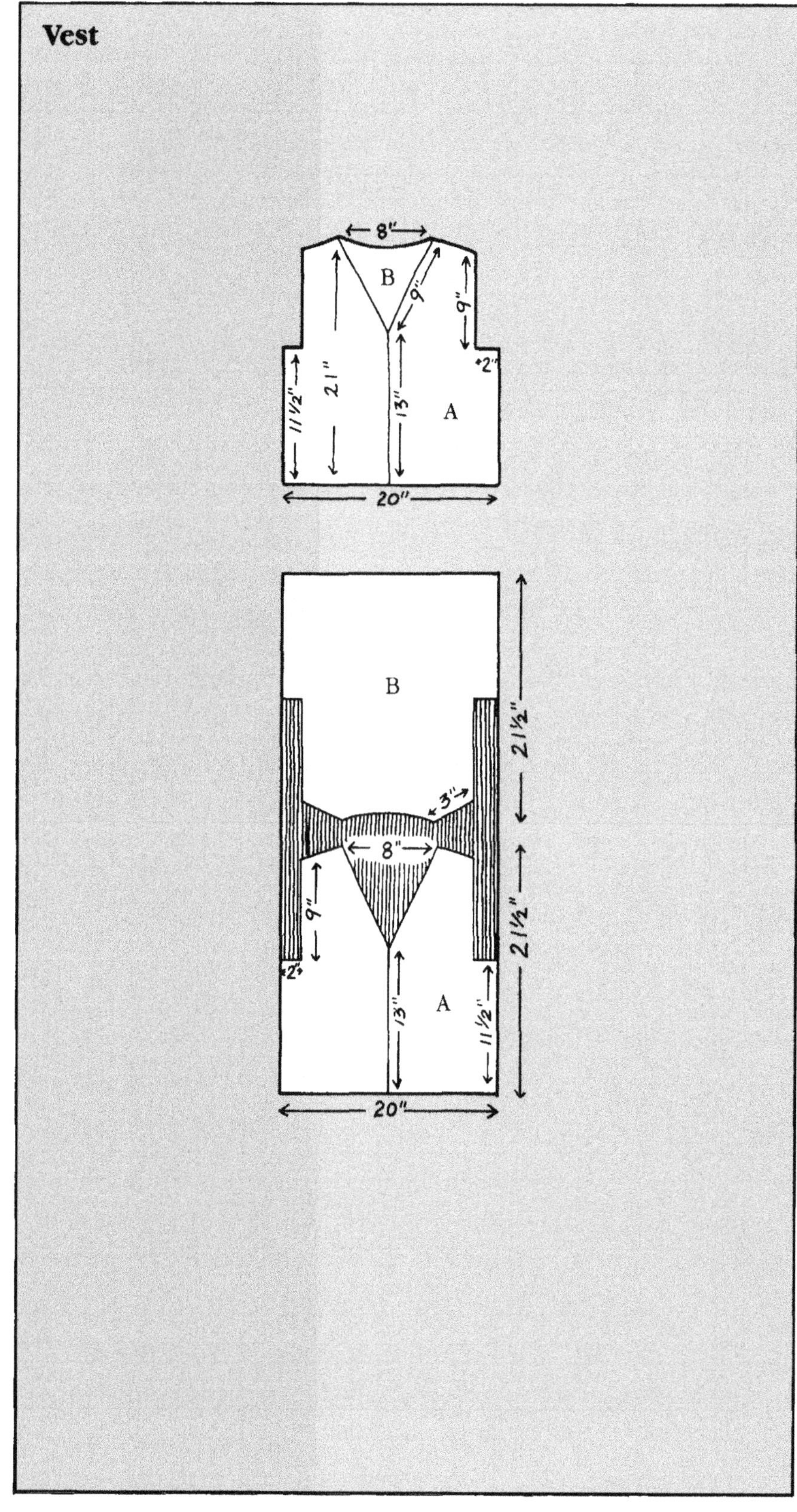
Vest
8"
B
9"
9"
2"
11½"
21"
13"
A
20"
B
3"
8"
21½"
9"
21½"
2"
13"
A
11½"
20"

Choli

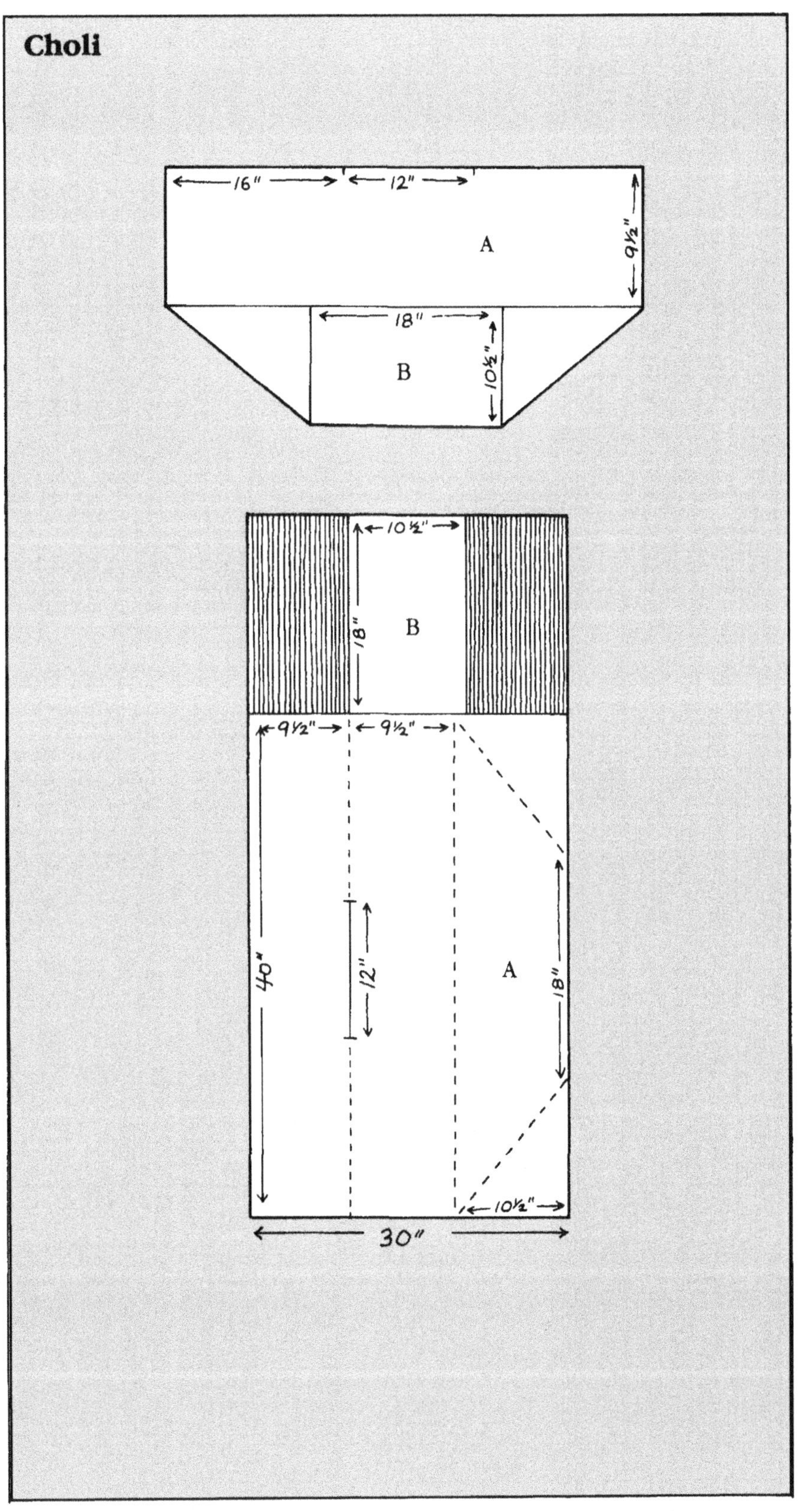

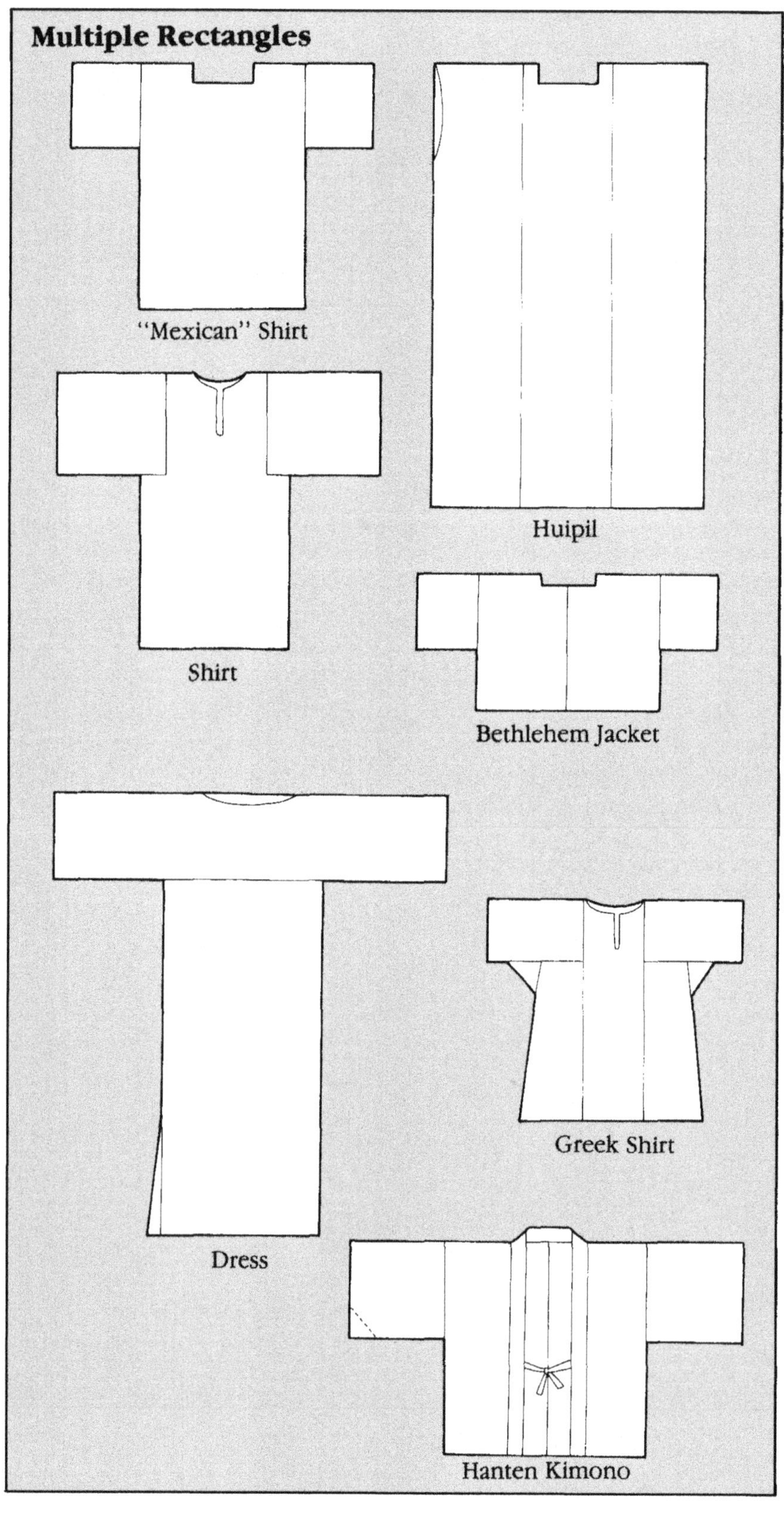
Multiple Rectangles
"Mexican" Shirt
Huipil
Shirt
Bethlehem Jacket
Greek Shirt
Dress
Hanten Kimono

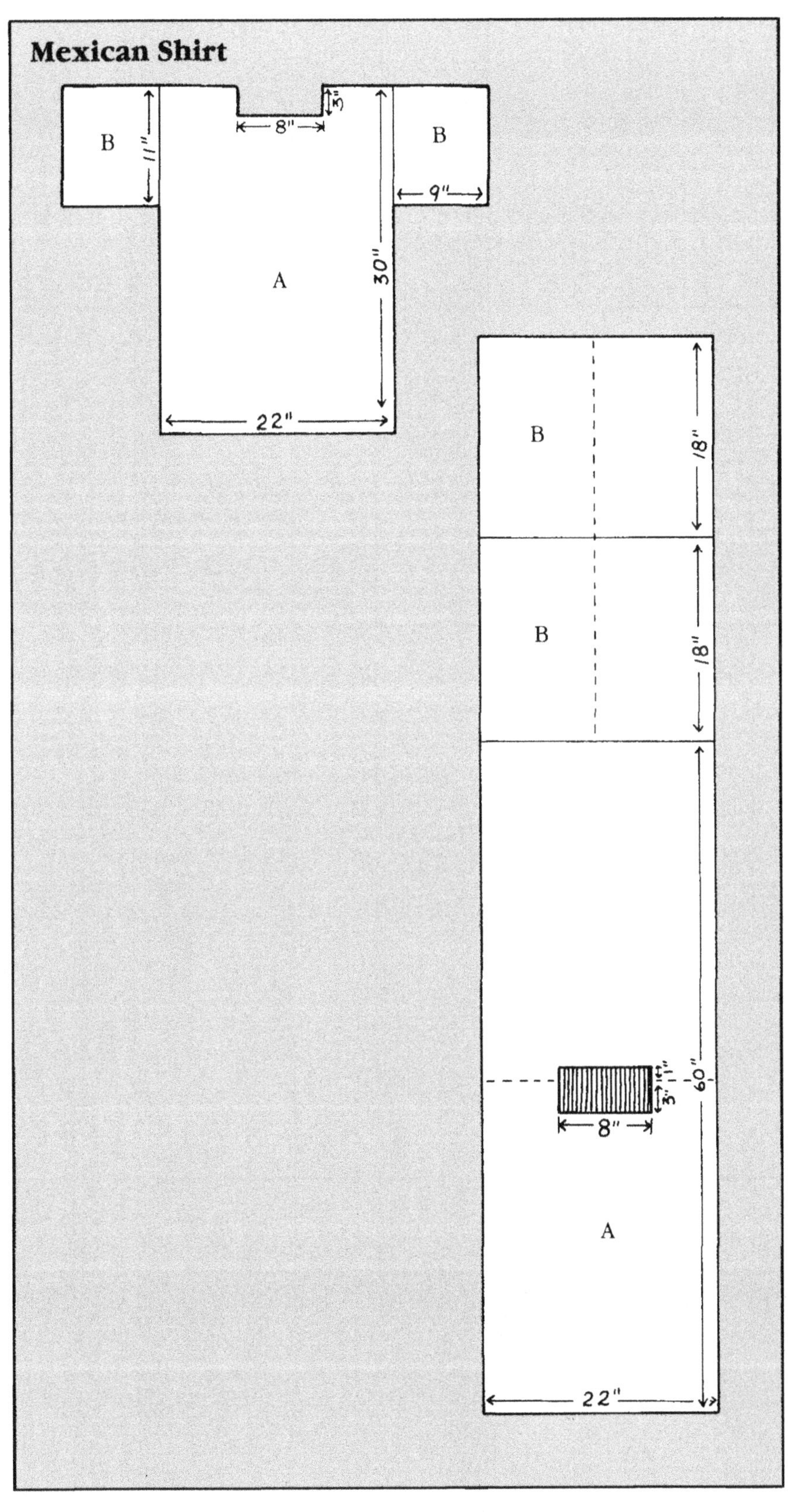
Mexican Shirt
B
11"
8"
3"
B
9"
A
30"
22"
B
18"
B
18"
60"
1"
3"
8"
A
22"

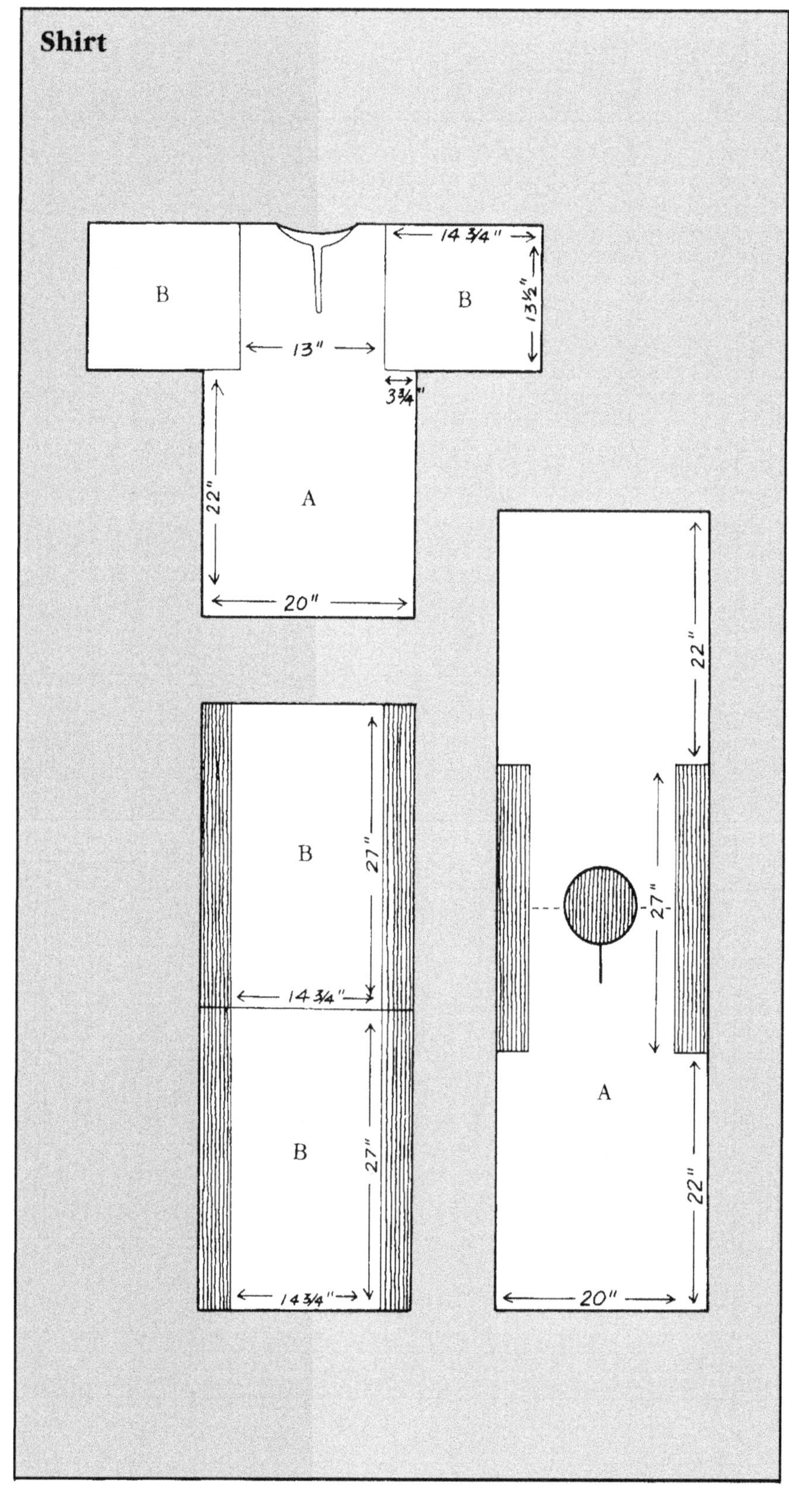
Shirt
B
B
A
14 3/4"
13½"
13"
3¾"
22"
20"
B
B
27"
27"
14 3/4"
14 3/4"
A
22"
27"
22"
20"

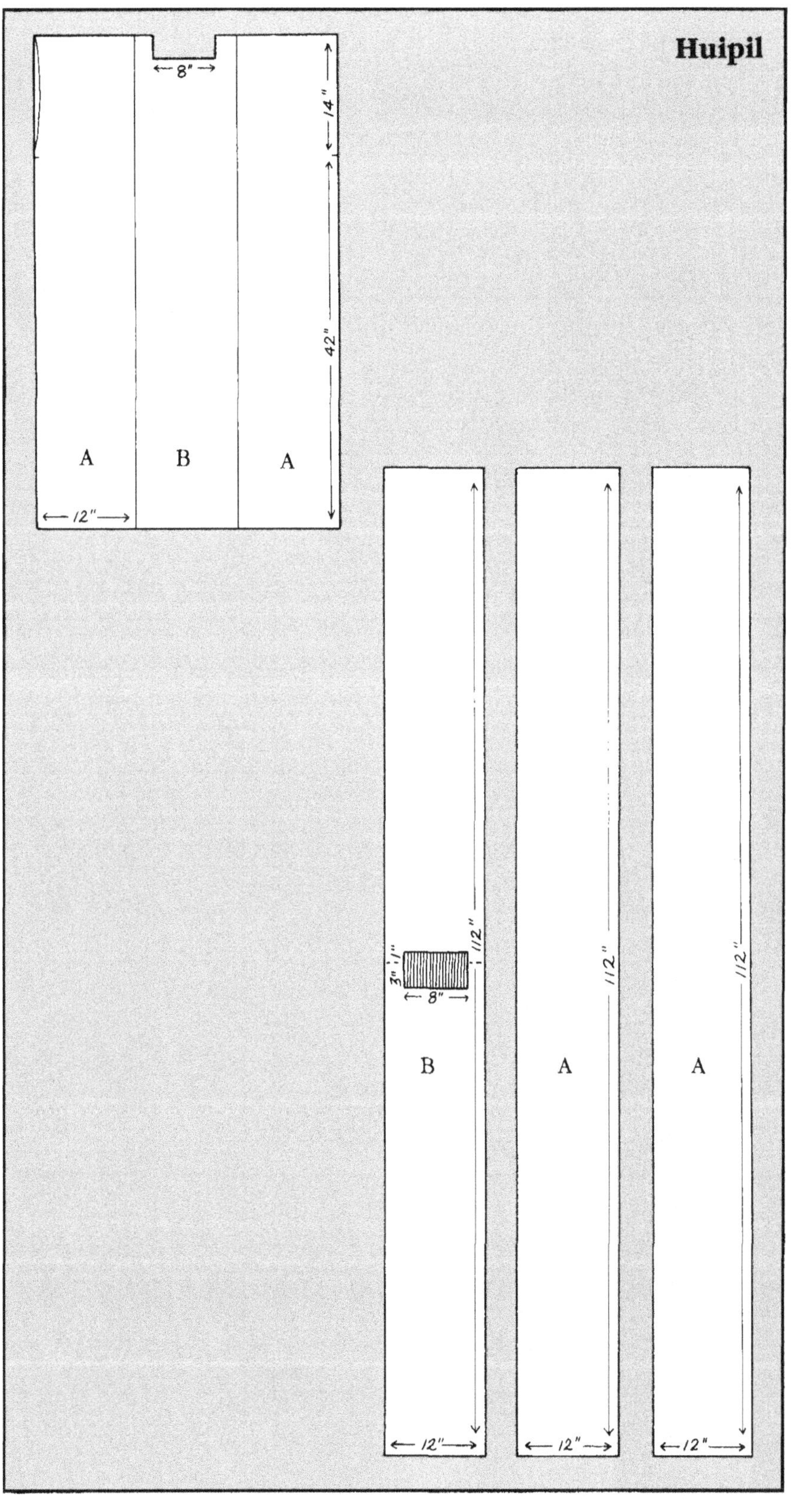
Huipil
8"
14"
42"
A
B
A
12"
3"
1"
8"
112"
112"
112"
B
A
A
12"
12"
12"

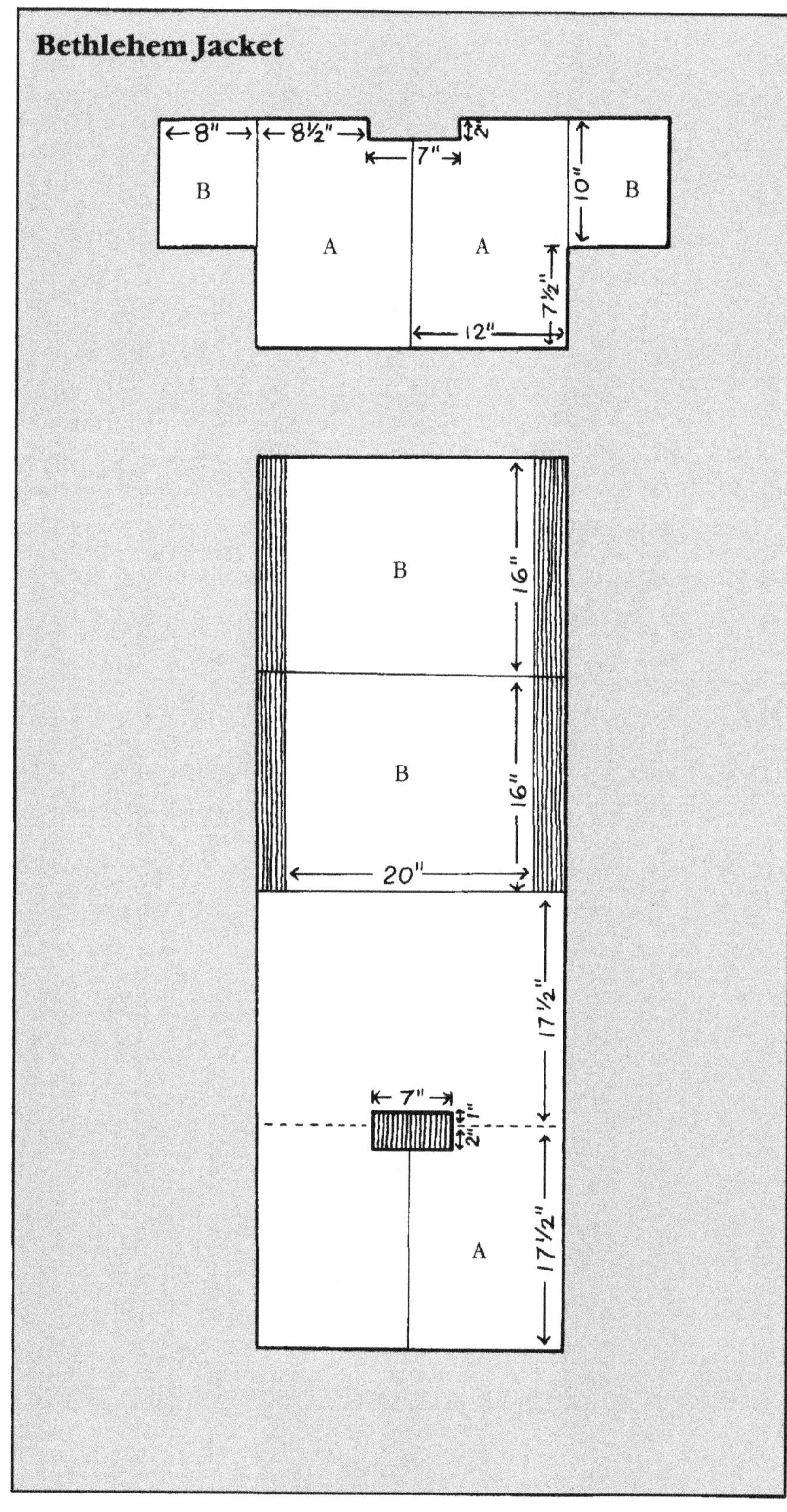
Bethlehem Jacket
8"
8½"
7"
2"
10"
B
B
A
A
7½"
12"
B
16"
B
16"
20"
17½"
7"
1"
2"
17½"
A

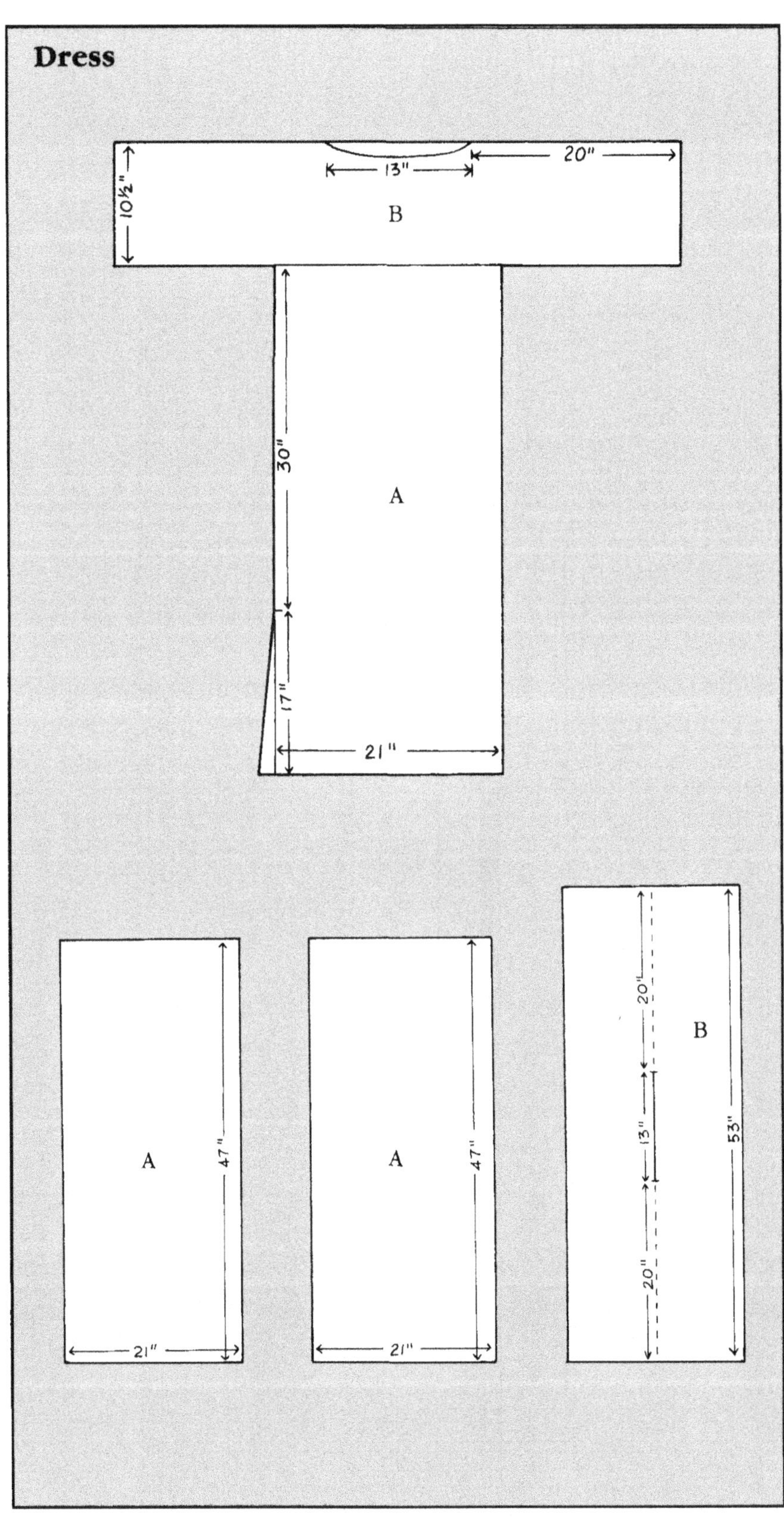
Dress
20"
13"
10½"
B
30"
A
17"
21"
A
47"
21"
A
47"
21"
20"
B
13"
53"
20"

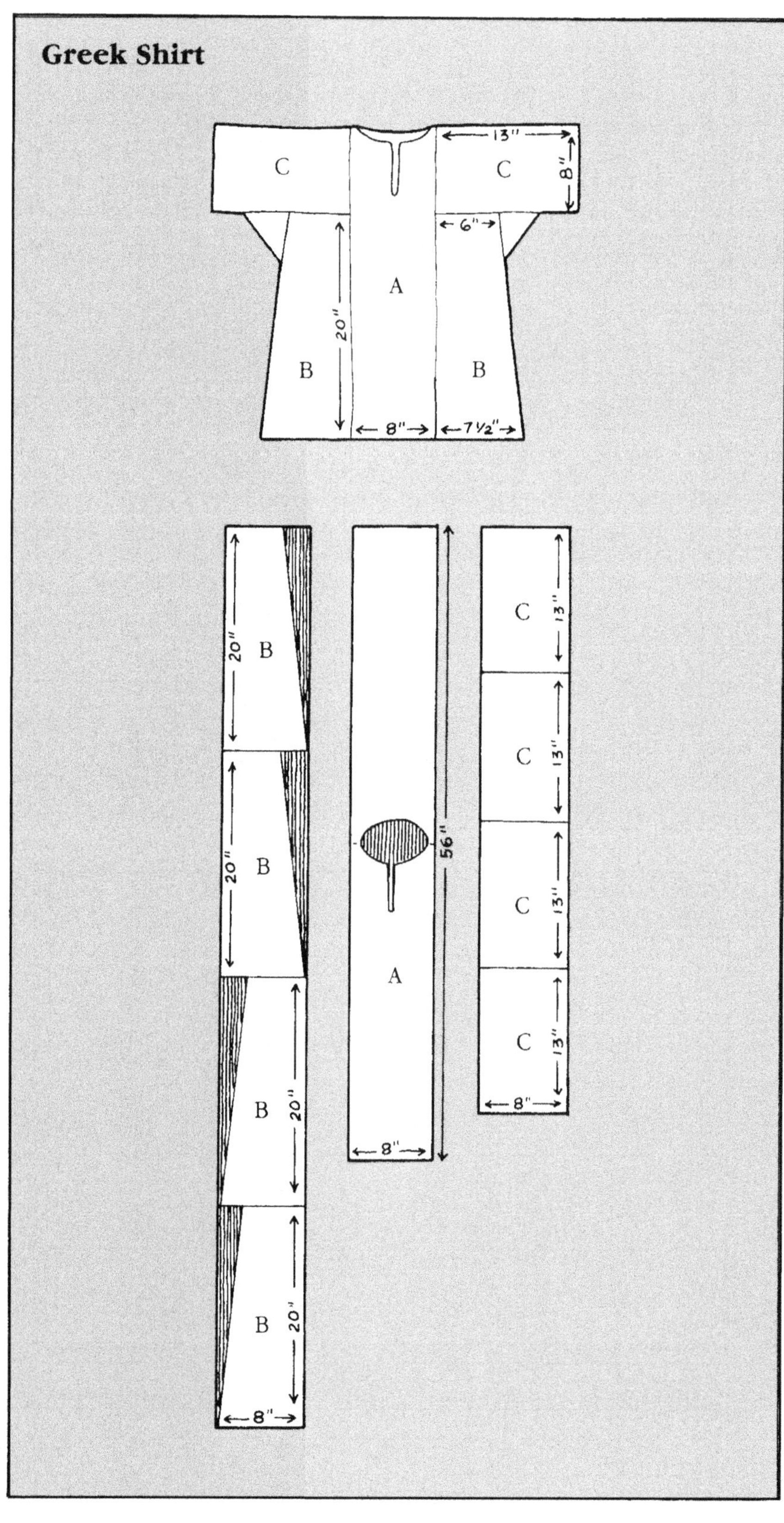
Greek Shirt
C
C
13"
8"
6"
A
20"
B
B
8"
7½"
20"
B
20"
B
B
20"
B
20"
8"
56"
A
8"
C
13"
C
13"
C
13"
C
13"
8"

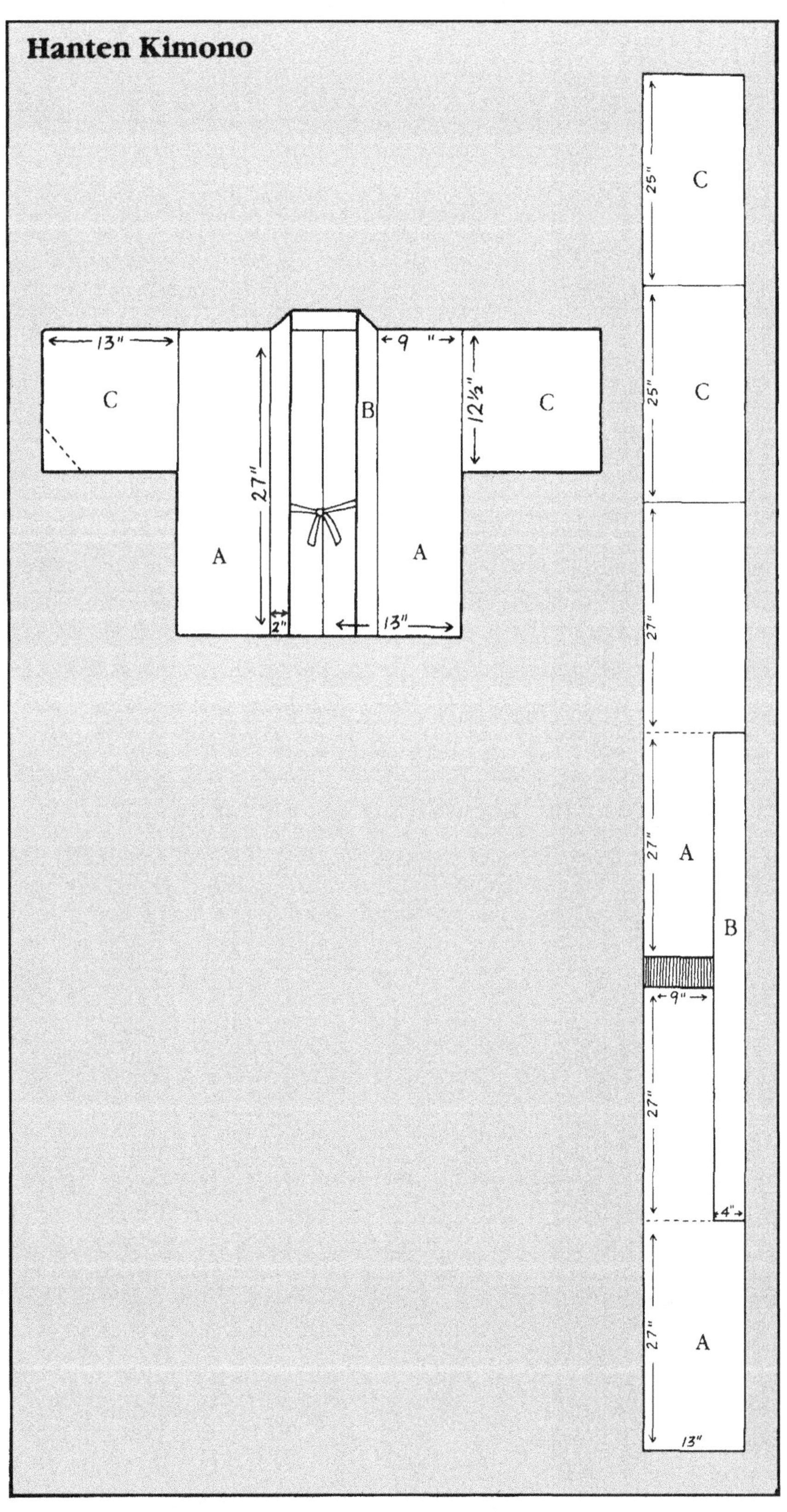
Hanten Kimono
13"
C
9"
12½"
C
B
27"
A
A
2"
13"
25"
C
25"
C
27"
27"
A
B
9"
27"
4"
27"
A
13"

"Everyone has a unique style waiting to be expressed"
Annette Hansen
Image Maker

"Women, even the strong and important ones, are timid about their clothes. People think there are rules for dressing they don't know about and there are no rules."

California designer

Chapter 2
The Type to Weave

We have reviewed the history of loom-shaped garments and related the shape of these to the widths of cloth that come from the loom. In order to create contemporary, wearable garments from handwoven rectangles and squares, it is necessary to do considerable planning and sampling. I have found that 20% of my time on a garment is spent at the loom with 80% spent on the following steps:

1. the history,
2. the type garment to weave,
3. the fit,
4. the edges and embellishment,
5. the fabric,
6. the pattern,
7. the fabric finishing,
8. the warp layout,
9. the record keeping.

These will not necessarily be done in this order, for you may be inspired by a wonderful yarn and start from the fabric; or perhaps a particular garment shape appeals to you, so that is your beginning point. No matter where you start, however, it is necessary to touch all nine steps to achieve a garment that is well-designed and comfortable, and fits you and your personality.

Clothing has had many functions through the centuries:

- to clothe (protect from the weather),
- to adorn (kings and ruling figures),
- to attract (low-cut gowns),
- to denote caste (social status),
- to classify people (nurses, policeman),
- to express moods (black for funerals, white for weddings in this culture),
- to impress (designer names on clothes),
- to pay tribute (cloth as payment for taxes),
- to pacify the Gods (witch doctor's clothing).

Our clothing is a self-created environment over which we have total control. We live, feel, act and die within clothing. The choices we make of style, fit, color and shape influence our physical bodies as well as our emotional, spiritual and intellectual selves.

Clothing is literally a costume and a subtle, complex communications system. Clothes tell people about you, who you are, the type of things you like and how you accept yourself—though you might not even be aware of it. If you walked into a room dressed exactly the way you are at this moment, what would you be communicating about yourself?

In one of the many image-building courses being done for the corporate world, Annette Hansen states that "in the first one-tenth of a second someone meets you, that person is deciding whether you are threatening or attractive, whether you are important enough to be with or not. In the next seven seconds, if you pass that first screening, your socio-economic level, educational level, success level and popularity are being estimated. This is particularly true in business."

Another authority states that if you have three salesmen competing for attention, the one who makes the best first impression has that little edge that's as "good as a mile". Attorneys have their clients dress for acquittal, for most lawyers agree that the way a person is dressed has great impact on a jury.

And in the media, the same importance of clothing emerges. As noted in *Time* magazine in 1982, "Clothes may make the man after all. At least a sweater may warm up his image. CBS anchorman Dan Rather, 50, who had struck some viewers as chilly after the avuncular Walter Cronkite, took to wearing a sleeveless, V-neck pullover on his newscasts some three months ago. Perhaps not so coincidentally, he has since reclaimed Cronkite's traditional top spot ahead of NBC and ABC. Rather is prepared to stay bundled up through the summer. 'If it takes wearing a sweater when its 112°,' he vows, 'we'll turn up the air conditioning!'." It was in May of 1982 that the Seattle Post Intelligencer noted in its "quote for the day": "You can tell how hot the weather is here. Last night Dan Rather was wearing a seersucker sweater."

Since clothes are indeed saying something important about you, you need to decide what it is you want to say.

You also need clothes that fit your lifestyle, draw attention to you in a positive way, clothes you can afford and clothes that make you feel good and reflect you. There should always be at least one thing about what you are wearing that is uniquely you. Most people are more than one personality type, and your clothes can and should reflect this. Don't be afraid of clothes, for there is no longer the problem of wearing the "wrong thing". Wear what makes you look and feel good.

"To be fashionable can be fun, but it can also be expensive."
Bernat Klein

Current clothing trends make it easier for those who weave and wear loom-shaped garments. You can have basic "uniforms" of pant suits, jeans or dresses, and add a second layer of clothing that is individually you. There are advantages to this approach to clothing. Fitting problems are minimized, for the second layer can hang more loosely, there is added warmth which helps ecologically, and it helps reduce the size of a wardrobe.

If you want to dress more effectively and with more style, it is necessary to understand the difference between fashion and style. Fashion defines the current trend or fad in clothing, while style is an individual type of behavior or dress. Style comes easily to few people and no one is born with it. If you want style, you must work to develop it. Style is unrelated to dress size and figure shape. To look good, you must feel good about yourself and be proud of your strong points. Decide to dress with style no matter what your size, for when you like yourself, you feel good; and when you feel good, you're beautiful. There's a popular catch-phrase that looking beautiful is 1/10th optical illusion and 9/10ths attitude.

There are some specific ways to dress more effectively. Analyze your own attitudes and preference for clothes. Take out of the closet that dress you bought three years ago and have never worn, and compare it to the outfit that you can always put on and feel wonderful wearing. List specifically what it is about each that you like and dislike as to color, fit, style, sleeves, length and so forth. Analyze your lifestyle and the type of clothes that will fit into it. Take a good look at your hair, body shape and coloring, for these may have changed since the last time you really looked at yourself. Fantasize a bit about how you would like to look. Use others as role models and determine what it is that they wear that causes you to be attracted to them. Seek advice from experts about what styles look good on you, ways to use make-up and what colors enhance your appearance. These are pieces of information that you can put together in your own way that will allow you to achieve the look you want.

There are styles that are slenderizing and you should utilize as many of these features as possible if that's the effect you want:

1. Vertical lines are the basis of a thin look, and narrow lines are even more effective than wide lines. A striped dress with a V-neck vest over it is very slimming, for there is a vertical on a vertical.
2. A straight waistband is slimming if it is not too tight and there are no bulges from underneath.
3. To look slim, it is best to avoid gathered, straight, circle or all-around pleated skirts. Pleats stitched down to hip line, gentle A-line, quarter-circle and wrap skirts all slenderize.

4. Well-fitted pants and pant suits that are not too tight yet aren't baggy, slenderize. An optical illusion of looking thin is achieved with a moderately wide leg that is straight or gently flared, for it keeps the hips from looking wider than the legs.
5. An illusion of slimness is given by layering blouses with a sweater or wearing a thin turtleneck under a sweater. Avoid bulky sweaters.
6. Jackets are very slimming, with an open jacket creating even more verticals.
7. Vests are ideal for a slender look, particularly those with V-necks and open down the front.
8. Full length coats and capes slenderize, but it is wise to avoid anything shapeless like a poncho.
9. One continuous color line, as in an A-line dress with interest focused near the face, is slenderizing.

Some further guides for improving your appearance

If you are TALL: DO

a. Use horizontal lines such as wide belts and circular trim.
b. Wear hip-length or three-quarter length jackets.
c. Mix-match contrasting colors.
d. Wear soft, rounded shoulders, dolman or raglan sleeves.
e. Wear heavy, bulky fabrics and large prints.
f. Wear box-pleated and full-gored skirts.
g. Look for large accessories—striking jewelry, big handbags.

If you are TALL: DON'T

a. Add to it with vertical lines, narrow belts.
b. Wear medium length or short jackets.
c. Wear narrow all-round pleated skirts.
d. Let exaggerated shoulders make you T-shaped.
e. Buy dresses with tightly fitted full-length sleeves.
f. Wear small-scaled accessories.

If you are SHORT: DO

a. Use vertical lines, princess styles, etc.
b. Go for boleros and short jackets.
c. Stay with small collars, round and short V-necklines.
d. Use self-belts or no belts.
e. Make sure your skirts are A-line or straight.
f. Wear soft fabrics.

If you are SHORT: DON'T

a. Wear garments with horizontal lines.
b. Cut yourself off with long jackets or figure-dividing lines.
c. Wear wide, contrasting belts or cummerbunds.
d. Lose yourself behind massive trimming like large belt buckles.
e. Wear large plaid and prints.
f. Wear box-pleated skirts.

If you are STOUT: DO

a. Cut the width with vertical lines (like buttons down the front).
b. Go for simple, uncluttered styles.
c. Wear dull-finished fabrics of medium weight.
d. Wear set-in sleeves, V-necklines.
e. Wear jackets not longer than 2″ below hipbone.
f. Wear narrow self belts or beltless styles.

If you are STOUT: DON'T

a. Wear anything with pronounced horizontal lines.
b. Wear round necks and collars.
c. Wear clinging or heavy fabrics.
d. Wear pleated or full skirts.
e. Wear pulled, droopy, dolman or tightly-fitted sleeves.
f. Add bulk with very long or very short jackets.
g. Cut yourself in two with wide or contrasting belts.

If you are THIN: DO

a. Look for horizontal and curved lines.
b. Wear two- or three-piece ensembles.
c. Try wearing bulky fabrics.
d. Wear semi-flare, pleated or A-line skirts.
e. Wear soft, rounded shoulders and necklines.

If you are THIN: DON'T

a. Let vertical line slice your width.
b. Accentuate it with tight-fitting clothes.

c. Wear clinging fabrics.
d. Expose bony areas, like shoulderbones, wrists, knees.
e. Wear sleeveless clothes, or tubes or strapless dresses.

Don't be inhibited by these "rules", but use them as guides in developing your own style and appearance. Analyze and experiment with different ideas and styles, and then decide what works for you.

As you plan your garment there are questions to ask yourself so that you can "program for success rather than program for failure." How much time do you have to give to this garment? If it is only a few hours a week, it might be wise to design a stole or one-piece huipil so that you can have it done in a reasonable length of time. Are you doing a one-of-a-kind garment or several pieces? If you need four vests for an upcoming fashion show, you might want to do a mixed warp or create patterns by treadling, while on a one-of-a-kind vest you might use tapestry or more complex techniques as the design focus.

"The whole designing process, as far as I am concerned, must start with the finished garment and has to work its way backwards."
Bernat Klein

Do you like to weave yardage or do finger manipulated techniques? Why design a coat with rya knots if tying them bores you? Focus on the fabric so once the loom is warped, you can enjoy the rhythm of the weaving. How much can you spend on this garment? If you are on a limited budget or are feeling guilty about all those yarns on the shelf, limit yourself. Instead of an all-silk top, what about combining silk with cotton in the warp or just doing the surface embellishment in silk? Decide that you will not buy one ounce of yarn, but will design a garment that uses only yarns on hand. What is your loom width? Usually any size garment can be created from assembling narrower pieces, but in some designs width can be a factor. What is the function of this garment? A coat to be worn to the store might differ greatly in design from one for special occasions. Is there a special purpose for this garment? Perhaps you just took a double weave workshop and need to practice those techniques, so you might design a double woven garment. If you have a surplus of handspun yarns, design something that is appropriate for those materials.

Some concepts that might help you in the designing of stylish loom-shaped garments: consider clothing as a statement of movement, with fringe on a sleeve or a slit on the side of a coat or skirt. Consider clothing as a special environment for jewelry, or consider the human body as an armature for a wonderful hanging and that hanging is your garment. Create a "wall banner, body banner" similar to the early Japanese kimonos where the robe was displayed on the wall when it was not worn. Celebrate life by dressing as though every day is an occasion. Put something of magic into your clothes.

To design, you must do some sketching and it doesn't matter if you can't draw. Sit down, close your eyes and imagine the garment you want. Keep your design simple and take some time to consider exactly what you want. Some of my pieces have been thought about as long as three years before they were woven. You must visualize what you want and get it down clearly on paper.

"It is time for individuals to wear designs that express themselves . . . comfort and individuality of clothing is of basic importance."
Geoffrey Beene

Decide the type of garment you want: shirt, jacket, dress, vest. Once the basic type of garment is determined, do a series of drawings on individual sheets of paper of the possible design choices. If you are doing a shirt, will there be a collar or no collar, sleeves that are full, narrow, long, short, cuffed, set-in, and what shape might neckline be? Do you want a hood? Should the body of the piece be to the waist or below the hip-line, and will it be full, fitted, flared or gathered?

Tape up these drawings and look at them for several days and start taking down the ones that you like the least. The ones that stay up the longest are probably the ones you will want to weave. This is designing by comparison, and it is difficult to do mentally. You need to look at your various ideas and then select one. Once the shape of the shirt is decided, draw a series of this shape on one piece of paper and do various design elements on each one.

Making a choice is sometimes the most difficult step, but keep all those other ideas. Start a notebook or file of clothing design ideas and include sketches, pull-sheets, historical clothing and photographs of garments. This type of resource will help develop your designing skills.

Shirt Ideas

Caucasus
Ukraine
Mexico
Panama
Egyptian Coptic
Sudan
Caucasus
Romanian
Russia
England
Spain
Ukraine

Shirt Ideas

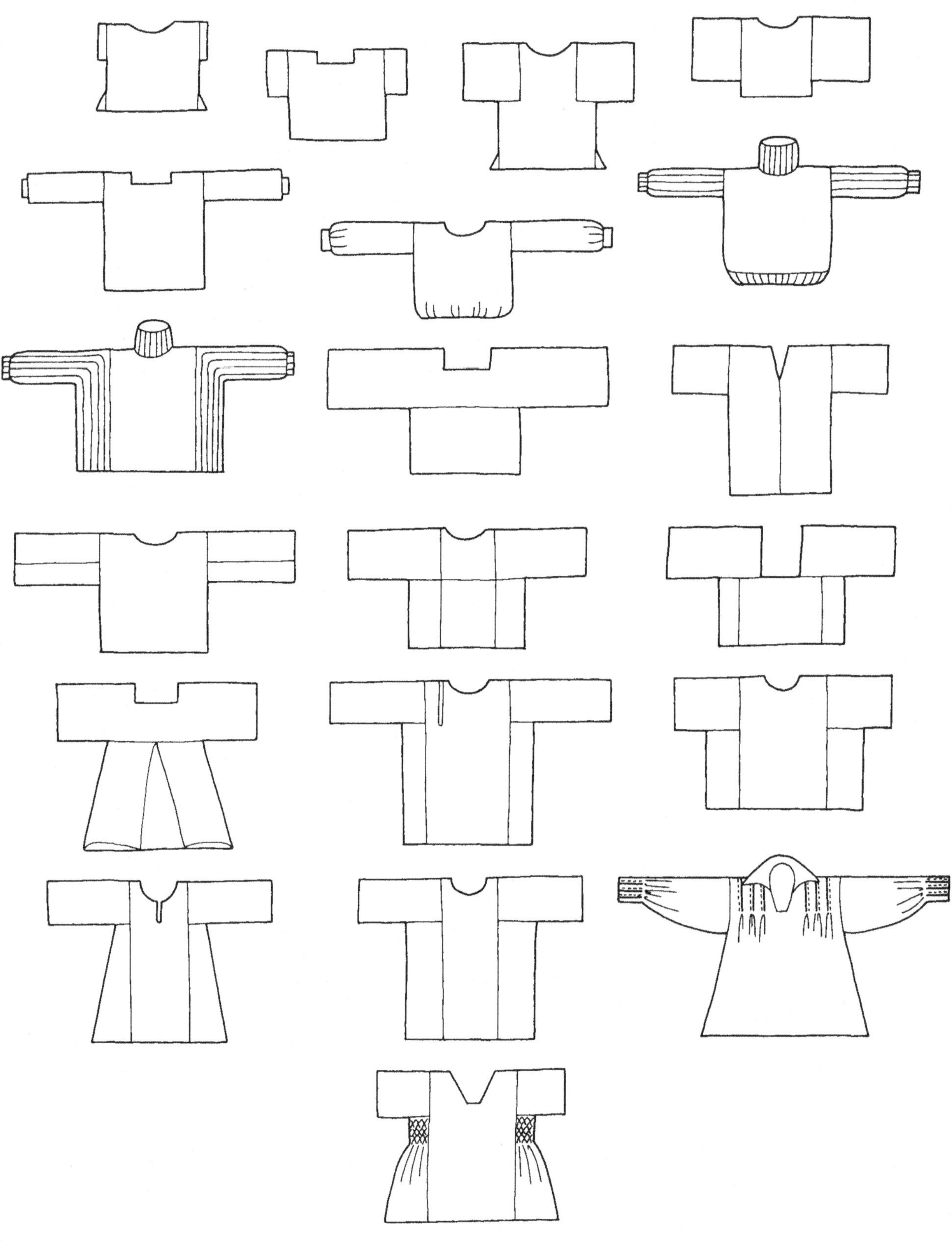

Design Elements on One Shirt Shape

Writer Joan Mills talks about her mid-life insights:
"I'd gone through life believing in the strength and competence of others, never in my own. Now, dazzled, I discovered that my capacities were real. It was like finding a fortune in the lining of an old coat."

"It occurred to me when I was 13 and wearing white gloves and Mary Janes and going to dancing school, that no one should have to dance backward all their lives."

Jill Ruckelshaus

Chapter 3
The Fit

The human body is a curved, sculptural form and with tailored clothes, the fabric is cut to shape, darts formed and curves sewn to allow the material to follow the contours of the body. In loom-shaped clothing, rectangular pieces of fabric form the garment and fitting problems may arise. Some of these are inherent in this type of clothing construction, but there are solutions and techniques that can be utilized.

Drape

The drape of garments is changed by the sizes and shapes of openings, of fabric joins, and the type of fibers and weave structures used. When a rectilinear fabric is draped over a sloping shoulder, vertical folds occur in the fabric. These will vary according to the degree of shoulder slope. The poncho is one of the simplest garments that has a slit-type neckline. When worn with the neck slit oriented vertically, the grain of the fabric is displaced by the neck and the shoulder slope, resulting in drape at the base of the neck slit in both front and back. If the slit is worn sideways, the drape falls from top of the arms.

Drape will also be affected by a front opening, as in a ruana, or underarm seams, as in an aba. Through observation and experience you can plan the drape into the design of a garment so that it works for your body shape and fabric weight.

Drape of Garments

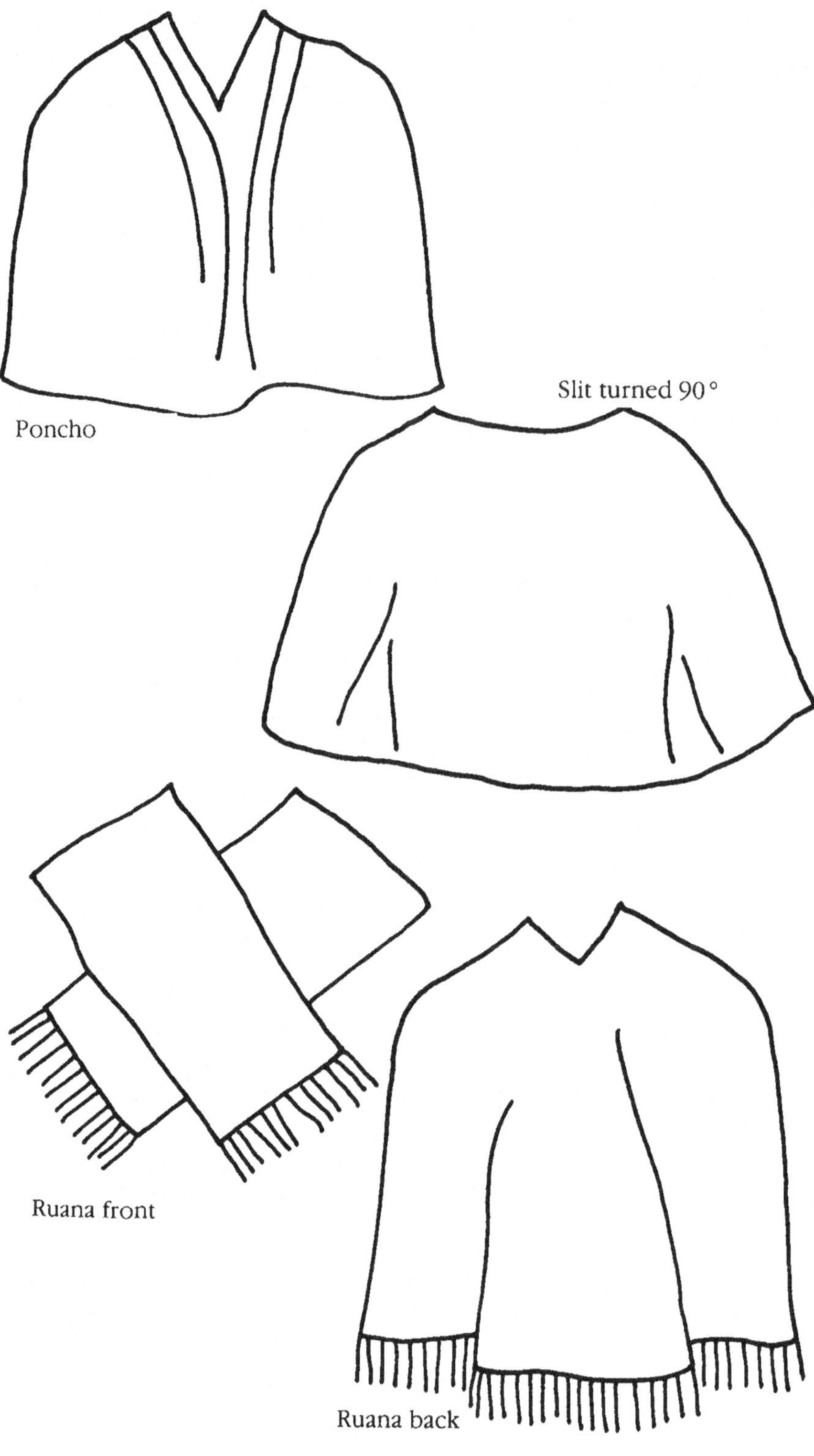

Shoulder slope and "wings"

If a garment is the same width as the shoulders, the slant of the shoulders will cause the fabric to form "wings" at the shoulder edge. In order to avoid this:

1. Make the garment wide enough so that a type of sleeve is formed when the arm is down.
2. Add a crocheted, knitted or woven band to extend the width of the garment beyond the shoulder edge.
3. Design the body piece so that it is an inch or so narrower than the shoulders.
4. If the fabric is lightweight, dart or fold over the extra fabric to create the necessary slope. This can be tacked down or embellished as a design feature.
5. Shape the necessary slope on the loom by weaving the garment in two pieces with a shoulder join. Hemstitch the weft edges (or secure them in some other way), put in about 12″ of filler yarn and when off the loom, cut the unwoven warps between the two pieces. Join the front and back pieces using pairs of warps and tying square knots, then thread the warp ends back into the fabric.

Shoulder Slope and "Wings"

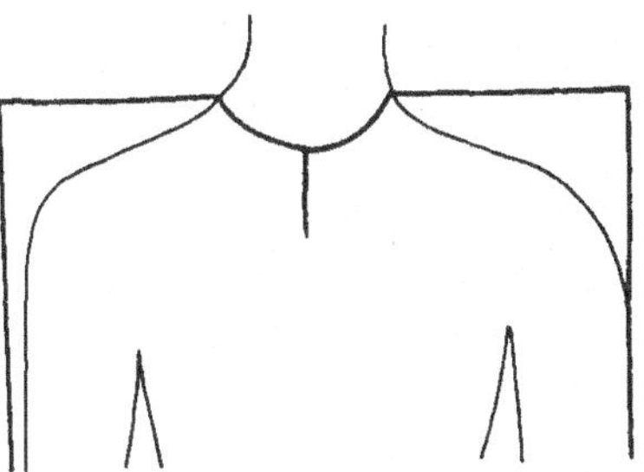

Shoulder Slope Shaping

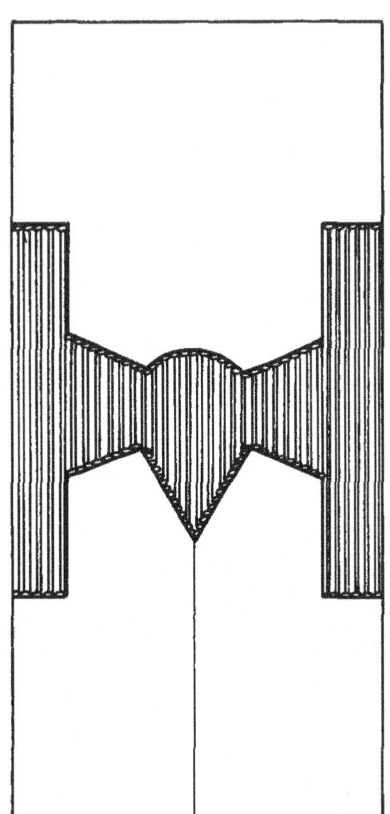

Basic Sleeve Shapes

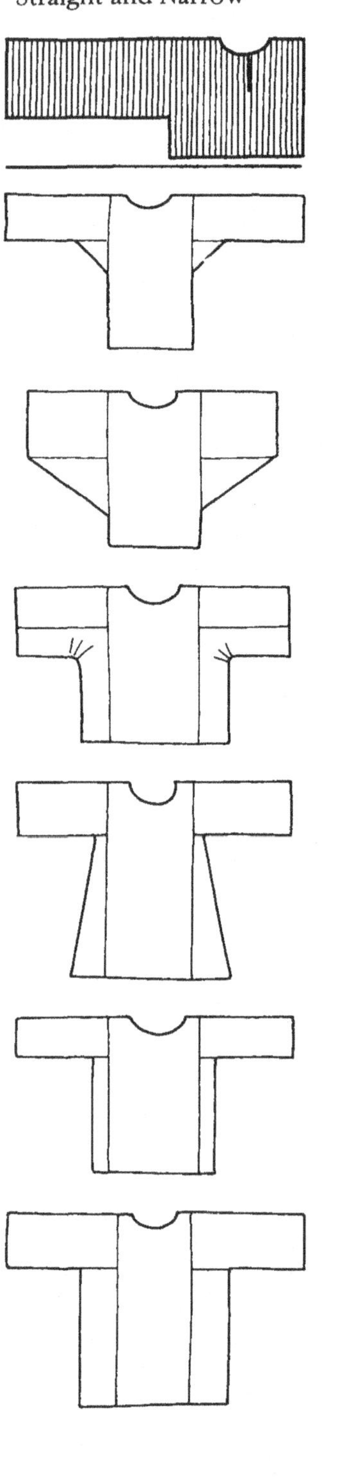

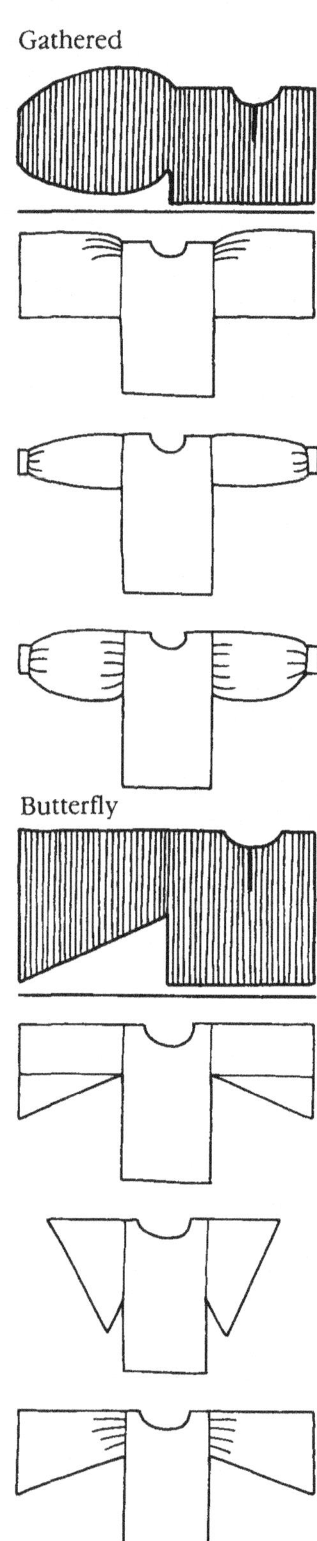

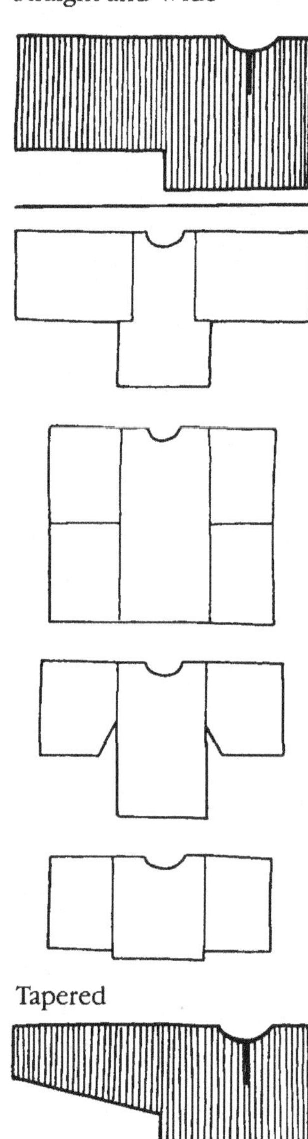

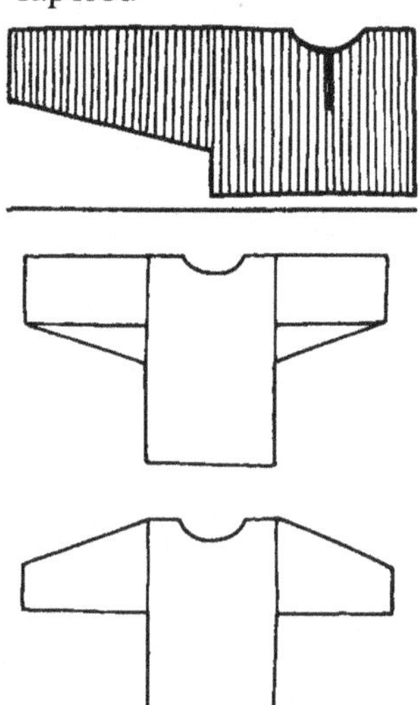

Sleeves

The basic sleeve shapes, according to Bennett and O'Connor, are straight and narrow, straight and full, tapered butterfly and puffed. The minimum circumference for a rectangle sleeve is 18″, with the average 20″ to 24″. This amount of fullness on a long sleeve is cumbersome at the wrist, yet necessary for ease of movement at the armhole. Reed and Buley suggest the following ways to reduce fullness at the wrist:

1. Turn back part of the sleeve to make a ¾ length, as 20″ at this part of the arm is not awkward.
2. Overlap the extra fullness at the wrist and add a button and loop.
3. Smock, tuck or pleat in fullness with or without a cuff.
4. Gather in the extra fullness with elastic or a draw-string. Plan a row of leno and add a ribbon for a draw-string. Weave in a narrow piece of elastic several inches wider than the sleeve and when the fabric is off the loom, draw up the elastic to fit and secure it.
5. Weave a shorter sleeve and weave, knit or crochet a long, tapered cuff.
6. Create a tapered sleeve by knitting or crocheting. Make a muslin pattern of a sleeve that fits you and then knit or crochet that shape by frequently laying your work on the muslin and increasing the knitting or crocheting as needed. Block to final shape when it is completed.

Reducing Fullness at Wrist

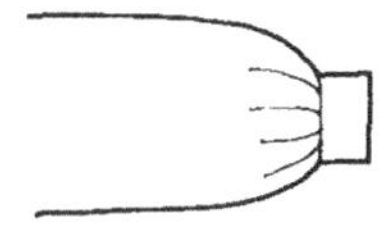

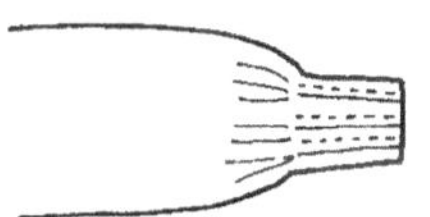

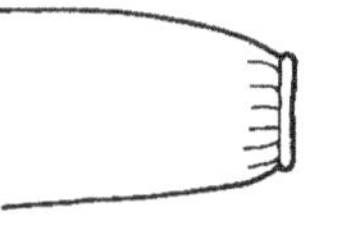

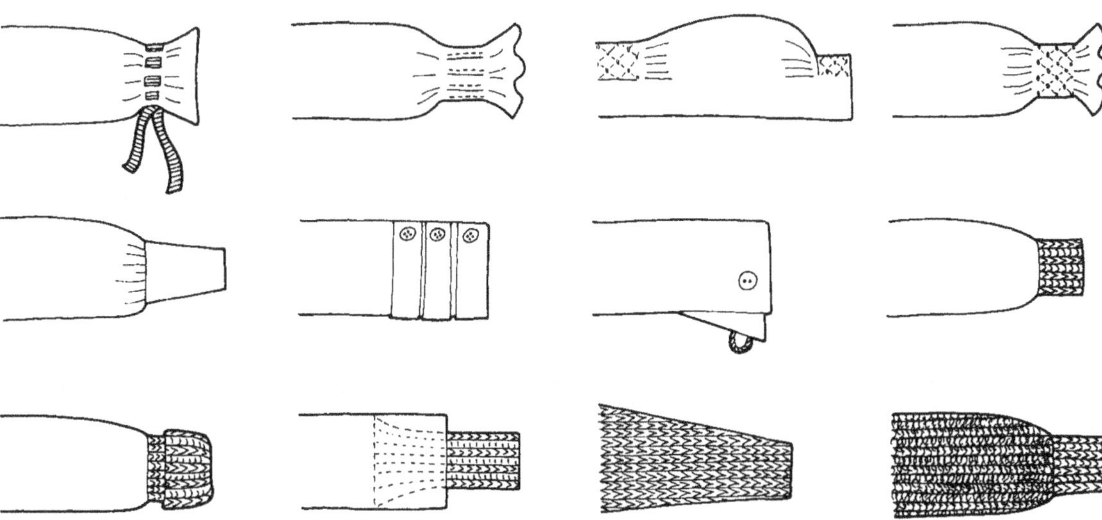

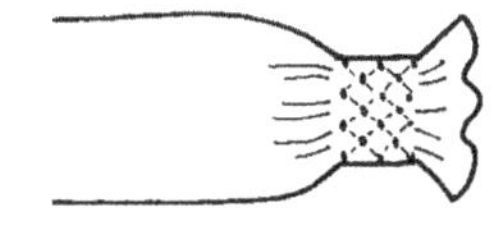

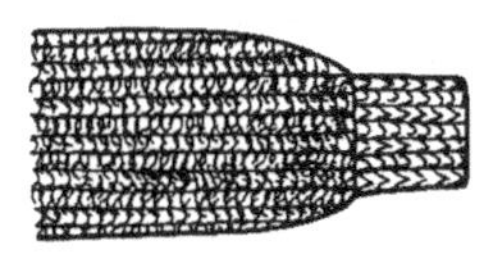

The additional fabric at the armhole created by a rectangular sleeve can be minimized if the sleeve is attached to the body piece beyond the shoulder line or as a set-in sleeve coming in from the shoulder edge.

A rectangular sleeve hangs at a diagonal when the arm is down, and one ways to avoid this is to narrow the sleeve at the wrist in one of the above ways. Also, a sleeve unit does not have to be joined under the arm. Consider a front or back join that is embellished as a design focus.

A Medieval-type sleeve can be achieved by weaving stripes on the sleeve unit and then stitching them into tucks at the top of the sleeve and at the wrist with the middle section left open.

Attaching Sleeve to Body of Garment

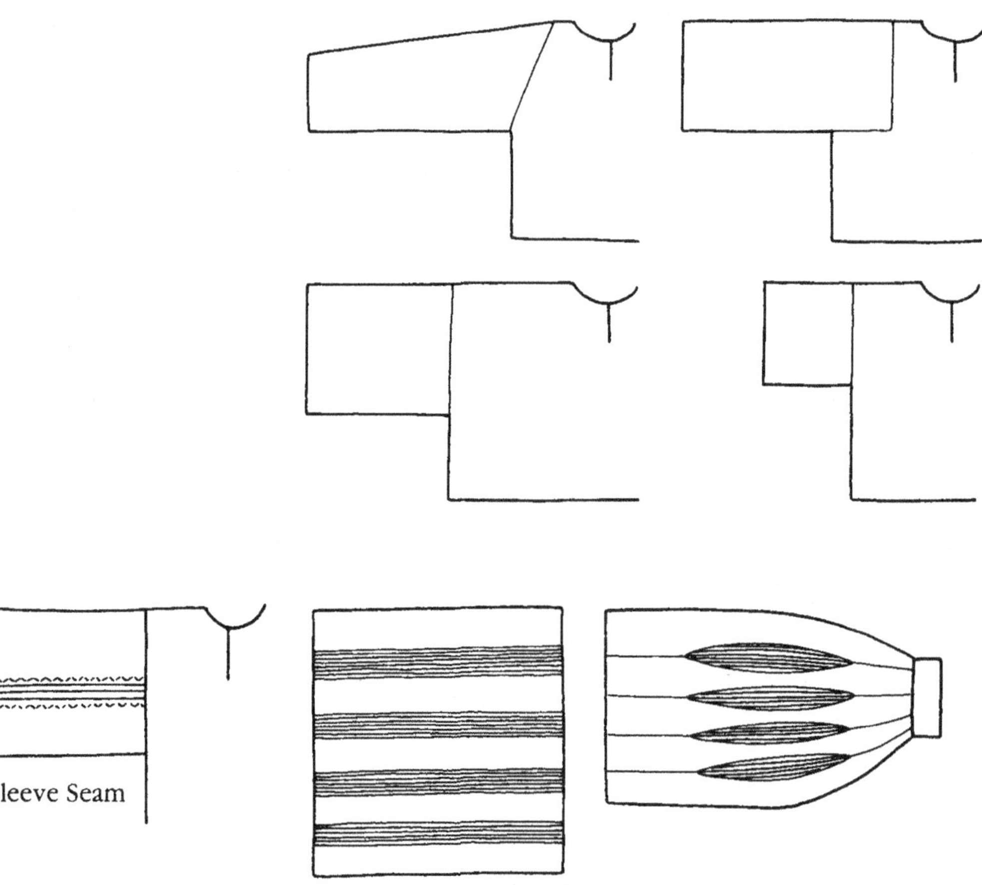

Medieval Type Sleeve

If you want a narrower sleeve, a gusset can be used to allow additional ease of movement. A gusset is a square of fabric generally 4″ × 4″ that is folded diagonally so it can stretch two ways. The use of the gusset reduces bulk under the arm, and the bias allows the sleeve to hang better. Gussets can be woven on cardboard, knitted or crocheted. It is simple to hand-sew a gusset in place that has four finished edges, since no seams are required. Each finished edge can be hand-whipped to the selvedge of the garment and sleeve. One rectangle can be folded to form a sleeve and a gusset as used on the Japanese Aino kimonos and jallabas of the Middle East.

The area under the arm can also be left open for freedom of movement, as found on the Japanese kimonos and some garments from Africa.

Gusset

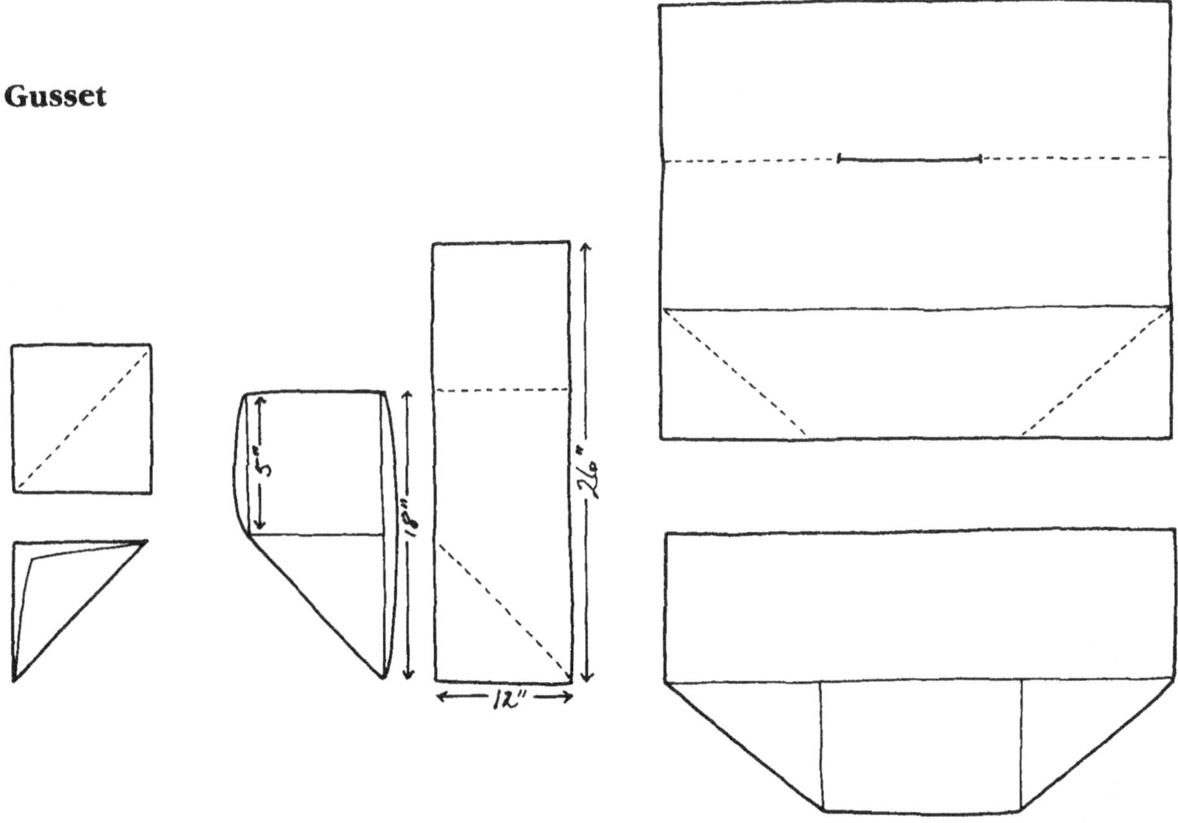

Accommodating Hip Width

Body circumference and hip/bust differences

Loom-shaped garments look best if they hang fairly loosely around the body, but this can be difficult to achieve if the hips and bust are quite different measurements. If the width of the rectangle fits one part of the body it may not fit other parts well. Some solutions to this problem are:

1. Design garments that end at the waistline with the width of the fabric accommodating the bust. This length is very flattering on most figures, for it focuses on the face rather than the hipline.
2. Weave the garment full enough so that it hangs from the shoulder like a caftan with the fabric width wide enough to fit both the bust and hips.
3. Weave the garment full enough to fit the hips and lightly belt it in at the waistline to create some shaping. This is satisfactory only with lightweight fabric and fairly slender figure types.
4. Weave an A-line shaped garment. This line is attractive on most every figure.
5. Use tucks or pleats at the shoulder area to narrow the shoulder width. This retains the fabric width for the lower part of the body.
6. Weave the bodice to fit and attach a wider skirt that gathers lightly to it. The gathers can be placed to the back of the garment to give a smooth line in front.
7. Add crocheted or knitted gores for additional hip width.
8. Vent or leave the sides open for extra ease.
9. Add woven, knitted or crocheted side panels.
10. Weave rectangles that are shaped for flared side inserts.

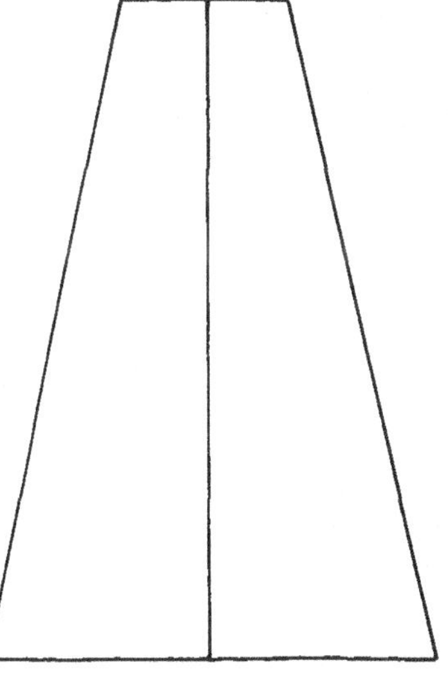

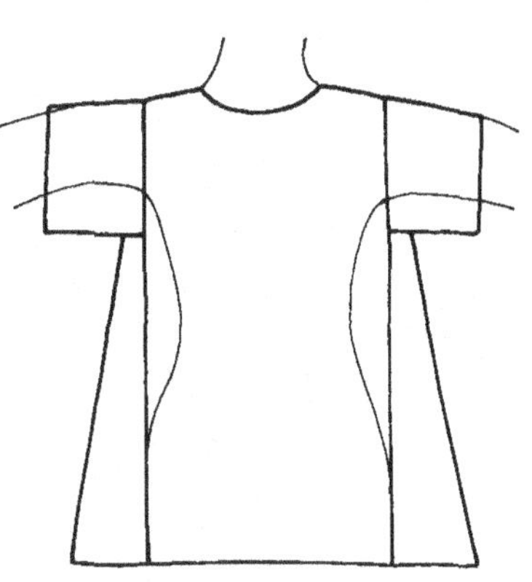

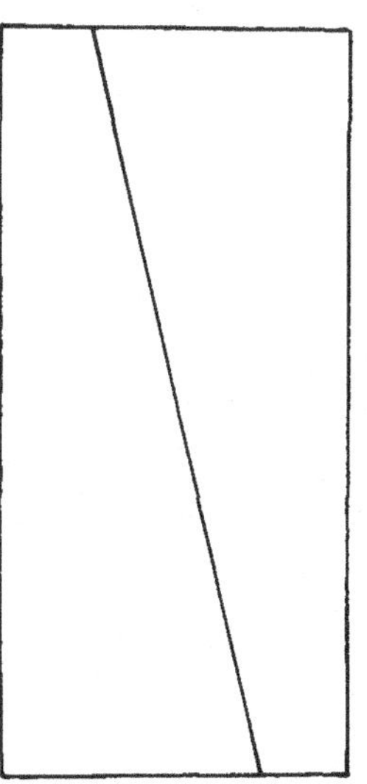

Adding Hip Fullness

Overlap

Loom-shaped garments that are open down the front will be more flattering if they hang open or have sufficient overlap. To create overlap:

1. Weave the fronts and back equal in width and overlap the fronts slightly in wearing. This works best when hips and bust are similar in size.
2. Add a decorative band (knit, woven, crochet, inkle) to one front for overlap or underlap.
3. Add rectangle(s) to the front(s).
4. Add rectangle(s) to the back(s).
5. Shape the front(s).
6. Weave the body of the garment with a join down the back and make the front pieces wider than the back so they can overlap.
7. Weave the body of the piece with a back join and leave slits for the sleeves. Place the slits so that the front widths are greater than the backs and can overlap.

Overlap

1.

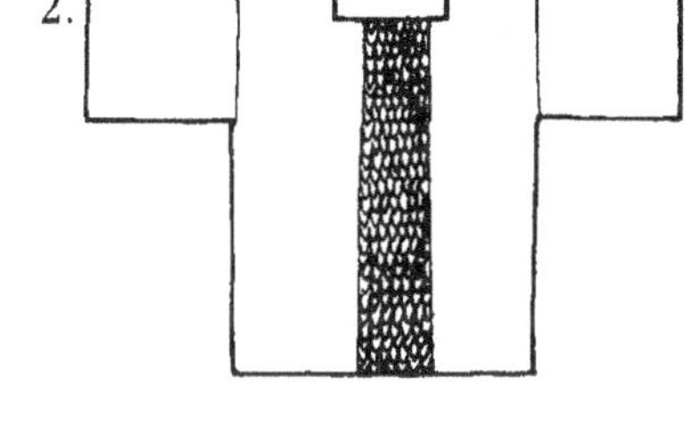

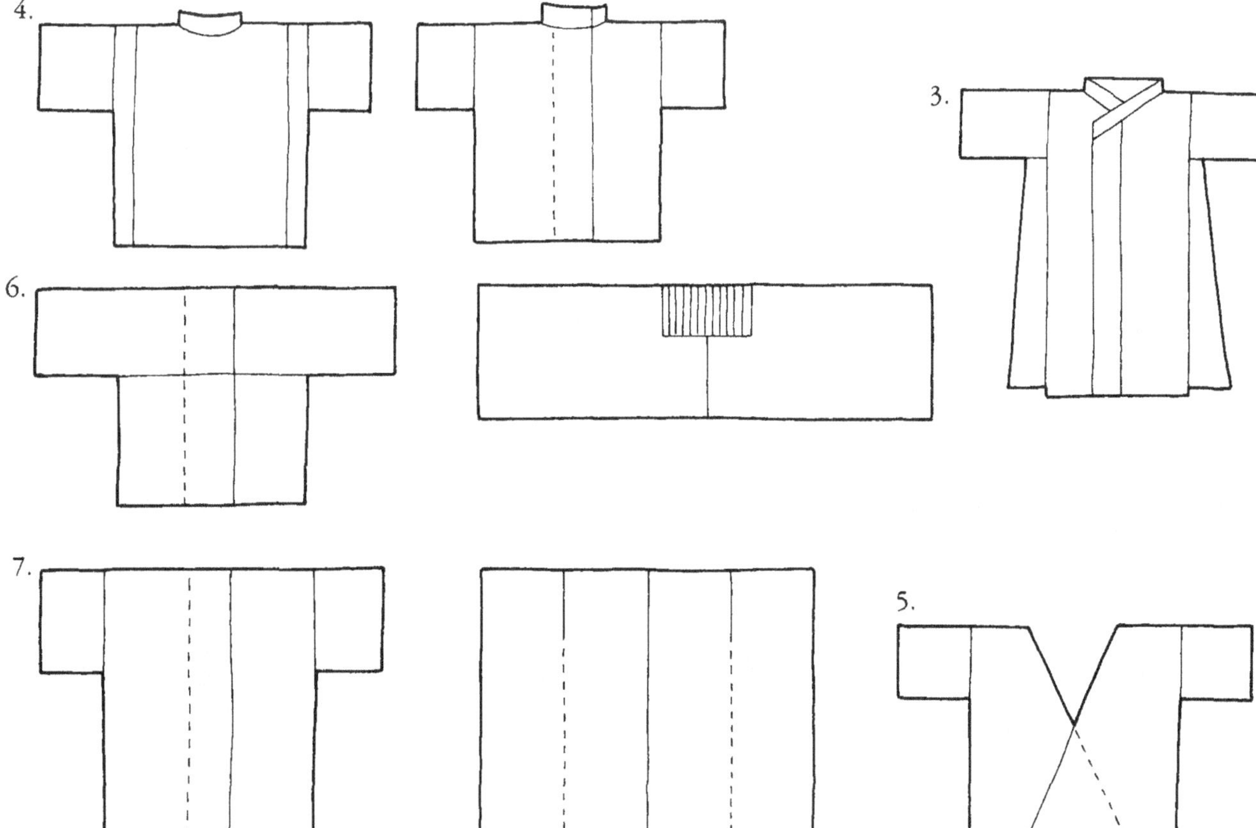

French writer Colette advised her daughter: *"You will do foolish things, but do them with enthusiasm."*

Length

A major dress designer recently stated: "Skirt length no longer matters. Choose and wear the length that is right for your body." The hemline of your garment is determined by your height, leg length and shape of leg. Once you have decided the most flattering length for you, wear that length and ignore any dictates from the fashion world.

For most women, 1″ or 2″ below the knee is an attractive hemline, while a long evening garment might be just above the ankle.

Hems

If hems are used as an edge finish on loom-shaped garments, coats and jackets should have 3″ hems and lightweight dresses 2″ to 2½″. The heavier the fabric, the wider the hem. If the hem curls, it can be weighted with crisp veriform.

Linings

Various factors determine whether or not linings should be used in garments. Linings are used to:

1. Hide something inside.
2. Make the garment easier to put on or take off.
3. Add support to the garment.
4. Give additional warmth.
5. Enhance the garment.

It is important to select the correct weight of lining for a garment, with the lining fabric never heavier than the garment. The amount of lining needed can be computed by laying out the garment pieces or by working to scale on graph paper. The lining must be about ½″ larger than the garment. When lining a coat or jacket, it is best to pin the lining in place in the piece while the coat is hanging and then sew into place. Consult the advice of a seamstress or refer to books on tailoring and sewing for additional information on this topic.

Pockets

Pockets developed from primitive bags, pouches and carrying cloths. As man needed both hands free, he hung the bag on a belt or fastened it to his pants or shirt. Pockets became part of the garment in the late 1600's. Regional variations of the use of pockets include the Lapplanders who use their caps and tightly belted tunics for carrying things, the Tibetans who cinch up a shirt as a pocket and the Japanese who use the deep sleeve of the kimono as a pocket.

Pockets

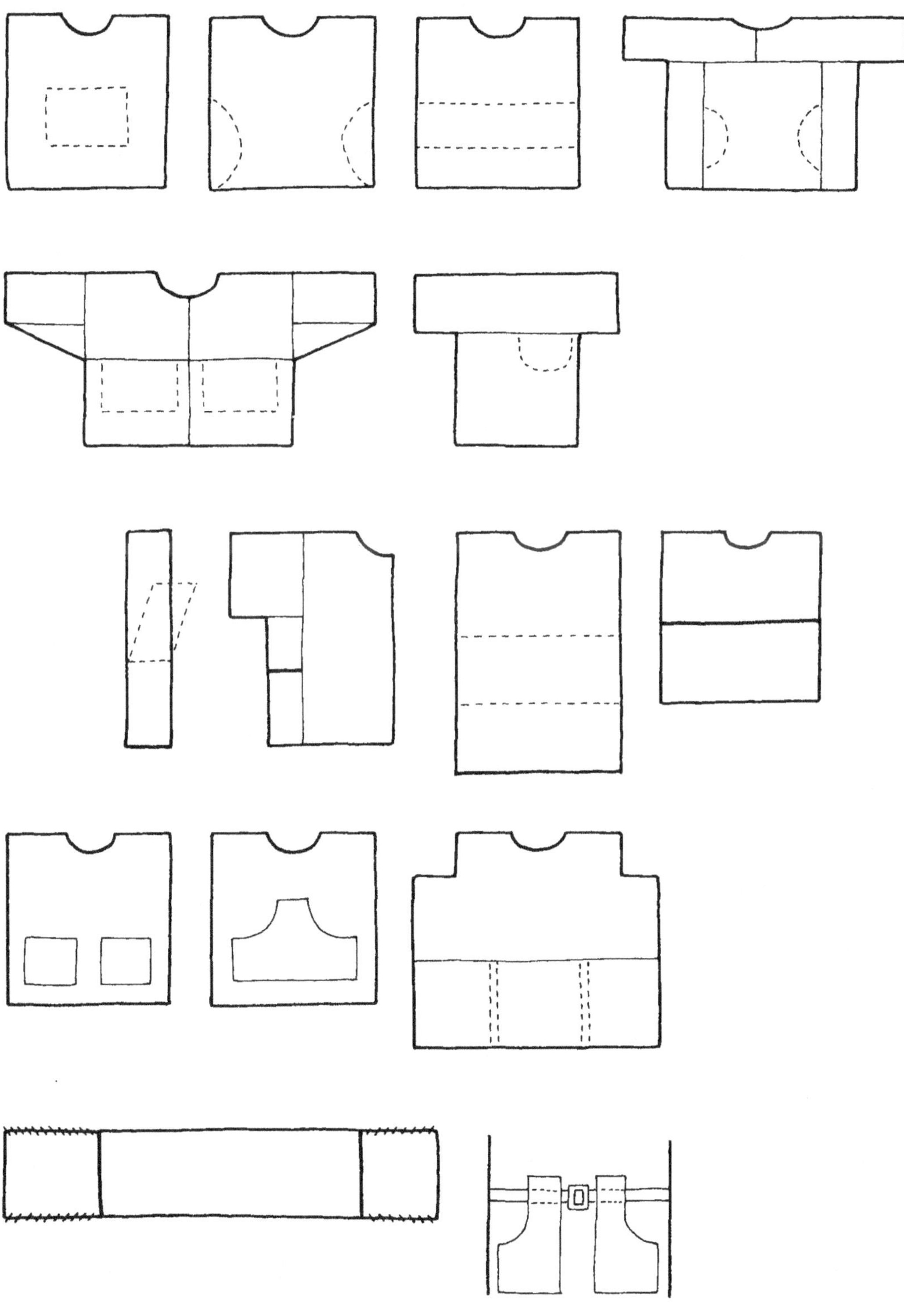

The pocket should be appropriate to the garment, and since it calls attention to the part of the figure where it is placed, it should be considered in the initial planning and fitting of the garment so that particular figure requirements may be taken into consideration.

There are two basic types of pockets:

1. Linings pushed to the inside through a seam or slot. Wherever there is a join, a pocket can be made from a lightweight lining material and inserted.
2. Self-applied to the garment. Wilson suggests, "A pocket can be woven on a small loom or cardboard loom. This can be a good way to introduce pattern variation or tapestry, or create an unusual shape using cardboard. These pockets are not too demanding in time and materials and are good little projects for experimenting with techniques."

Some ways to create pockets:

1. Insert the pocket into a vertical or horizontal seam join.
2. Weave the fabric longer than the body and turn this up, with or without fringe.
3. Apply pockets. Closures might be buttons, flaps or ties. Use the pocket top as a belt or sash loop. Chaudiere and Kapitan suggest that you can insert pockets in a scarf if you don't want them in a coat or jacket.

Hoods

Hoods can be traced back historically as far as 500 B.C., with a continuous evolution to the present day. The fit of the hood may be close to the head and face, loose on the head and face, or open and face-framing. In relation to the garment the hood can be:

1. A continuous part of the garment.
2. Set into a slit.
3. Set into a shaped neckline.
4. Set on away from the neck edge.
5. Separate or detachable.

The basic rectangular hood has appeared throughout history and is the simplest type of hood. The size of the rectangle is based on the height and width of the head. According to Plummer and Shapley, in their extensive discussion of the subject; the accepted minimum dimensions for half this hood are 10″ × 14″. This can be woven as two rectangles joined at the top and back, as one piece 20″ × 14″ joined at

Hood Dimensions

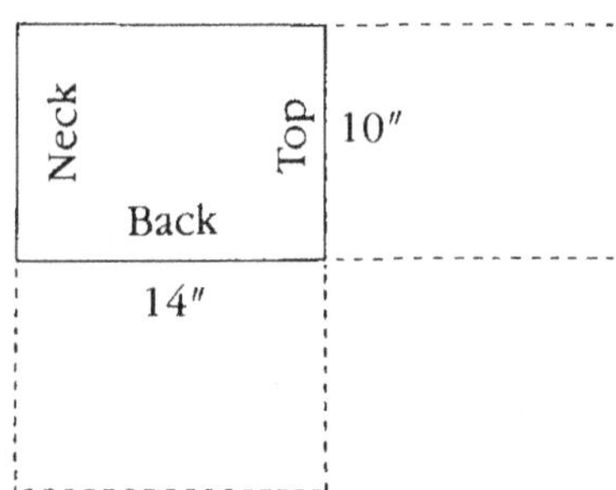

the top, as one piece 10″ × 28″ joined at the back, or as a combination of narrower strips making a whole, either separate from the garment before joining at the neck or continuous with the garment eliminating neck seams.

To determine your hood size:

1. Measure around the head to determine the width of the hood.
2. Measure from the shoulder next to the neck over the top of the head back to the other shoulder.
3. Cut a piece of muslin to these measurements and try the hood on and make necessary adjustments. Hair length and style can affect the size.
4. The size of the garment neckline is then determined by the width of the hood.
5. Dropping the hood 1 ½″ at the neckline sometimes makes a better fit.

The hood can be used on a slit as well as a shaped neckline. The basic hood (10″ × 28″) fits neatly into a 10″ neck slit, about minimum for a pullover garment with "give", and also about minimum for a garment open at the front. It fits smoothly into a shaped neckline with a 20″ circumference, which is quite comfortable for garments.

Varying the width and/or height of any hood will affect its appearance, not only on the head but also when it is off the head lying back on the shoulders. Increasing the width of the rectangle allows the hood to come forward farther on the face, protecting more against the weather while obscuring vision somewhat. A soft fabric may collapse on the forehead, especially when wet, unless it is faced, lined, turned back and/or stuffed.

Increasing the height of the rectangle creates a fold like a jowl at the shoulders all the way around, opening the hood and framing the face. This hood is flattering to most people, but less warm and more easily blown off in a wind. Off the head it will form wider lapels, and the point of the hood will rest lower on the back.

If the top seam of a rectangular hood is left open and trimmed with buttons and buttonholes, a zipper, or short braids, it can lie like a sailor collar on the shoulders until it is buttoned, zipped or tied up into a functional hood.

Hood Measurement

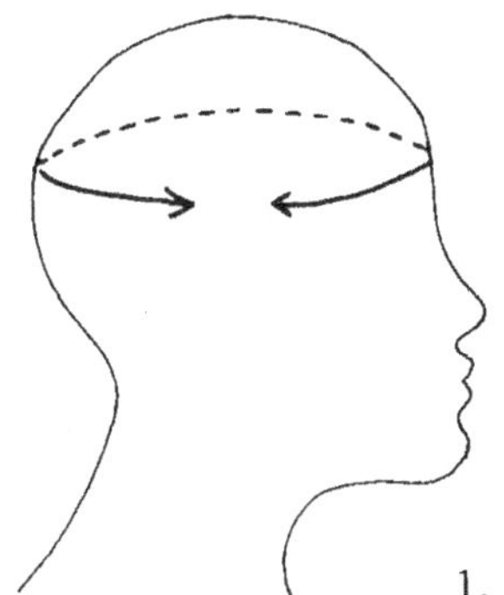

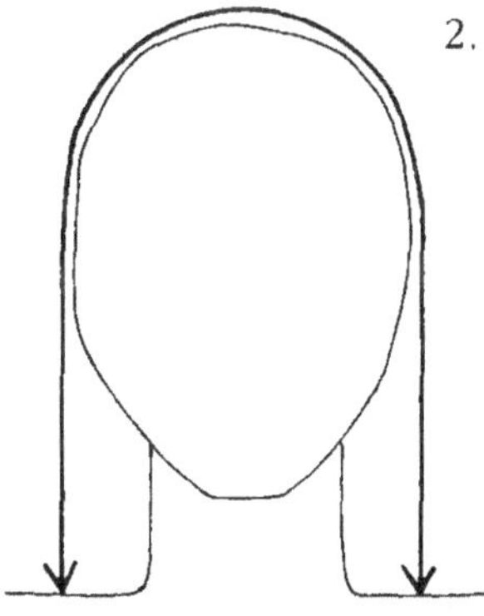

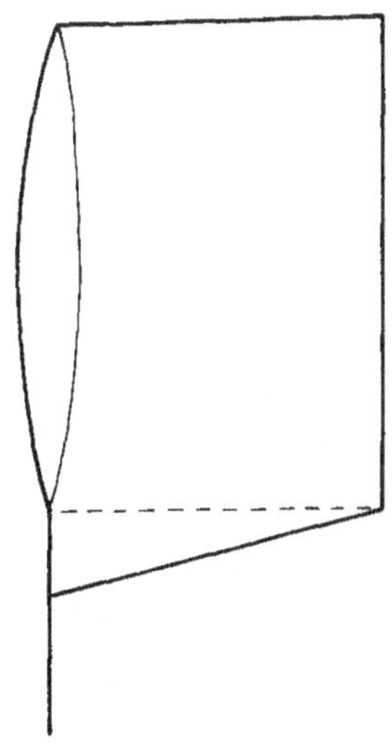

The peak of the rectangular hood is not appealing to everyone. If heavily tasseled, the peak will fold over when the hood is on the head, but extend down when the hood is on the shoulders. The peak can be folded to the back and stitched down with its tassel, or the point can be inverted and stitched across inside the hood.

Hood design ideas:

1. Knit a cowl collar long enough to make a hood and attach it to the neckline.
2. Weave a hood and then add a knit or crocheted band around the edge for shaping.
3. Gather the hood into place at the neckline if using light-weight fabric.
4. Use a drawstring around the hood to hold it in place.

Collars

Collars can be utilitarian or decorative; they tend to focus attention on the face. Collars can be added to garments using woven, knitted or crocheted bands. The simplest style collar is a long, narrow rectangle. Its width must correspond to that of the neckhole, which can be measured with a tape held edgewise. The collar can be of varying heights, and if it becomes too high to stand on its own, it can be folded down.

Collars and Hoods

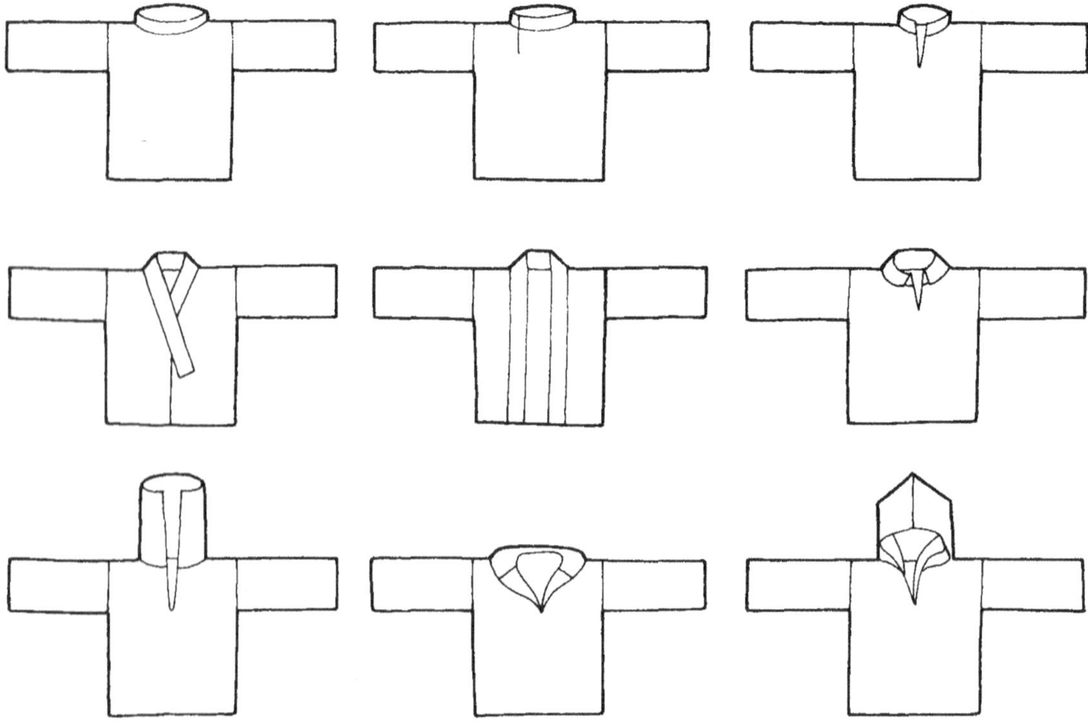

Adapted from Hamre and Meedom, *Making Simple Clothes*, Borgens Forlag, 1980.

Necklines

The style of neckline affects the appearance of the face, neck and shoulders because attention is focused on those areas. Necklines can be divided into three general types: round, V-shaped and square; and each can be used for particular effects.

1. Round necklines will accentuate a short neck, but can be flattering if made deep enough to be more oval than round. A shallow, scooped neckline will add length to the neck and appear to slim the throat and face. This type also works well if you have broad shoulders or are small bosomed. A key-hole neckline can be created by adding a front slit to a round or oval opening; this style is very flattering on most people.
2. V-necks add more length to the neck and face and are one of the best lines for any type of figure. This shape has great versatility and can be adapted to any garment, body or fabric. For the slimmest appearing line, keep a V-neck narrow.
3. Square necklines are good for those with short necks and narrow shoulders. Although rather severe, this shape is attractive on large women.

In *Weaving You Can Wear,* Jean Wilson and Jan Burhen suggest making a banner of necklines using an old sheet or piece of muslin. The dimensions can be written directly on the cloth and can be tried on when designing a garment to see which neckline is the best size and shape for the garment and the particular body. Small changes in the width and length of a neck opening can make a great difference in how a garment looks and fits. The opening must be large enough for the head to go through comfortably, but not so large that it appears sloppy or hangs off the shoulder. An average circumference for pullover garments is 24″, but a neckline with a front or back opening can be much less than that amount.

The placement of the neckline in relationship to the shoulderline is critical to how the garment feels, how it drapes and how it "rides" when worn. The position of the neckline depends on the wearer's posture. The farther forward the neck is carried in relation to the rest of the body, the farther the neckline has to be shifted. When a warp slit worn horizontally is used for a neck opening, it should be to the front of the shoulderline. If the warp slit is to be worn vertically, it is usually woven with the longer portion of the slit toward the

Necklines

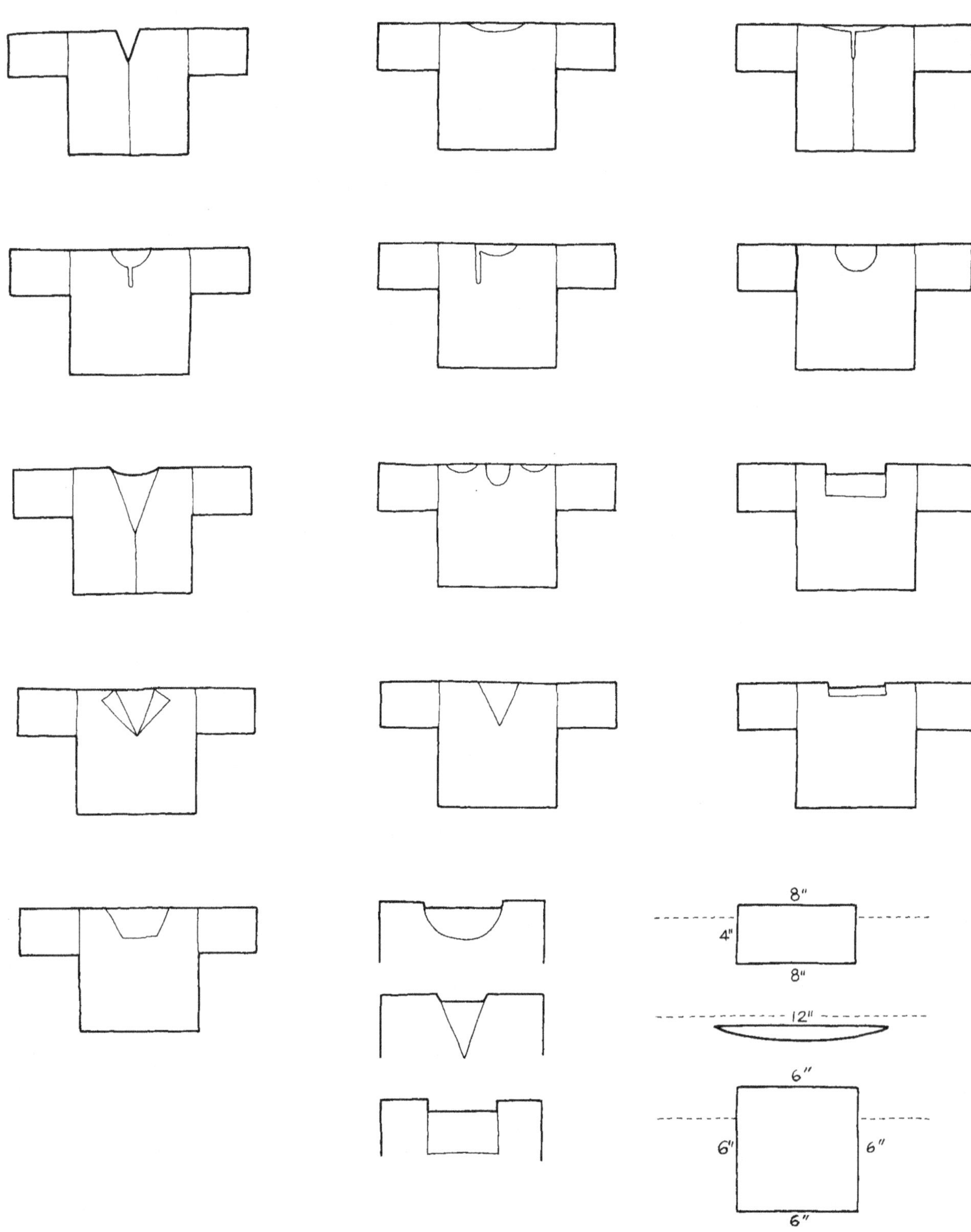

Adapted from Hamre and Meedom, *Making Simple Clothes,* Borgens Forlag, 1980.

front. With other neckline styles, at least 1″-2″ of the neckline should be to the back of the shoulderline.

The neck opening may be left unwoven and when off the loom, these warp ends can be threaded back into the body of the garment with a large needle. This helps to eliminate bulk and the problems of raveling if the fabric were cut. Square and rectangular necklines with facings are easy to weave to shape on the loom. Three shuttles are used, one for the neckline facing and one each for the two shoulder areas. The edge of the facings can be hemstitched while on the loom or machine stitched when off the loom. The unwoven warps between the facings are cut when the garment is off the loom, and these ends may be used as a decorative fringe, cut off or needled back into the facing to finish the edge. The facing may be turned to the outside as a decorative trim or be used as a hidden reinforcement for the neck when turned to the inside.

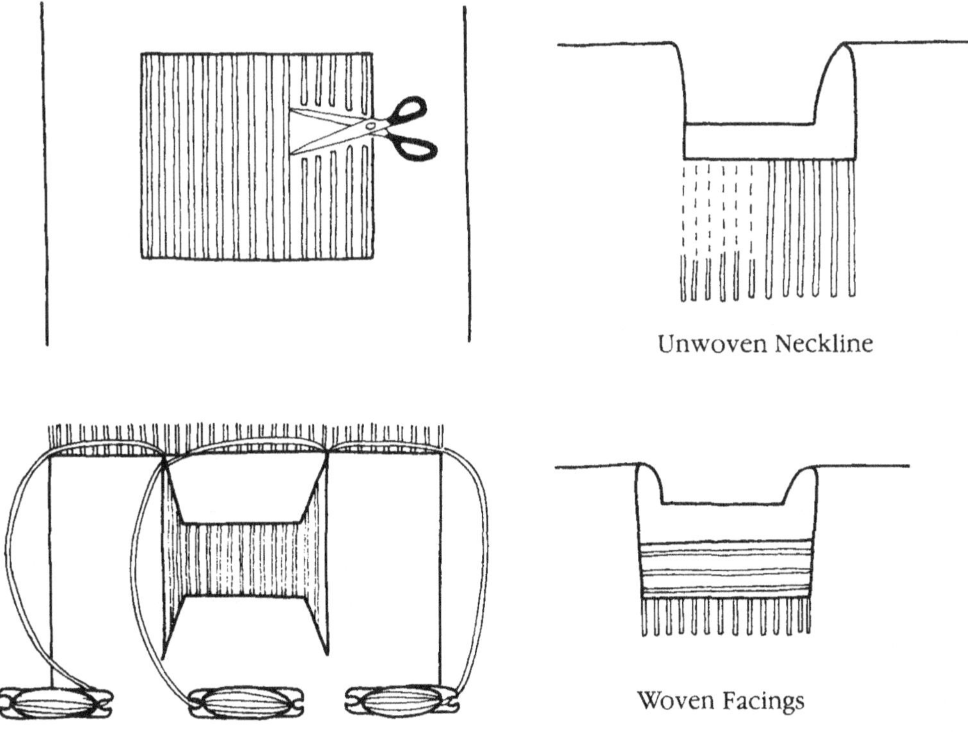

Unwoven Neckline

Woven Facings

There are stress points on some types of necklines and these need to be strengthened. On a slit-type neckline the ends of the slit can be reinforced with stitchery or arrowhead tack. On a key-hole neckline, leave two or three unwoven warps in the vertical opening. When the garment is off the loom, these unwoven warps can be cut and darned back into the cloth for additional strength.

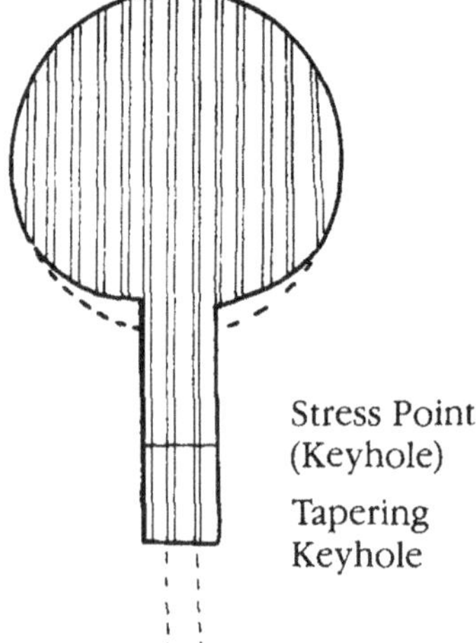

Stress Point (Keyhole)

Tapering Keyhole

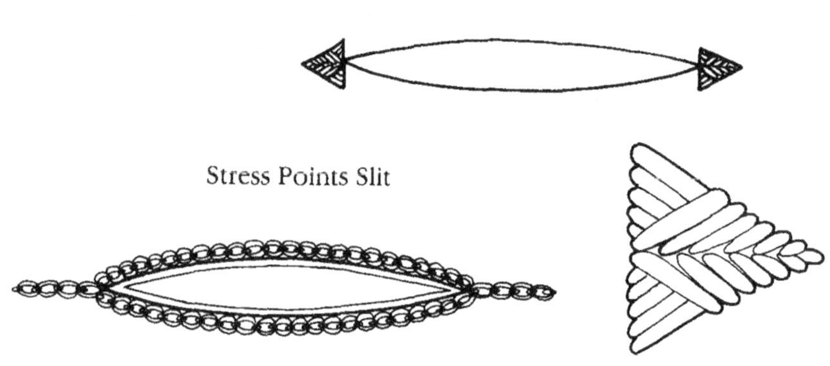

Stress Points Slit

To make a neckline shape to fit you:

1. Take a 12″ × 20″ rectangle of paper, fold it in half lengthwise and mark the fold. This represents the center of the garment. Fold down crosswise about 4″ from the upper edge and mark this line for the shoulder line. Mark the intersection of the two folds. Measure the distance around your neck and divide by 3. This equals the diameter of the neckhole. Center that measurement on the shoulder line. Mark ¼ of this diameter to the back of the shoulder line with ¾ to the front for an oval pullover neckline.
2. Cut out the opening and try on. If it is too tight or won't go easily over the head, trim the front part a bit larger until it fits comfortably.
3. Cut the neckline out of muslin and make any corrections as to size and shape. Note that the front point of a key-hole neckline may have to be tapered to lie flat along the base of the neck.
4. Transfer the shape and dimensions to your banner of necklines for future reference.

Making Neckline Shape

$\frac{\text{width around neck}}{3}$ = diameter of neck

¼ of diameter to back of shoulder
¾ of diameter to front of shoulder (oval neckline)

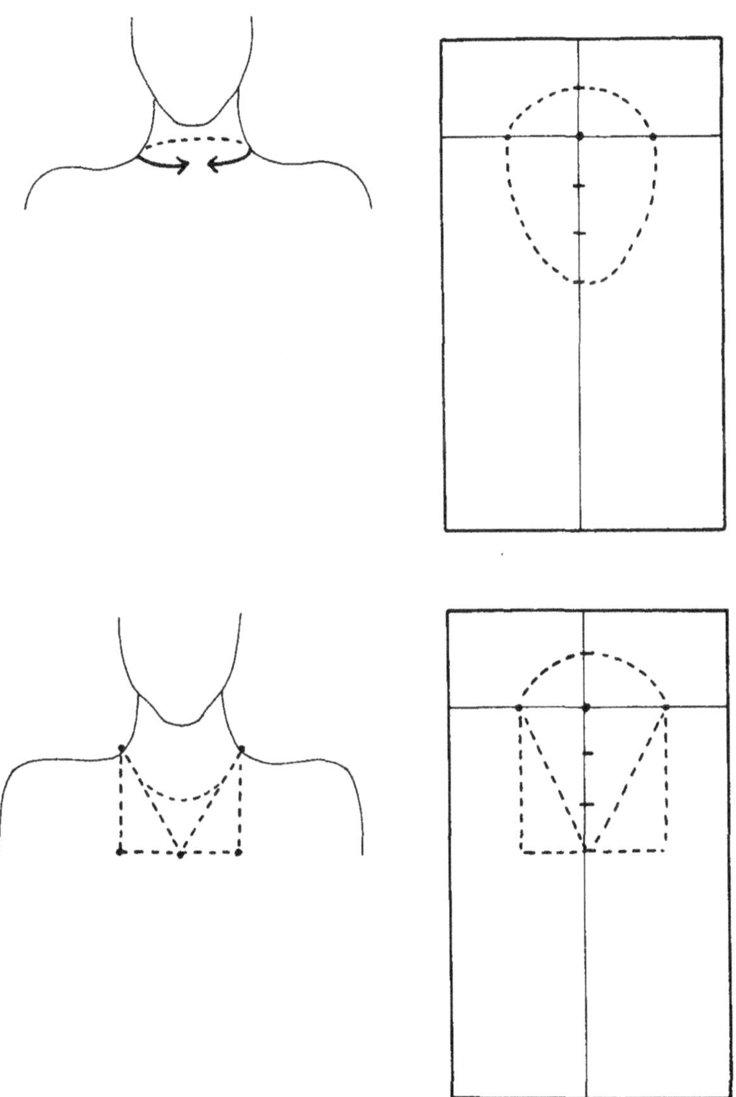

"A woman who has no daughter
To guide her or tell her this or that
Will have a strange looking living room
And wear a peculiar hat!"

Anonymous

"If people are to work with paint, clay or fiber, they must learn how to use tools, how to make what they have conceived, how to temper creativity by patience. It is this last capacity which is perhaps the most difficult and most important to cultivate. Craftsmanship requires the ability to keep the pulse of creativity beating slowly over long periods of time."

Sir Misha Black
Crafts *Magazine 1976*

"The hands are like a tap to turn on the creative stream that connects the heart and the head."

Mary Crovatt Hambidge
(1885-1973)

Chapter 4
The Edges and Embellishments

Edges and embellishments deal with the finishing of the garment, and as defined by Baizerman and Searle, mean any "manipulation or addition applied to a woven piece once it is taken from the loom." This finishing must be an integral part of the total design of the garment, and it is therefore essential to determine the finishing techniques before going to the loom. The design features of selvedges and allowances for fringe, joins and hems must be planned before weaving. Finishing can emphasize the materials used in a garment, enhance the piece, introduce a new material or color, or be a way to camouflage edges and joins. As Barbara Wittenberg states, "let us never forget that no matter how beautiful the fabric we weave, it is all in vain if the finished work is not as fine as the fabric." Often the hours to complete the finishing of a garment far exceed the weaving time, but it is this very finishing that can make a piece unique.

The areas that need to be considered in finishing are edges, joins, embellishments and closures.

Edges: Fell Edge

Cloth has four edges: two selvedges and two fell edges. The concern at the fell edge is to keep the weft from becoming unwoven. There are temporary methods used to hold the weft in place until the final finishing can be done and these include slip knots, glue or ending the weaving with rags or heavy yarns that are later removed.

Weaving Warp Ends Into the Cloth

The permanent methods of securing the weft are darning in, knotted or hemstitched fringe, machine stitched edge, and hems. These can be decorative in addition to holding the weft in place; they can be the final step in the finishing process or the foundation for further finishes.

Weaving or darning the warp ends back into the cloth is a technique that protects the weft and makes an attractive plain edge. The extra warp in each channel sometimes creates distortion of the fabric, but this can be used as a design feature and a means of adding weight at the garment edge. If the warp ends are very short, a needle or crochet hook can be first darned into the material, then threaded and pulled into place. For a fabric of very fine yarns, weaving one warp end back into the cloth every inch or so will provide a very inconspicuous finish. To prevent clipped ends from working through to the right side of the fabric, trim the inside darned warps to a ¼″ fringe and when the garment is steamed, these ends will fray open which prevents them from working through the material. The warp ends can also be darned to the right side of the material, left long and embellished with bells, beads or knotting.

Tying warp ends into knots is one of the most common ways to secure wefts, but as illustrated in Peter Collingwood's book, *Techniques of Rug Weaving*, there are ways other than the familiar overhand knot. The Phillipine edge is a series of continuous knots that run without interruption from one selvedge to the other. The knots can be tied from right to left or left to right, but the knots will shift unless the garment is turned over for each new row and the knots always made from the same direction. One row is quite secure, but several rows can be tied.

Phillipine Edge

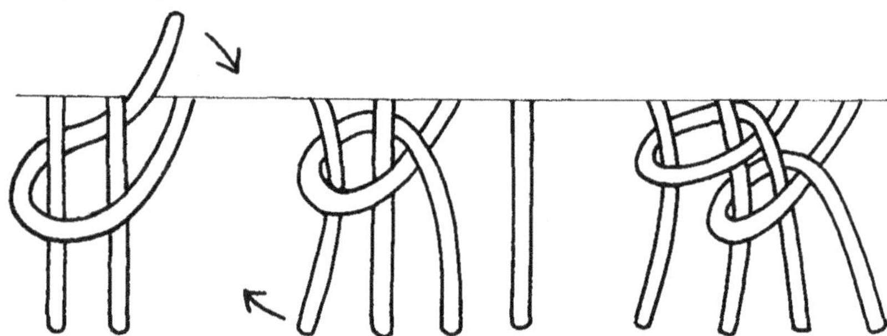

Hemstitching

A long strand of weft yarn or matching sewing thread may be used for hemstitching wefts. The stitching is easier to do while the work is under tension on the loom, but can be completed off-loom. If working on-loom, leave an end of weft at least four times as long as the width of the piece at the right side when you begin. After weaving several inches, go back and do the edge stitch. The number of warp ends and weft rows covered by the stitches is determined by the weight of the material and effect desired. Hemstitching is one of the most secure edge stitches because it sews into the fabric and encircles the warp. There are a number of ways to do this stitch and any one of them is suitable.

The Cavandoli knot is two half-hitches, one above the other, and can be wrapped around any number of warps.

Cavandoli Knot

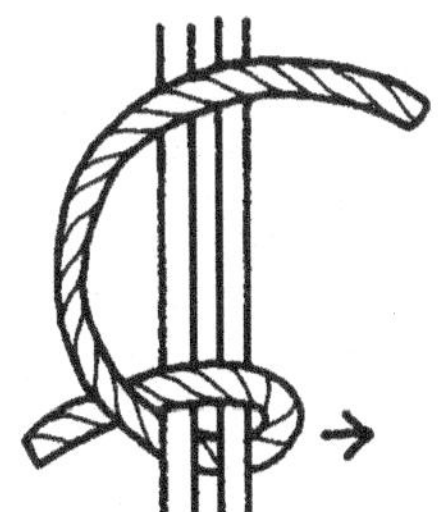

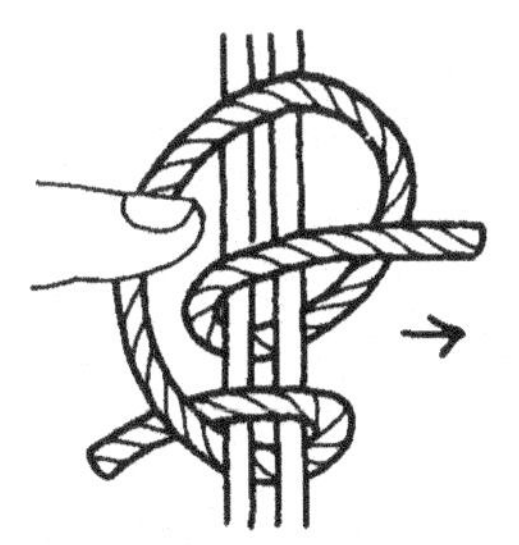

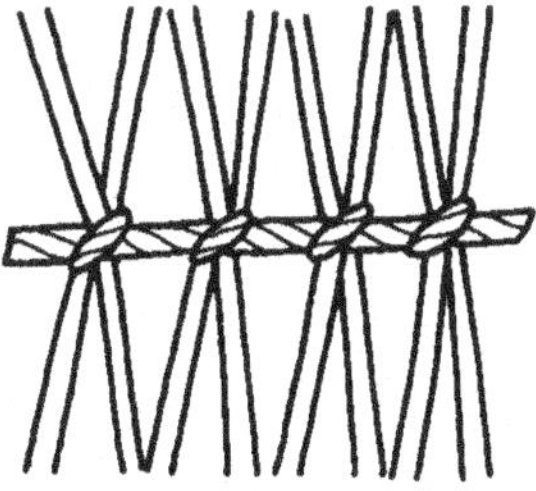

"Mistakes are like rocks in the path
Against when we stump our toes
That we may be more clearly
Awakened to see the road ahead."
Mary Crovatt Hambidge

The buttonhole stitch works well in securing wefts; it was originally used to bind the raw edges of blankets to prevent raveling and is therefore also known as the "blanket stitch". The many variations possible with this stitch make it ideal for garment finishing.

Buttonhole Stitch and Variations

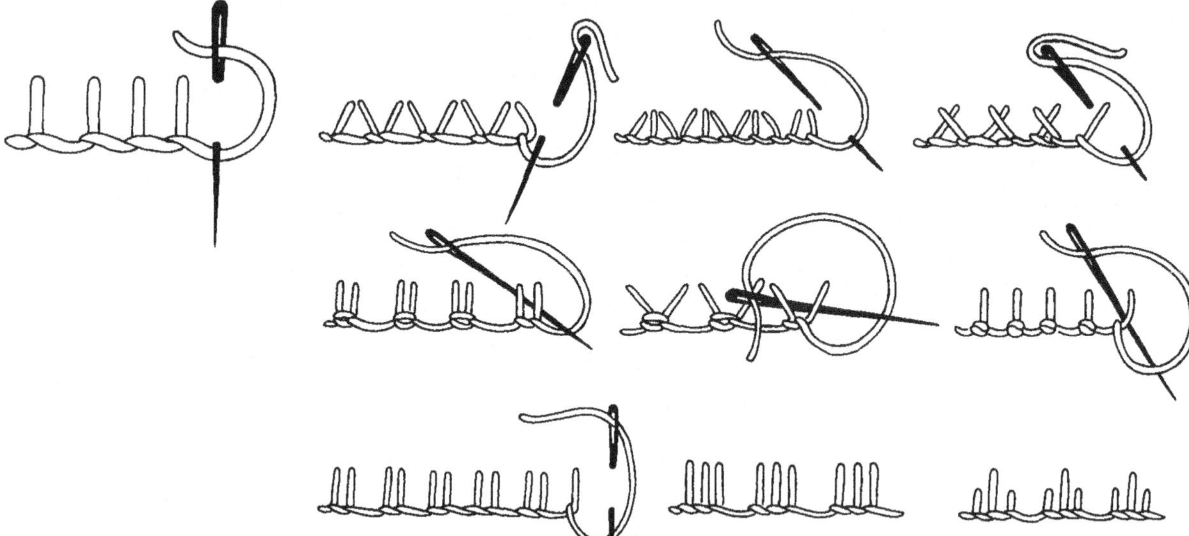

Warp that is left hanging as fringe can be treated a number of ways to prevent it from unplying and wearing away, make it more attractive and have it add to the overall design of the garment. Warp can be treated with series of overhand knots, plaiting, plying and braids.

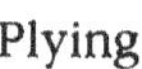

Plying

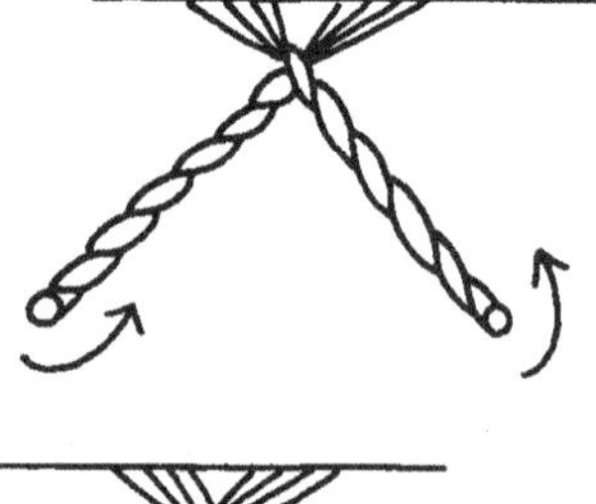

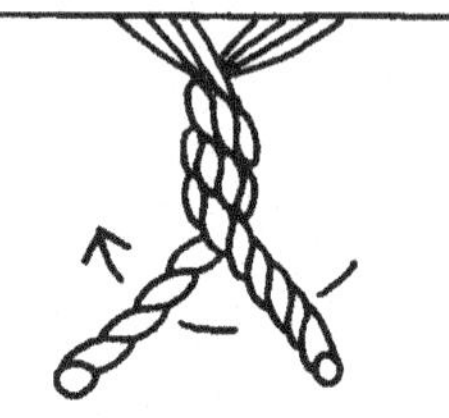

If the thickness of the warp threads is not sufficient for fringe or warp treatment, fringe can be added to a garment using another material. Weave a heading and place a row of rya knots where the fringe is needed. The edge of the heading can be turned under and hemmed into place when the garment is off the loom.

Jean Wilson suggests that fringe can also be made separate from the garment and then sewn into place.

When machine stitching is used, the thread should match the color of the fabric, and the stitches should be set close together. Machine stitch two rows close to each other, and close to the edge of the weaving. If the fabric is not too heavy turn ¼″ of the sewn raw edge to the right side of the fabric, and machine stitch a third time. This edge can then be covered with stitchery, crochet, commercial binding, a knit bias band or a couched cord.

Joins

The join that holds two pieces of fabric together can be inconspicuous or decorative, as long as it meets the basic requirement of being secure. Joins can be handstitched, woven or crocheted, and if machine stitching is used, it should not detract from the garment and should be hidden in some way.

It's usually the selvedges that are joined in loom-shaped garments. A selvedge must be planned and woven with care since a straight, firm edge is an integral part of the total piece. Selvedges can be plain or treated in some decorative manner; for example, create selvedge stripes by using contrasting colors or different weights of yarn along the edge when warping. If you're planning a stitchery join, you can place a warp of a slightly different color or weight a short distance from the edge. This will provide a visual guide for your needle when doing stitchery. Ideas for a wide range selvedge treatments are presented in Jean Wilson's *Joinings, Edges and Trims*.

Warp Guideline for a Joining Stitch

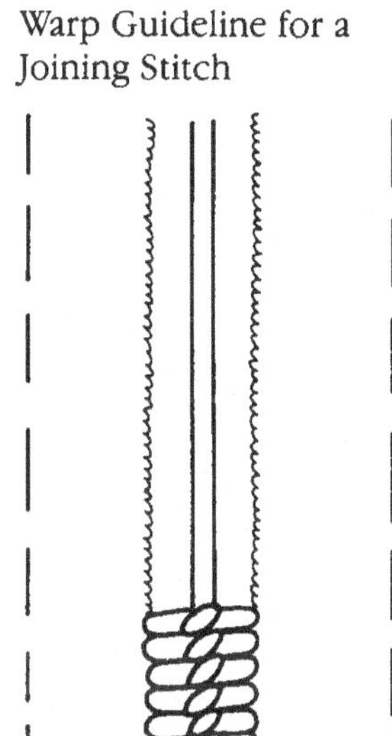

Plan the way the garment pieces are woven so that when they are assembled, a raw edge joins to a selvedge rather than a raw edge to a raw edge. The selvedge can then be laid slightly over the turned back edge and handsewn in place, making a type of felled seam. This reduces the bulk of a traditional seam, provides a smooth finish on the inside and gives the appearance of a selvedge-to-selvedge join on the right side.

Lacing

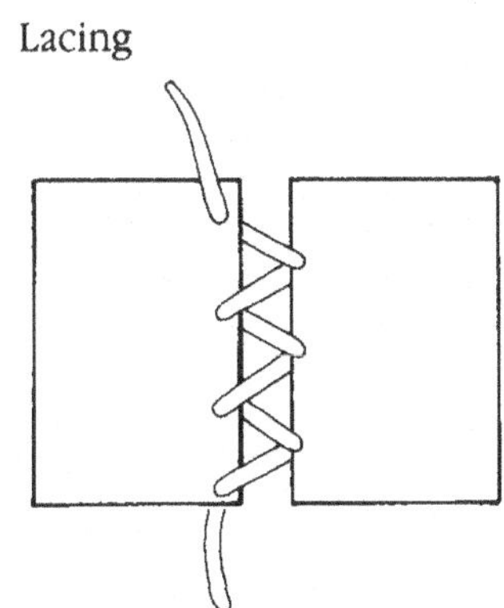

Lacing can be used to join garment pieces. An invisible join can be achieved by using a strong sewing thread compatible in color to the fabric. The stitches should be quite close together with the sewing thread catching the loops of weft. Every inch or so, pull the sewing thread tightly to gather the fabric a bit, and then smooth it out. This will produce a secure, inconspicuous join. If the edges are first embroidered or crocheted, the lacing stitch can be used to join the pieces. The lacing thread can be the same as the edge thread or contrast in color or type. Lacing can also be used as permanent basting to hold two pieces in place prior to being embellished with decorative stitching. When using lacing to baste, the stitches need not be too close.

With adaptation, almost any embroidery stitch can be used as joining stitch. Some stitches, such as buttonhole or chain and their many variations, are applied to the edges and then laced together. Stitches such as the raised chain-band, Romanian stitch, and the open chain are best done over a join that has first been basted with the lacing stitch. This holds the edges together evenly while the stitchery is being completed.

Embroidery Stitches as Joining Stitches

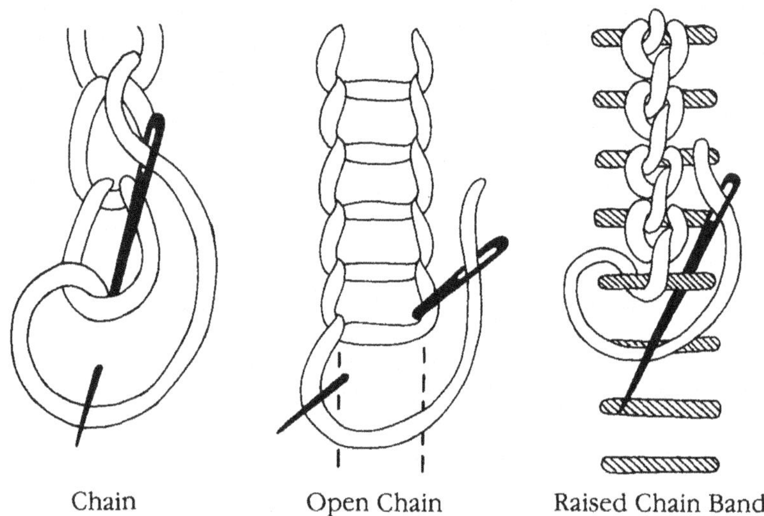

Chain Open Chain Raised Chain Band

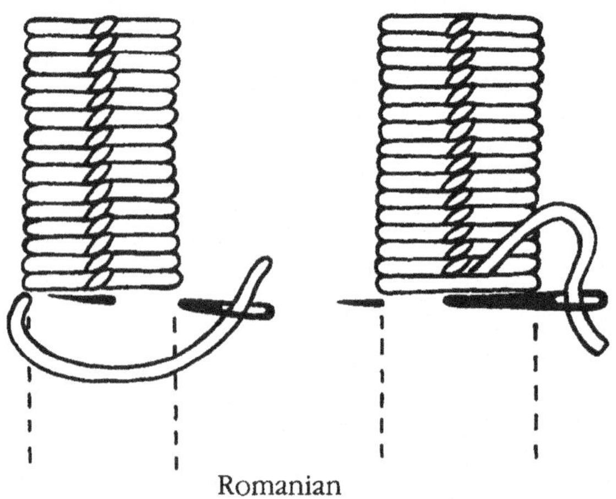

Romanian

Insertion stitches fill space between two edges in a lace-like effect. It is easier to keep that spacing uniform if the two edges are basted to a narrow piece of firm backing. The spacing is then held even while the insertion stitch is being completed.

Keep a sampler stitchery cloth in a basket with a needle, yarn and simple embroidery book. This will help provide the incentive to experiment with new stitches and to be creative with familiar ones. As Constance Howard, an expert in the field of embroidery, has noted, "You need one or at the most two embroidery stitches in your repertoire for with creative use, these can serve you a lifetime."

When assembling the garment pieces, plan how to do the majority of the joins with the garment flat on a surface. As you work, the pieces can be kept even by gently easing or stretching the fabric.

Insertion Stitch

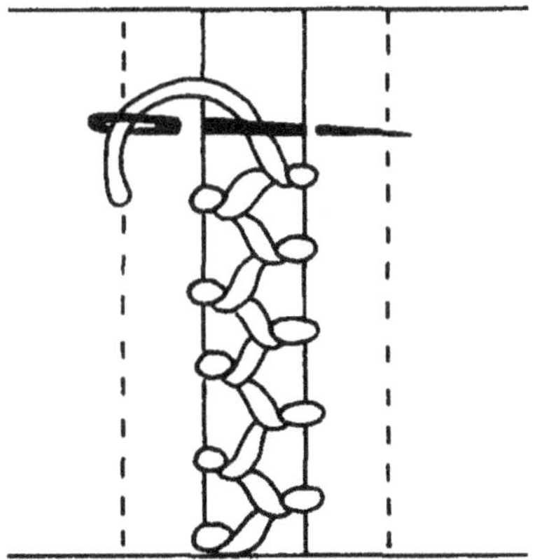

Assembling Garment Pieces

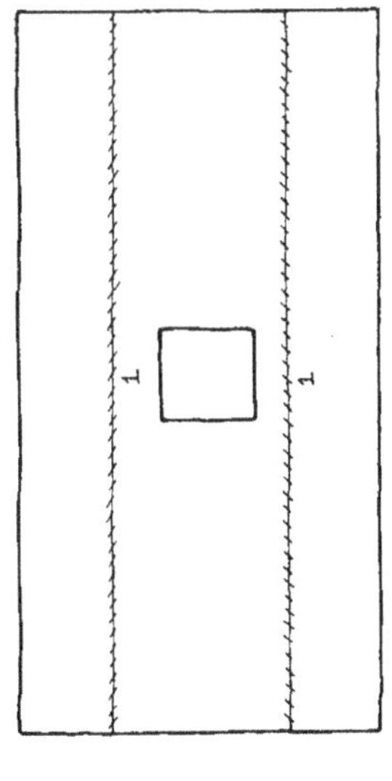

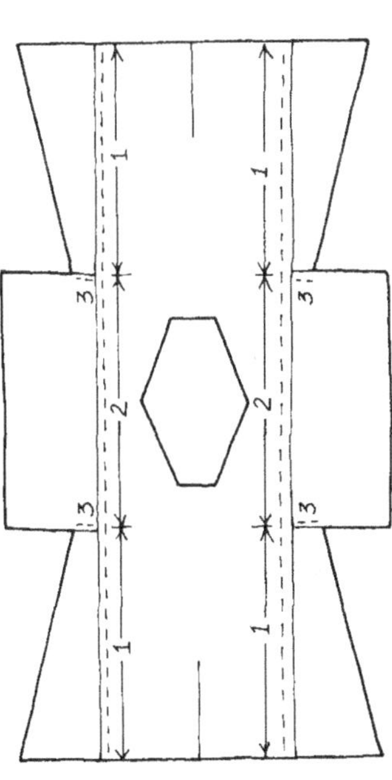

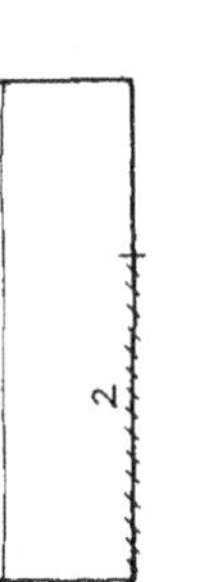

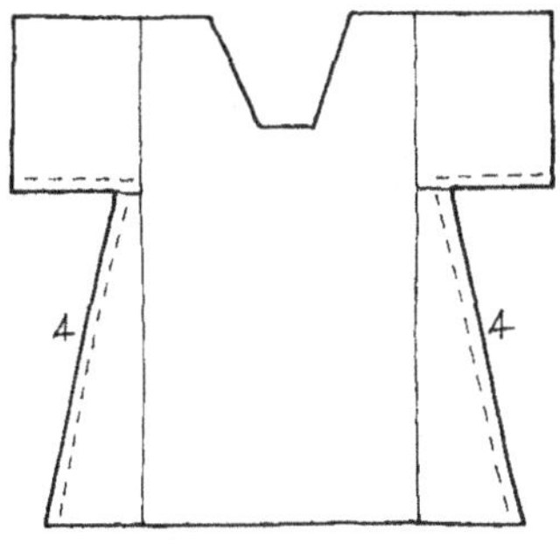

Embellishments

Embellishments are those additions to your garment that make it more beautiful and unique. Embellishments range from tassels and pom-pons to surface stitchery and beading. Materials used might include leather, bone, beads, ceramic, feathers, metals and yarns. Whatever your choice, the embellishment is an integral part of the total design of the garment, and must be planned prior to weaving.

Ethnic pieces and historic garments are rich in ideas. Sketch or photograph the details that make the piece unique. Learn to look closely to see what people in other cultures have done to add meaning and caring to their work. A "magic box" of treasures could be an additional source of inspiration. Start collecting buttons, old jewelry, small tassels and beads and keep them in one special container . . . a magic box. Everyone needs a bit of fantasy in her life, and your box may provide you with just the embellishment idea you need.

Closures

The closures on a garment may be the main design feature or be inconspicuous, but they should be functional and do what they are supposed to do—keep the garment closed yet easy to open.

Historically, closures have included tying material over the shoulder, drawstrings, belts, girdles, lacing and loops. People have used pewter clips, various hooks and eyes, snaps and such found objects as bones and thorns. Pins of all types have served as closures ranging from those found on kilts to fibulas and different styles of brooches. Even leather straps and buckles have been utilized to keep two pieces of material together. Crocheted, knitted or woven cords that were embellished with fringes, beads and tassels have been used for centuries as fasteners.

Buttons of pewter, wood, bone or fabric are appropriate for handwoven garments, and the buttonhole can be a woven slit or a loop of yarn that is wrapped or crocheted. Crocheting a chain of yarn and handsewing it as an edge finish with loops formed for the buttons is a practical and attractive type of closure.

The type of closure for a garment, according to Cram, is influenced by the function of the garment, the type, weight and color of the fabric, the number of closures, the visibility of the closures, whether the garment will be washed or dry-cleaned, and the importance of the closures to the total design of the piece. The final choice of closures is determined by what is practical and appropriate for the garment.

"She folded her work and put it right,
and said, dear work, good night, good night."

"Nobody can make you feel inferior without your consent."
Eleanor Roosevelt

Chapter 5
The Fabric

Fiber Selection

You should use the best quality yarns you can afford in handweaving. It is a waste of time and money to create a garment using inferior materials, for there is no way to make a garment look, wear or hang well unless the fiber selected is of a high quality. It is better to limit the number of garments you weave than to compromise on the fiber. No matter how skilled you are as a weaver, you cannot produce a successful garment using inferior materials.

The fiber that you select for a garment is determined by climate, cost, garment design, intended use, and the preferred method of cleaning. If you know the properties of various fibers, you will be able to use them appropriately in weaving garments. I will discuss natural fibers and some of the yarn types that I most enjoy weaving into special fabrics.

Wool

Wool is among the fibers longest in use by man. It is a protein fiber and one of the most versatile materials for the handweaver because of its many excellent properties.

Advantages	Disadvantages
Excellent insulator.	Moth problem.
Dyes easily.	Felts if improperly washed, so must be washed with care.
Not easily soiled..	Harmed by strong alkalis.
Absorbent.	
Will full and felt.	
Does not wrinkle.	
Breathes.	

A 7/2 weight wool set at 12 ends per inch (e.p.i.), woven in tabby with 12 wefts per inch (w.p.i.) makes a comfortable medium-weight fabric for loom-shaped garments.

Fibers from other animals—mohair, cashmere, camel hair and angora—are not as plentiful as wool and so are more expensive. Each shares some of the properties of wool, but none is quite as serviceable.

Silk

Silk, like wool, is a protein fiber, but in its most characteristic form is made of a continuous strand, unlike the shorter, individual fibers of wool.

Advantages	Disadvantages
Very strong.	Harmed by strong alkalis.
Dyes readily.	Does not wear as well as other fibers.
Has luster & translucency.	Expensive.
Elegant in look & feel.	Maintenance difficult.
Drapes well.	

Cotton

Cotton comes from a plant and is one of many cellulosic fibers.

Advantages	Disadvantages
Comfortable to wear.	Low elasticity, wrinkles.
Cool.	Mildews.
Washable.	Shrinks.
	Dries slowly.

A 10/2 pearl cotton set at 24 e.p.i. and woven in tabby with 24 w.p.i. makes a medium-weight plain fabric very compatible with stitchery or areas of treadled pattern.

Linen

Linen is a bast fiber and comes from the stem of the flax plant.

Advantages	Disadvantages
Stronger than cotton (weaker than silk).	Wrinkles.
High absorbency, cool to wear.	Subject to abrasion. If always folded on same line, the fibers will break.
Use & ironing increase luster.	Mildews.

Cottolin

Cottolin is a blend of cotton and linen ranging from 60% cotton and 40% linen to a 50/50 combination.

Advantages	Disadvantages
Cool to wear.	Shrinks.
Washable.	Expensive.
Dyes well.	
Wrinkles don't show.	
Has a pleasing textured surface.	

A 22/2 cottolin set at 20 e.p.i. with 20 w.p.i. and woven in tabby makes a comfortable weight fabric for loom-shaped parments. When designing a warp, consider combining cottolin with a comparable size silk or pearl cotton.

Rayon

Rayon is the first man-made cellulosic fiber; many do not consider it a synthetic because its characteristics are so similar to those of natural fibers.

Advantages	Disadvantages
Comfortable to wear.	Shrinks.
Lustrous.	Stretches.
Little wrinkling.	Weaker when wet, so must be washed with some care.

A supple warp-faced fabric can be woven using 12-cut rayon chenille as warp, double sleyed in an 8-dent reed with the warp ends single through the heddles. Select a fine yarn for weft and use a light beat.

Rags

The recycling of cloth into rag wefts has limitless potential for the garment weaver. Old jeans, discarded clothing, drapery lengths or purchased yardage can be used. The width the rags are cut is dependent on the effect you want, the desired weight of the woven piece, and the sett of the warp. The only way to determine these is by making a sample. Yarn wefts can be used with the rags, and the fabric can be woven in tabby or threaded to a pattern.

Rags can be cut a variety of ways; one way to cut lengths of material is to fold the fabric in half selvedge to selvedge and double again. Cut the strips straight across, not on the diagonal, and they will be as long as the fabric is wide. Overlap 1″ for each new strip and make any color changes at the selvedge. If using commercial yardage, select a 50/50 polyester-cotton blend or a lightweight cotton broadcloth. A variety of warps are suitable for rag weaving, from 3/2 cotton set at 12 e.p.i. to a 20/2 worsted at 24 e.p.i. Machine wash in warm water using the regular cycle, and expect at least 5% shrinkage in the warp and 15% in the weft.

You can purchase or cut your own bias strips (usually 5/8″ wide if using light-weight cotton). Using a 20/2 warp set at 14 e.p.i. with 10 to 12 rows of bias rags per inch produces a velvety terry-cloth finish after machine washing. Take-up and shrinkage will be from 10% to 15%. In any type of rag weaving, a better drape will be achieved if the rag wefts hang vertically.

Creating a mixed warp

The choice of warp yarns depends on the strength of the yarn and the effect you want in the fabric. Plied yarns are usually recommended for the warp and are easier to use, but a firmly twisted single is also satisfactory. Note that singles tend to curl more and are somewhat difficult to beam. If a yarn seems to fray easily, double sley rather than single sley the warp. The abrasive action of the metal sides of each dent against the thread is greater than two yarns rubbing against each other. For example, if you are using a wool set at 12 e.p.i., double sley it in a 6-dent reed with each warp single through a heddle. Loop, bouclé or mohair yarns will be easier to work with if they are alternated in the warp with smooth yarns and are single-sleyed. This prevents them from catching on each other.

Your warp may be a combination of fibers and the weft can be different from the warp, so long as the final fabric meets your needs.

A warp of mixed fibers adds interest to fabric, saves weaving time once the loom is warped, and is a way to use up odd amounts of yarn. Any combinations of fibers can be used in the warp if they are equally strong and give the desired effect, and if the various yarns are alternated throughout the warp and not bunched in groups. If ½″ of silk warp is followed by 1″ of wool and ¼″ of rayon, tension problems can result which will increase as the warp is woven. Wool, cotton and synthetic yarns can shrink and stretch at different rates, both in the weaving and finishing of the fabric, causing a rippling effect like seersucker. Sometimes this can be minimized by pre-washing the skeins of yarn before warping, but if you don't want this effect, you must sample first to see if your yarn combination is compatible or use all of one type of fiber and plan to dryclean the garment.

If you warp the loom from the front (through the reed, then the heddles and then to the back beam for winding), there is an easy way to create a unique mixed warp. Determine the length and width of the warp for the garment you are going to weave. Assemble all those yarns that you want to combine in a mixed warp fabric, being certain that you have enough. There can be any amount of each yarn, just so the total will be sufficient. Select the reed that accommodates the thickest of those yarns. Make a warp of each yarn, but do not measure more than for one warp end in every other dent. Tie the cross, go to the loom and sley that chain. If there are only ten ends of that yarn, space them about equally in the reed—don't count or measure, just do it by eye. Remove the lease sticks, for the reed now maintains the thread order. Take the next yarn and make it into a chain and sley it as an independent chain, spacing it across the reed. Continue with each yarn separately. Place finer yarns together in a dent; this means that in some dents you might have one warp end (the thickest one) and in others two or three ends. If you have a number of fine yarns and want to avoid more than three ends per dent, hold two together as though they were one when you measure, which will cause them to ply together after a fashion. When putting that pair in a dent, make a slip knot in the end to keep them together. When it is time to thread the heddles, every yarn goes in its own heddle except those that are slip-knotted. They stay as one throughout the warping. Check the density of the warp by placing your hand under the warps in front of the reed to see if there are enough yarns to give the degree of warp emphasis that you want. If not, add a few more. When the reed is sufficiently filled, thread each warp through the heddles and gently wind on, shaking out the yarns as you go rather than combing them with your fingers. It does take more care to warp this way, but the resulting fabric is worth the effort and you will be able to use up odd amounts of yarn. Sometimes there may be only two or three warps of one yarn, but if the color is compatible, they will add interest to the fabric. To emphasize the warp, weave tabby, twill or a warp-faced twill. Select a fine weft of medium value to the hues in the warp, i.e., not the darkest or the lightest of the yarns in the warp. A light beat also accents the warp yarns, allowing the weft to disappear visually.

Weaving such a mixed warp in this way makes sampling for shrinkage and yarn compatibility impractical, so dry-cleaning is recommended.

If you are hesitant to try this technique on a garment, practice it making a series of scarves. You will gain experience in how close to set the warps and how various colors and types of yarns interact.

Weft-faced fabric

Various amounts of yarns can also be used up in creating a weft-faced fabric. Gather together all the yarns you want to incorporate into a garment. There can be any amount of each yarn and the fibers can be different, although it might be wise to avoid linen because of its lack of elasticity. The basic criteria are that there are sufficient yarns for the garment you design, and that you like the combination of colors and textures. The warp used should be compatible in color to the weft yarns, fairly fine, and set far enough apart that the different sizes of wefts can be beaten down to cover it. If the warp does show in some areas, it will then not distract from the surface of the fabric. A 3/2 or 5/2 pearl cotton at 6 e.p.i., or an 8/4 carpet warp at 12 e.p.i. might be possible choices if your yarns are medium weight. Line up and rearrange the yarns until you have a sequence that is pleasing to you. If you want to begin and end with the same yarn, weigh and divide it in half. Warp the loom for plain weave and using tabby, begin weaving with yarn A. When you are running out of it, or are tired of it, introduce yarn B on a second shuttle or butterfly. Carry the second yarn along the selvedge and gradually increase the shots of B while reducing the number of shots of A. Then weave with B until it is nearly gone and start introducing yarn C. If you want the same sequence of yarns in the front and back, divide all of them in half before you begin;

parts of a garment have to be identical. This technique uses up any accumulation of yarns but eliminates counting or measuring, for it is your eye and the effect you want that determines the choices.

Fabric design

Fabric can be designed with certain characteristics and these need to be considered in planning your garment.

If you want the material to be water repellent, weave tightly, use wool in the grease, weave the fabric warp- or weft-faced, or brush up the nap, since a rough surface repels water better than a smooth finish.

For drapability, use a twill threading. Plain weave is also very drapable, but will show wrinkles more because the surface is flatter than twill. Any of the weave structures with a skip spacing in the reed, lacy weaves such as leno, or lightly beaten fabric will drape well.

Durability of fabric can be achieved by using quality fibers in a tightly spun or plied yarns, and weaving a smooth surfaced material with minimal floats.

Fibers with crimp, like wool, produce a fabric that will wrinkle less than smooth, non-resilient fibers like linen and cotton. Combining fibers can help reduce wrinkles. Color and weave structure can hide creases, and a loose fitting garment will wrinkle less than one that is tight.

If you want a light-weight fabric you must use fine threads, for the smaller the diameter of the yarn, the thinner the fabric, other things being equal. A light beat is also important in achieving a finer weight material.

To create a heavy-weight fabric, use heavy or thicker thread, increase the warp sett, and beat more firmly. Weave structure will also affect fabric weight; given the same warp, weft and sett, a plain weave give a sheerer fabric than, say, a twill.

The surface appearance of the fabric is an integral part of garment design. You may want a plain, dull material as a background for other embellishments but if you want a textured surface, one that has a play of highlight and shadow, other ingredients are involved, such as thread choice.

I like to categorize threads as plain, bumpy or velvety. Within each group, these threads are shiny or dull, large or small. Textural effects result from the way these threads are combined as to type, size, proportion of each, color, and interlacement. Contrast is "the spice of design", and if you want an exciting fabric, contrast must be involved. For maximum texture, contrast shiny yarns with dull yarns, thick against thin, and smooth versus rough. One or a combination of these contrasts can be used to achieve texture, and the more these relationships are exaggerated, the greater the visual effect.

The woven pattern is an integral part of fabric design and a wide range of pattern drafts is available to the handweaver. These can be used for subtle texture or as the focal point of a garment. Do not, however, overlook the simple beauty of tabby and twill. Some 90% of the garments I have woven in the last ten years are woven in tabby. The simplicity of the structure allows emphasis on the yarns, surface embellishments and color.

How you handle the beater will help determine your fabric weight. The more shots of weft per inch, the heavier the fabric. You should measure the number of wefts per inch regularly to be sure that you are maintaining a uniform beat. This is especially important when weaving tabby. Particular care needs to be taken when shaping narrow areas on the loom. The tendency is to beat too hard, because the weight of the beater is greater in relation to the width of the fabric than in wider sections.

If the warp is sticky and it is difficult to get a shed, spray the warp regularly with hair spray. This coats the side hairs and they are less likely to tangle. A twill treadling, where pairs of warps are rising together, will be less sticky than plain weave. Clearing the shed by bringing the beater forward, changing the treadling, and letting the beater go back, will help open the shed.

The sett of the warp is determined by the thickness of the yarn, the amount of fulling desired in the finished cloth, the weave structure (tabby, twill or pattern), and the design and function of the garment.

The only way to avoid costly mistakes in weaving is to sample. The sample can be woven, unwoven and woven again until just the right effect is achieved. If the warp turns out to be an unfortunate choice, or if the sett is wrong, it is certainly less costly in time and money to weave another small sample. All those heartbreaking mistakes can be avoided if you weave a small sample of every project before making the final warp.

Designing with color

Colors can be combined in such a way that each makes the other more exciting, and brings out qualities in the other that you wouldn't see if you were using one alone. There is a vocabulary that describes the properties of color—hue, value, intensity, tint, shade, tone; and formal relationships—monochromatic, analagous, complementary, triadic—that will help you make color decisions until you begin to internalize your personal color aesthetic. As you read about these harmonies in the many available resources, and use them in your work, you will gain more confidence in making unusual and pleasing color combinations. Here are some other factors that affect color in weaving:

Texture. A rough texture appears darker than a smooth one because of the shadows on the fabric surface. A brushed surface will also appear darker, as will a fabric that drapes and creates shadows in its folds. Yarns look darker if they are looped or woven in a cut pile than if they are woven flat. A smooth surface reflects light and thus looks lighter. A fiber that packs down easily will look different in color than one that rides on the surface of the fabric; the weight of a fabric affects your perception of its color.

Light. Daylight and artificial light change color, as does the amount of light present. Check your color choices in the kind of light in which your finished piece will most likely be viewed.

Proportion. The distance from which an item is viewed influences color. The larger the area of color, the stronger the color will appear. And weaves with small warp and weft floats, such as plain weave, will not show the color of the warp or weft as much as will a weave with long warp or weft floats, even though both use equal quantities of the same two colors.

Interaction. If warm and cool colors are used equally side by side, the warm colors will appear larger and nearer, for they tend to "spread" or "advance". Adjacent and surrounding colors affect color, too. The interaction of colors in the warp as they cross colors in the weft can change those colors, particularly in a balanced weave. Spaced denting in the reed can create a different color effect than regular denting because weft spots become prominent in the extra spacing. Two colors, such as blue and yellow, same size and kind of yarn, produce the illusion of green; but if either is heavier or shinier, that color will predominate.

The principle of dominance is important in designing the fabric for your garment. The resulting material will have more unity if one element is exaggerated and the others are subordinate to it. If dramatic texture is to be the dominant theme, perhaps the textile should be woven of white threads or very muted colors. If exciting color effects are desired, the amount of texture contrasts should be limited. If a striped fabric with many changing areas is the ultimate goal, color and texture contrasts should not be quite so dramatic as they could be in a striped material with a simple arrangement of area. A simple design capitalizes on the materials used, so plain threads show patterns well. The adage of fancy yarns in plain weaves and plain yarns in fancy weaves is basic to designing fabric. If you want to visually blend colors, minimize these contrasts and keep the value of the colors similar.

Ideas for color in weaving can come from a variety of sources. Consider using:

- Fabric or wallpaper swatches.
- Colors that are combined in a variegated yarn.
- A color wheel for working out possible color scheme.
- Nature.
- Photographs and slides.
- Tear sheets from magazines—advertisements, photographs, fashion layouts.
- Paint chips.

You learn about color by working with it, and you can practice the theories of color by wrapping yarns on cardboard and needle-weaving samples or small items such as evening bags or pockets. Plan an extra amount of warp when warping the loom and use that for experimenting with color and treadlings. Weave a series of small items such as purses, scarves or belts to gain confidence in color.

Color can be a slenderizing feature in garments. You need not use only dark colors if you have a large build, but do remember that light, bright color will accent a problem area and call attention to it. If you are wide hipped, don't wear a light skirt and dark top; and if you are top heavy, a light top with dark slacks will accent that feature. A *total* look that is light and bright is effective whether as a dress, slacks and top, or coat.

The slenderizing secret of color is contrast, for this breaks up the horizontal line and creates a vertical line. This means more than just a light top and dark skirt. A green shirt with light collar and cuffs, a dark jacket with light knit collar, or a white dress with dark buttons, dark, thin belt and dark jacket, or a tweedy jacket over an A-line dress all provide contrast. Try to keep the dark color to the outside of the ensemble and build up the bright or light colors toward the center. Wear a dark top over a light turtleneck; and if the top has a V neckline, even more verticals are created.

Color techniques that can add interest to your fabric include mixing several fine wefts on the shuttle and using them as one. If they are closely related in hue, very subtle color effects occur. One of the weft threads can be dropped and others added for a gradual color change. Use surface embellishment such as stitchery to add color. The color of the warp can be totally changed by the weft that crosses it if the values are compatible.

Two quite different colors can be made harmonious if they are bridged by a neutral, for this ties the two hues together. Depending on the colors involved, the bridge might be whites, browns, blacks or grays.

If you are not ready to explore color while also trying to create successful loom-shaped garments, simply use neutrals in your weaving. The beauty of white on white and the range of soft browns and grays cannot be surpassed. I worked only in neutrals when I first began to explore loom-shaped garments. As I gained experience with various yarns and pattern drafting, I then added color by weaving in monochromatic color schemes in warp- or weft-faced fabric; or I introduced color through stitchery. I am now ready to explore the interaction of a weft color across a warp color. Color will be there when you are ready for it.

Fabric planning can be approached two ways. A particular garment shape can be the starting point and from that all other decisions are made—selection of warp and weft yarns, sett, the colors and the pattern to treadle. Or you might begin with the yarn, that one you couldn't resist buying. From it you design a garment that will be compatible with the weight, size and type of that particular fiber. Either approach requires decisions, choices and samples. Success cannot come from "happy ignorance". You must have a plan and a goal, but also remember that "a plan is something to deviate from." Always be open to that sudden inspiration or better idea as the garment is in progress. Making your garment and fabric plan is like following a roadmap—you decide on your destination and how to best arrive there, but then you can take all kinds of side trips that can enrich the experience. You still end up at the destination . . . a wearable piece of clothing in a fabric that is right for the garment design and for you.

Portfolio

Weaving notes for all designs in this section can be found in the Appendix, page 159.

The moment I saw the Royal Ontario Museum research on the Hungarian szur, I knew, that one day, I would weave myself a coat of that type. The cultural significance was so special: each rank of herdsmen was designated by the embroidery; the coat was used as payment for serfs and herdsmen; and for young peasant boys, the szur was his life-long attire, used in courting and draped over his coffin. Since the fabric from the looms was too narrow to go around the body, side pieces were added but with all coat segments rectangular. This garment

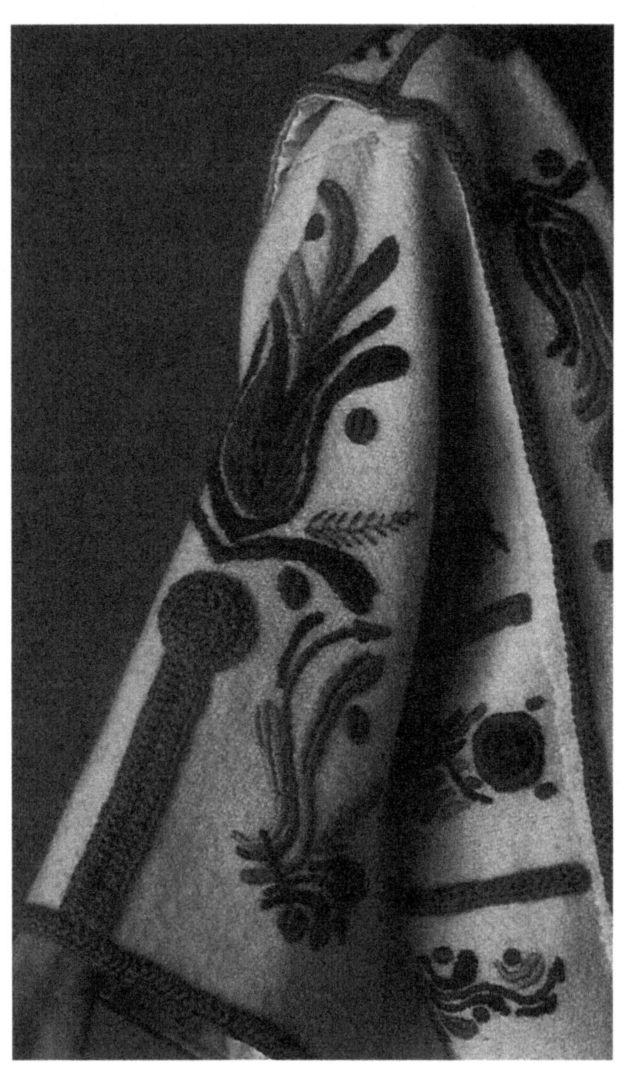

was so important in Hungary, that the weaving guilds between 1816 and 1817 produced fabric for 407,600 coats. One szur maker, unassisted, could make 200 to 300 szurs in a year. A decorated szur took much more time. In the 1800's, a master szur maker took nine days working from 4 a.m. to 9 p.m. to complete one richly embroidered szur.

I know that the handwork on my coat took at least that long but every stitch was fascinating and I felt great inner peace as I worked. I used waste canvas for transferring the pattern and removing that took almost as long as doing the embroidery! Finding the right wool to full meant several months of sampling and more sampling . . . I wanted fabric that was lightweight, had the appearance of felt, yet had a soft hand. I ended up using a 7/2 wool and it took nine yards of loosely woven material to produce the six yards of felted fabric required for my coat.

The choice of color for the stitchery was a careful process. I wanted subtle blends that would become more intense the closer one viewed the work. The colors, I felt, should represent the richness of the earth, pastures and fields where the coat was originally worn.

The edging braid was made by crocheting a chain and then couching it into place. The roundels, used historically to reinforce stress points, were also crocheted. The China silk lining added the final elegant touch. I continue to be emotionally involved with this piece.

> ". . . once it was important to weave cloth to clothe the body and even though machines can now do that faster and cheaper, handweavers are still at it. They weave now for its own sake . . . to clothe the soul."
>
> *Woven Works*

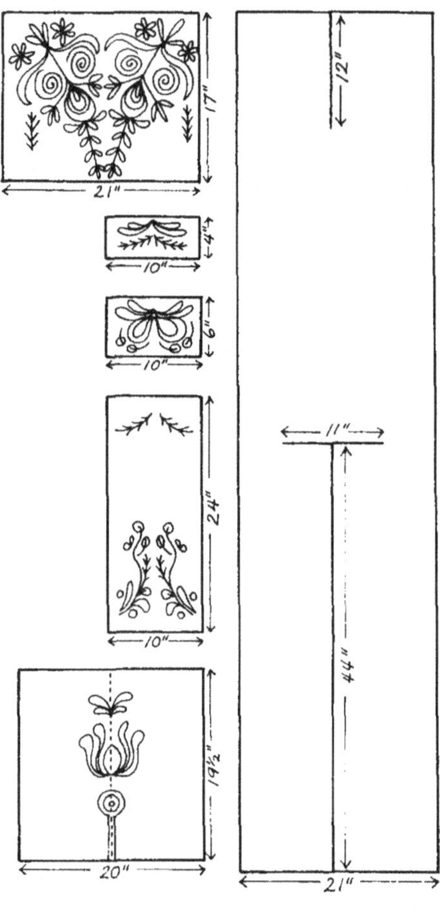

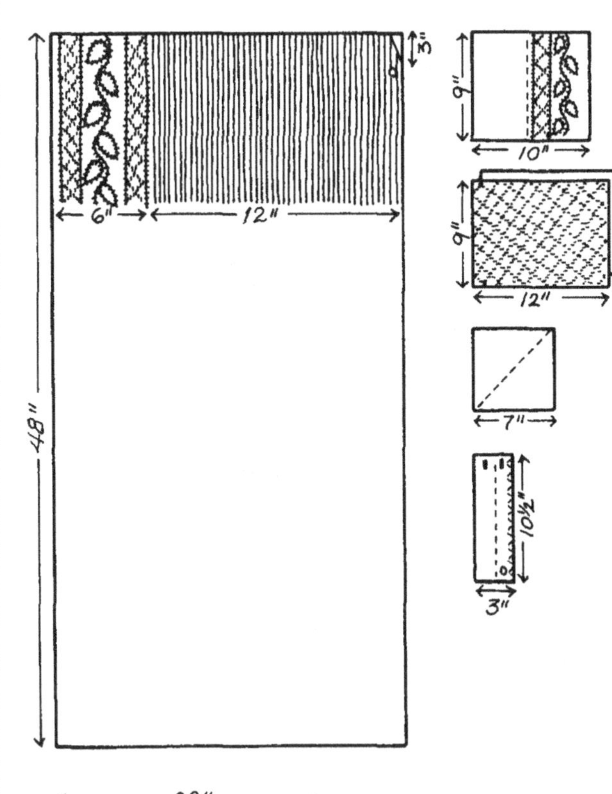

Smock

The smock is certainly one of my favorite garments for it is the epitome of all the advantages of using rectangles and squares for clothing. Traditionally made from three yards of fabric, the smock utilizes every inch of fabric and puts the selvedge edges to maximum use. Although the basic cut was always the same (so that the farmer's wife could "cut by eye" and not need a pattern) each smock was distinctive because of the surface embellishment. The fullness of the garment is controlled by gathers but there is total ease of movement due to the smocking . . . the original stretch stitch!

I knew that the weight of the fabric was critical so that it would gather easily. I selected cottolin combined with a pearl cotton of a similar size for the warp, cottolin weft. It was a challenge to weave in the draw-threads since all design decisions and smocking placement had to be made before going to the loom. I attempted to capture the feeling of the original workingman's smock, which focused on the embroidery and smocking stitches as the design features, so I used a neutral fabric with contrasting thread color.

(Warp layout on page 153.)

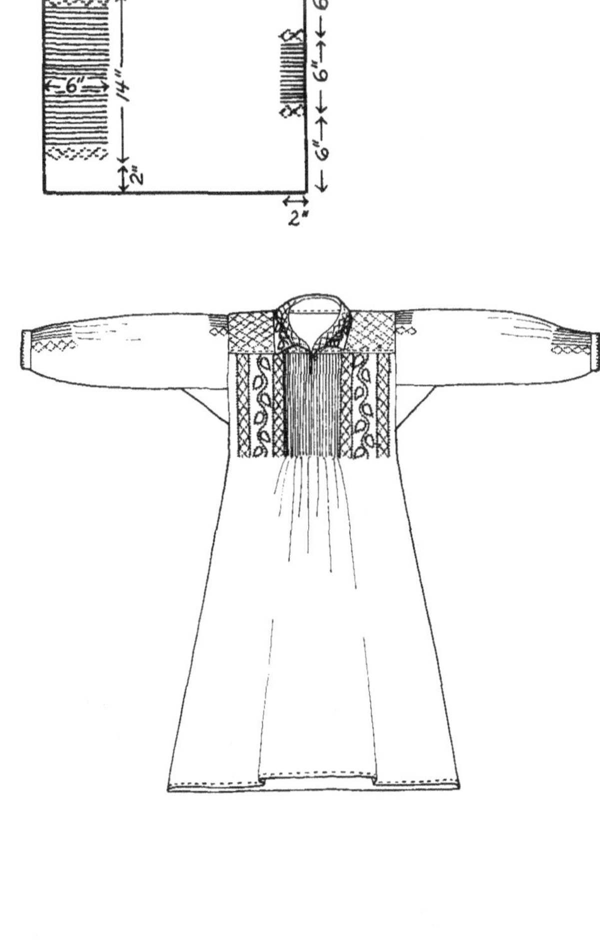

Silk Aba

The silk aba was inspired by an illustration in Tilke's *Costume Patterns and Design.* I was intrigued with the open work for shoulder ease and gusset, the use of various widths of panels to produce the final shape and the lightweight fabric created with weft-faced silk.

It took *two* years to find the right weight of silk wefts in white and beige that would produce the fine fabric I wanted for the aba. The panels were individually warped to the necessary widths and then joined together with lacing. The stitchery was done in natural dyed silks (left from an earlier project) and I used needle lace for the open work. Jill Nordfor's book, *Needle Lace and Needleweaving,* provided the inspiration for this feature. The herringbone stitch was worked over the shoulder area and then wrapped in tiny buttonhole stitches. The "gusset" areas were done in spaced buttonhole filling. Although I don't normally compute "how long it took", I know that the needle lace segments required some 60 hours to complete and I did finish the garment for a scheduled exhibit!

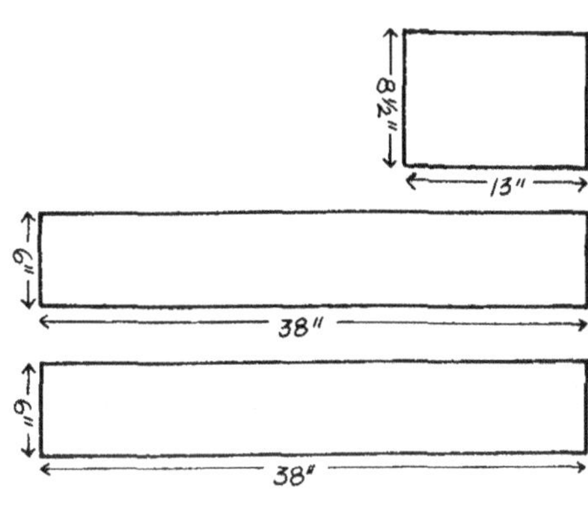

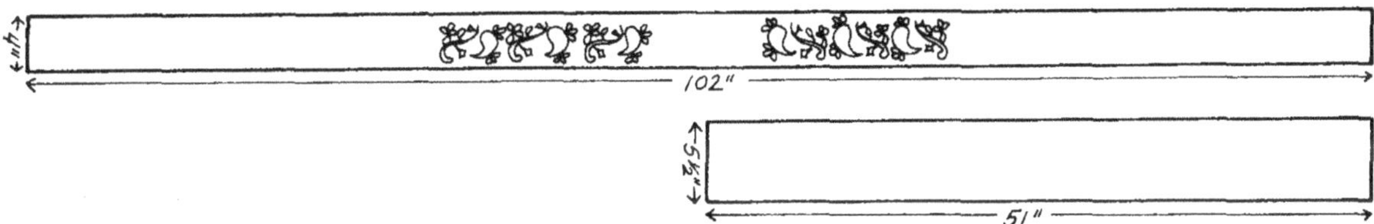

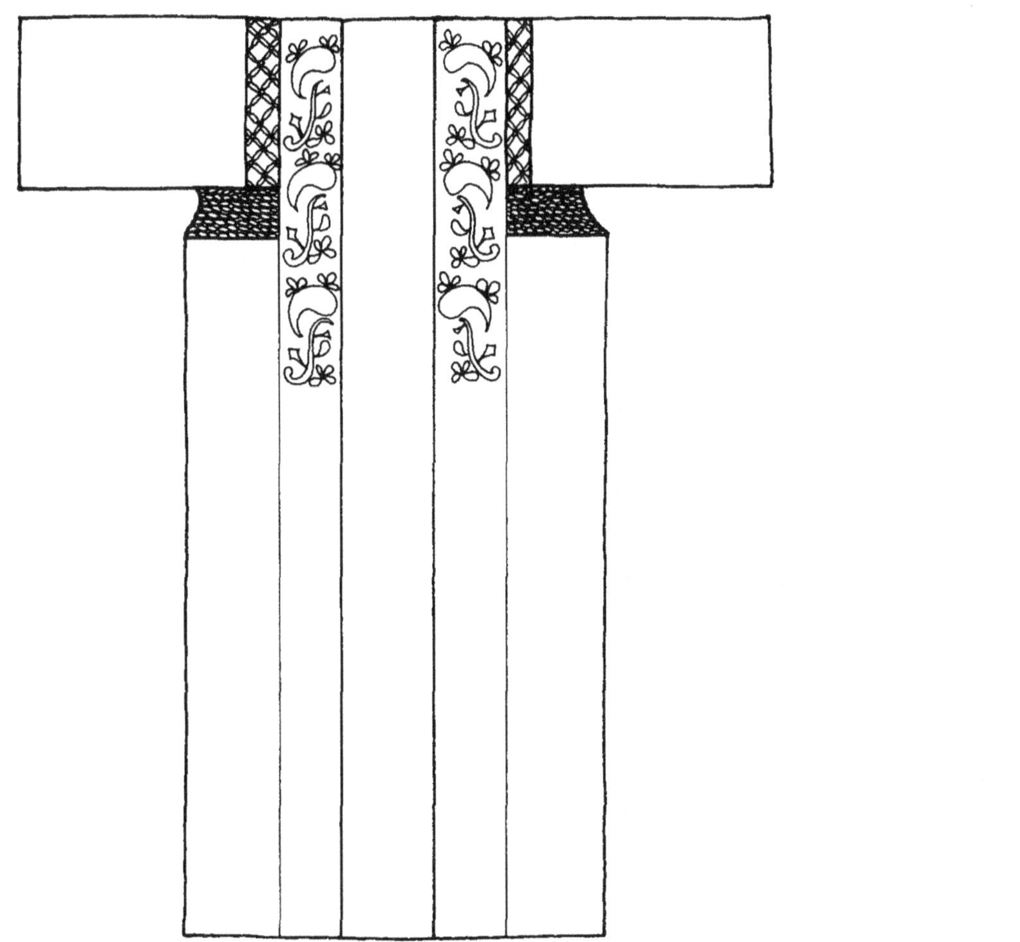

Akha Jacket

A photograph of the Akha jacket led to the weaving of this garment and a four-week journey to Thailand to find the people who created it and wore it.

Although the original garment is embellished with applique, I decided to use stitchery since it is handwork I enjoy. I chose cottolin for the fabric for it weaves into a garment weight I can wear the year round. I knew how difficult it would be to keep the lines of stitchery straight so I pre-planned and treadled in equally distanced lines across the back panel and on the sleeves. I then spent summer evenings, while the family watched tv, filling in the spaces with stitchery. The color choice was difficult and I literally spent days with yarn samples trying to make a decision. I wanted a contrast of "shiny versus dull" so decided to use pearl cotton . . . it also came in a wide range of colors and was durable for embroidery. The full intensity colors looked rich against the black fabric and though I began with several more colors than used, they seemed to eliminate themselves as I began working. I felt that repetition was important so once I had a few rows designed, the rest of the bands flowed from those. I made stitchery and color decisions as I worked and if it "didn't look right", I took it out and tried again. The authentic Akha jacket has wonderful adornments so I made Greek braid (an international touch) with bells and Middle Eastern buttons added for sound and magic.

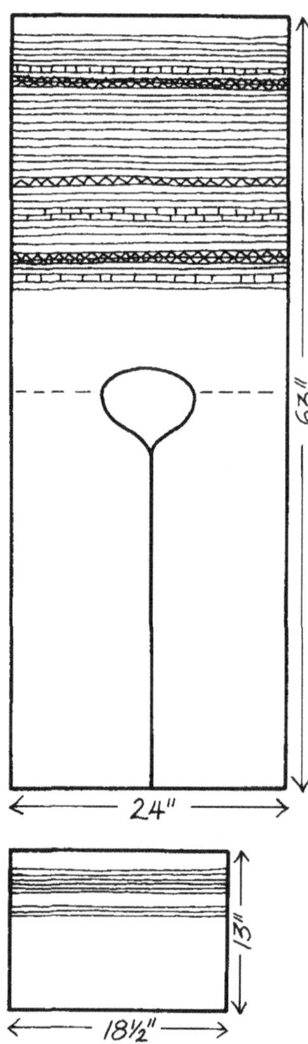

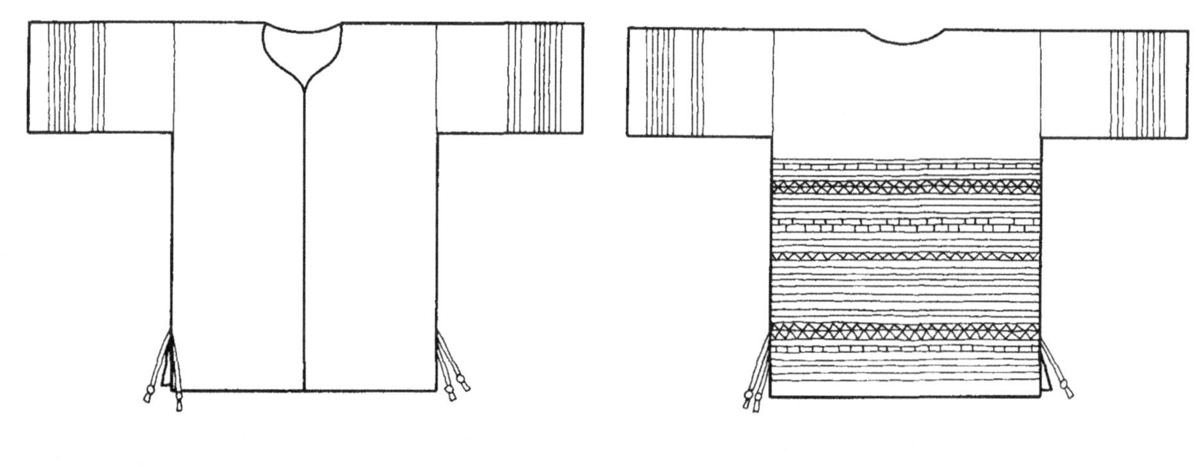

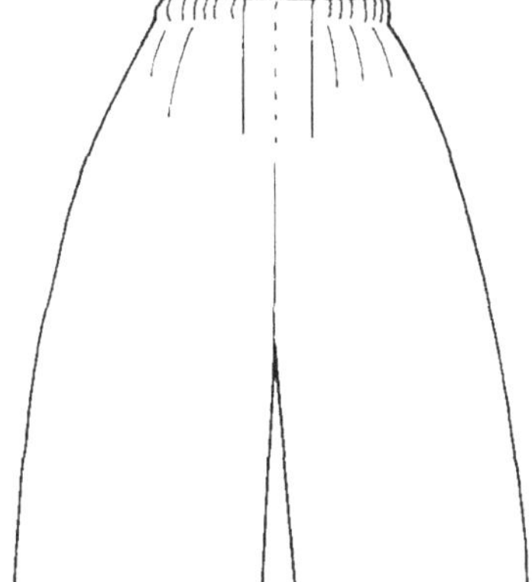

Culottes

As I researched clothing, I realized that nearly every culture has had some type of pants, worn by men or women, and typically made of two rectangles for the legs and with some type of gusset in the crotch for ease of movement. Thus my "pants period" began. I assembled drawings, pictures and photographs of pants from all parts of the world. These culottes were designed using just two rectangles (no gusset) and wide enough to accommodate my hips. The shape was narrowed in at the waistline with an elastic band and a box pleat further reduced the "bulk" in the front of the pants.

As a means of expanding my knowledge of color, I have used Malin Selander's color studies as a learning guide, taking inspiration from her woven color and combination of threads. That was my color source for these pants.

The horizontal bands on the legs evolved because of a treadling error undiscovered until the fabric was off the loom. I spent two days trying to resolve how best to disguise the mistake and chose to sew on the added strips of woven material. The width of the band was determined by the amount of fabric left from the project!

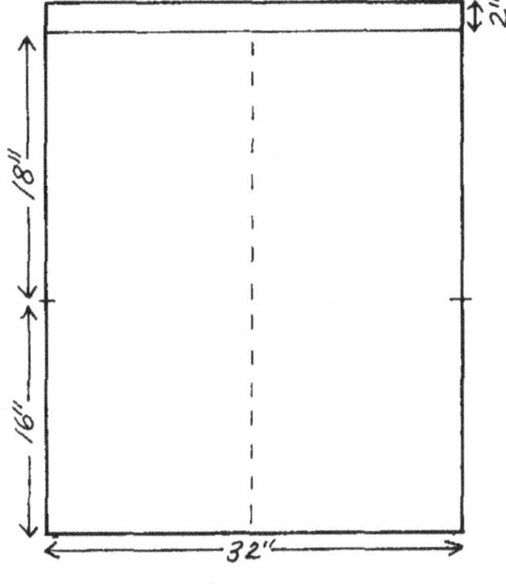

Portuguese Shepherd's Coat

When *Weave with Style* was published, I was fascinated with the entire book, but the photograph that most intrigued me was the one of the Portuguese shepherd in his coat made from a sheep skin. I thought about how to recreate the essence of this garment over a three-year period, knowing eventually I would weave it. Then I met Buckwheat, a wonderful angora goat who lives with Sally Bill on Lopez Island. I purchased Buckwheat's sheared mohair one spring and the concept began to develop. I have had a long-term love affair with unspun fleece used for surface texture, for I really dislike twisting a soft, free mass of fiber into a straight, rigid yarn. There must be something philosophical about that within me! It seemed so logical to use the unspun mohair laid into the warp to look like the natural fleece worn by the shepherd. I also wanted the inside to be as beautiful as the outside . . . a way to express how we all conceal our inner selves with an outer layer or cocoon, yet within is the butterfly waiting to come forth. I used my handspun silk for the filler yarn between the rows of mohair to create a lining of silk. It seemed only right that natural dyes be used with these magnificent natural fibers. I realize now that my color choice came from a visit, years earlier, to the canyons of Sedona, Arizona. I had never before seen those warm pink hues in nature . . . the feelings were obviously internalized and later expressed in the colors I chose for the cloak. The link of a Portuguese shepherd to contemporary life continues. A functional garment becomes elegant through the use of fiber and color.

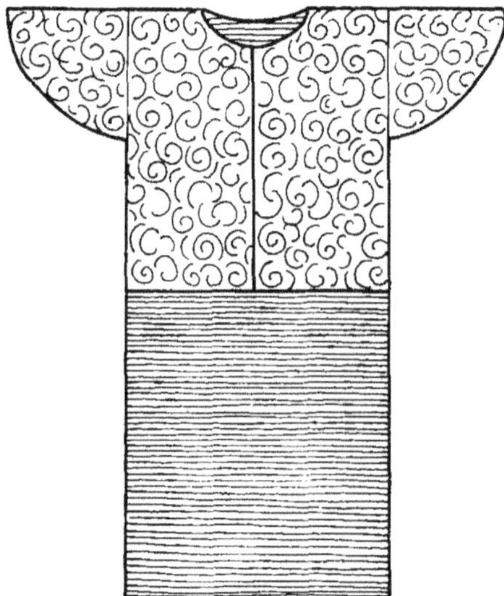

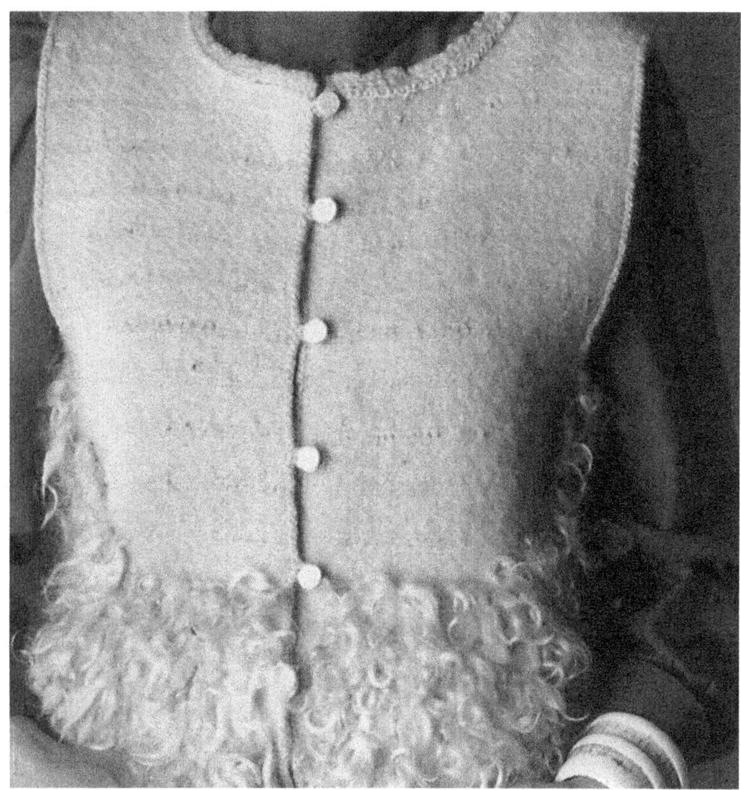

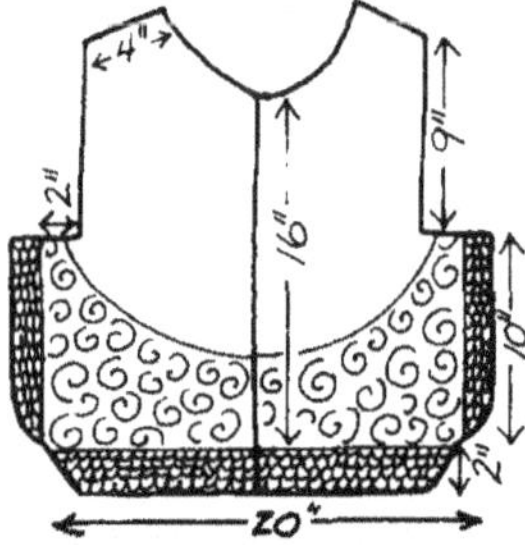

Sweetie Pie

Ah yes, Sweetie Pie . . . that is the name of the Angora goat (again, belonging to Sally Bill on Lopez Island) that provided the mohair. I was, at this point, beginning my exploration of felted fabric and wanted to simulate the historic vests of embroidered tanned hides with fleece inside. I also wondered if you could rya knot mohair into place (which doesn't mat like wool), loosely weave a garment shape and throw the entire piece into the washing machine and have it work. I decided there was only one way to find out so I loom-shaped the vest (20% larger to allow for the shrinkage I get in felted fabric), knotted Sweetie Pie into place leaving extra space between the knots and the rows to allow for the fulling and put the fabric into the machine. It worked, the vest fit perfectly and the fabric felted just like the sample. But there was one minor problem. *All* of Sweetie Pie whipped out of the cloth during agitation. It did mat some, so I spent hours needling back into the fabric new ryas of mohair. I abandoned the entire project when I got to the fronts of the vest and the flat area is now referred to as a "subtle design area". I worked in white on white just to save time in dyeing the mohair. Crochet was used to pull in the waist area and the edges of the vest were finished with a crocheted chain couched into place and also used for the button loops.

Nimsha

Nimsha happened because of the problems with Sweetie Pie. I was determined to felt fabric with mohair, rya knotted into place. The original design of this piece began with two rectangles seamed up the back with two additional rectangles as sleeves (type of ruana with sleeves). All surfaces, except those under the sleeves, were to have been knotted mohair. I dyed the fleece to match the Harrisville warp and weft, but midway into the weaving, I realized I didn't have enough fleece. I knew that I could never match the color a second time, and after sheer panic, came up with "plan B". There would be no fleece over the shoulder areas and no fleece on the sleeves. When the fabric was felted I had more material in the sleeve lengths than planned and realized I could use the field kimono sleeve and therefore not waste any fabric. The short length of the jacket, combined with this sleeve, gave a raglan look I liked. I extended the sleeve length with crocheted cuffs and overlapped the front panels for a fitted look.

I kept the mohair in place during felting by folding the length of woven fabric in half, right side to right side but with a piece of cotton cloth sandwiched between. The edges were basted together and then the piece was fulled in the washing machine. The fleece stayed in place and the wool felted as planned.

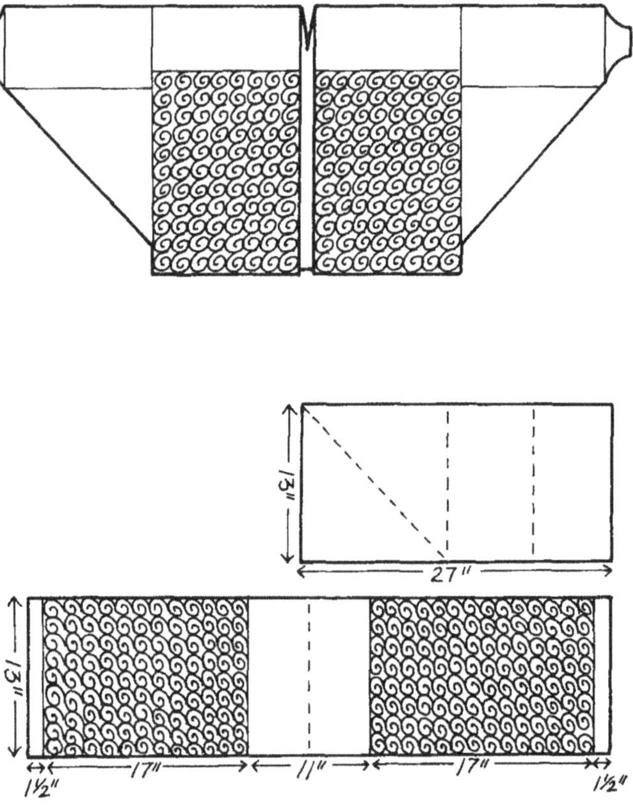

Batikari

A west African shirt made of 4″-wide strips with gores for hip fullness was the inspiration for batikari. I continue to be fascinated with narrow woven pieces that can be assembled to create a larger whole. It is ironic that the first thing I wove on my new 52″ loom was the 22 yards of 4″-wide strips for this dress.

Many of the African garments are indigo dyed so I chose logwood from the blue color family. I had odd amounts of cultivated and tussah silk left from earlier projects. These I used to exhaust the dye bath and to experiment with the effects of various mordants with logwood. I lined up the balls of dyed silk in a color sequence I liked, numbered each and transferred these numbers to a pellon pattern the size I needed for adding width to my dress. I wasn't about to cut fabric gores, but having just learned to crochet, that seemed a logical way to obtain the triangular shapes. At Little League games all one spring, I crocheted gores, changing colors when indicated on my pattern. The gores were handsewn into place by lacing the edges to the crocheting that had been done along all the selvedges of the fabric strips.

There were several "happy surprises" with this piece: the tussah used for the dress does not wrinkle so it is ideal for traveling . . . the color changes in the gores produce a subtle tapestry landscape which I find pleasing. However, I did not allow for the extra width created from the crocheted selvedge edges, so the dress is a bit larger than I would like. However, there will be future "editions" of batikari which will depict the colors found in the sunrises and sunsets in this area.

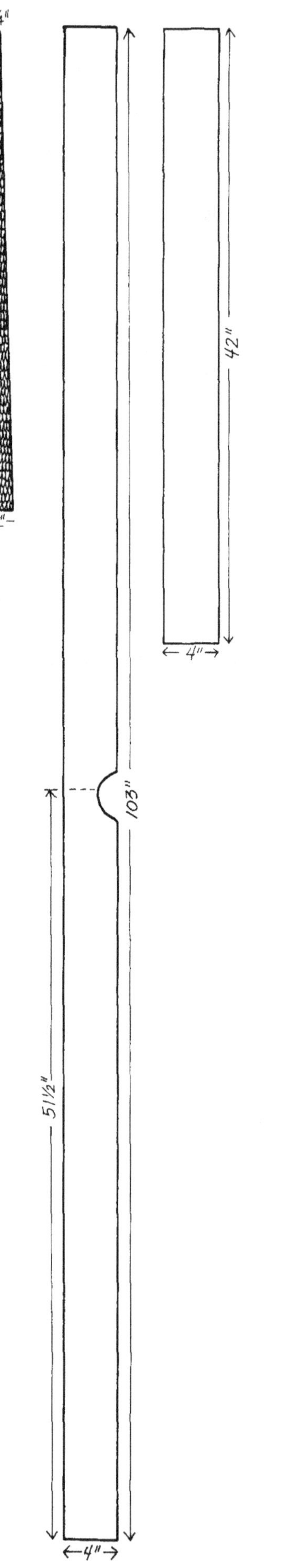

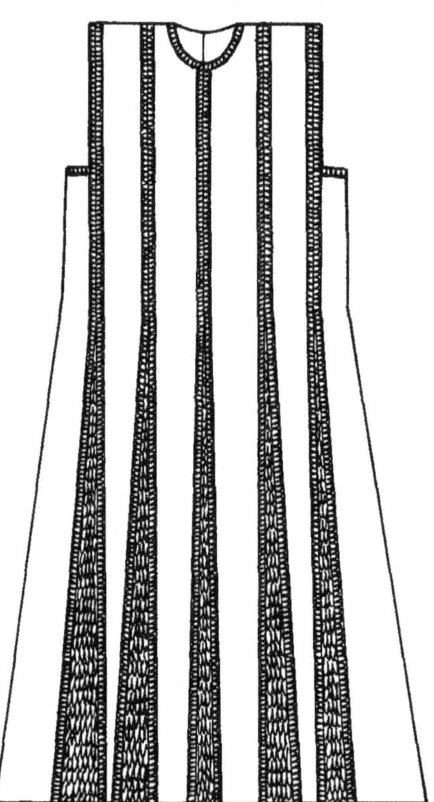

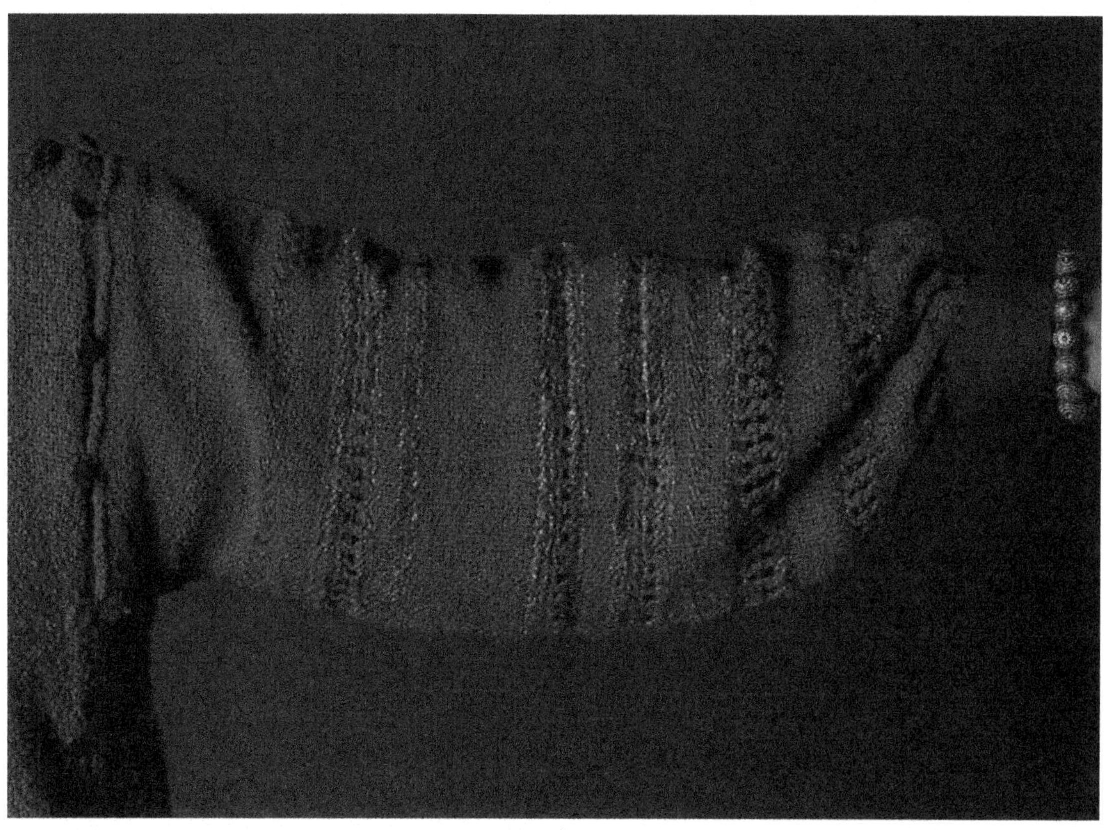

Grey Sky Shirt

Grey Sky Shirt was born in a yarn store. I saw one cone of grey silk boucle and before I realized what was happening, I had it in hand and was selecting soft pinks, greys and off-whites that seemed to belong with it. The yarns came first—my personal response to the colors I see in the sky where I live, and then the garment design followed. It had to be a small woven piece for there wasn't much grey boucle. I decided to repeat the Purple Plum top but couldn't decide whether to do long sleeves or over-sized shorter ones. I chose both! I now realize that I had seen an African shirt with large sleeve extensions and had admired an interpretation of this by Judy Thomas of Seattle, where the sleeves could be removed. I was not conscious of those things at the time I was designing the garment.

"Whatever we look at with delight
Whatever we see that gives us pleasure
Though we may think we have forgotten
The next day
Will influence us all our lives."
George Santayana

Grey Sky Shirt practically wove itself . . . it just flowed from within. The only problem was finding the right button and slacks. Even that was finally resolved. A weaving that was meant to be.

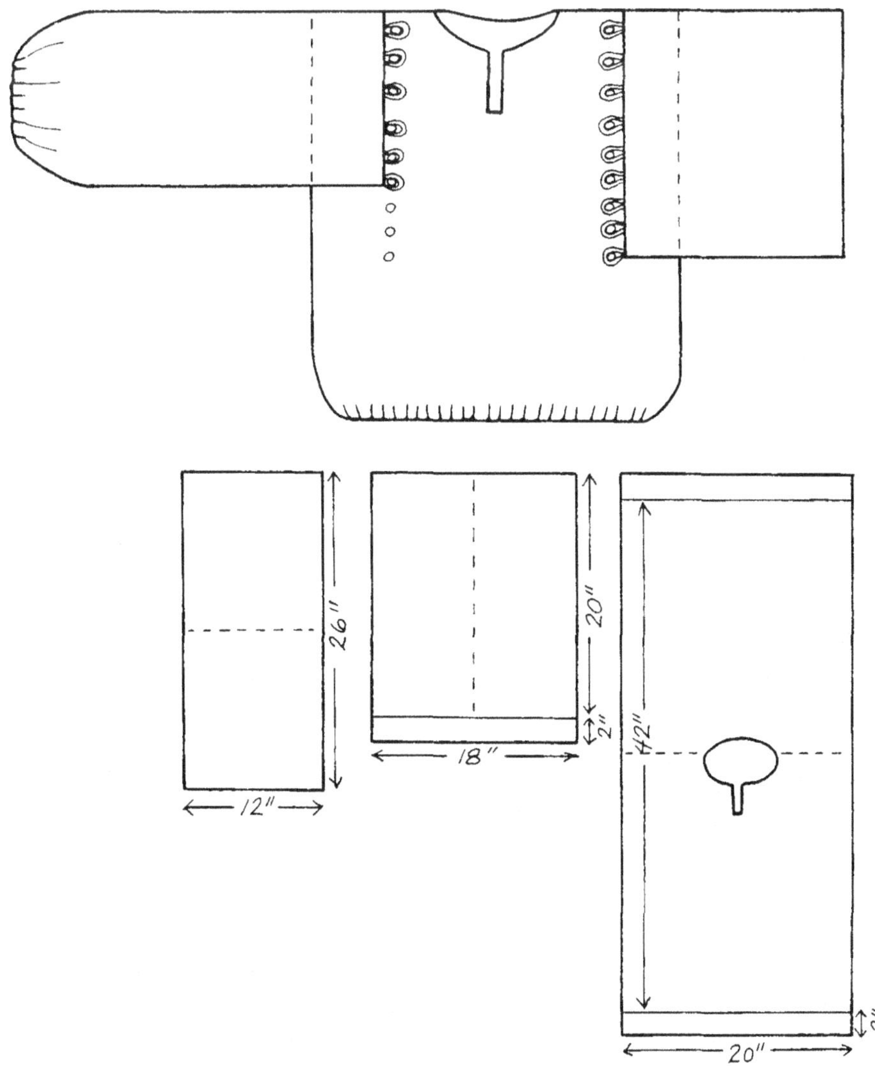

Aba

This style of aba has haunted me for years and again the idea came from Tilke. Something about the flow of the robe and asymmetrical tapestry spoke of the "men of high stature" who originally wore it. Feeling that I could be a "woman of high stature", I decided to interpret the piece as a special occasion evening coat.

Finding the right fiber for weight and appearance was not easy. I sampled on and off for a year but when I came upon Harrisville singles, I knew I was close to the answer. Once I had the sett determined and decided I didn't like what happened with fulling (this garment will never see water) I had to make a color choice. Royal purple seemed appropriate although my purple is a bit more subtle. I finally made the decision, only to learn I had to special order the quantity I needed so another six weeks of waiting dragged on. The warping was miserable with yards of singles twisting on one another. The silk tapestry area was another set-back, for I couldn't find the "right" colors. I finally started throwing skeins of silk in the dye pot until I had the colors I wanted. *Then* I discovered that the silk wouldn't cover the wool warp, but by treadling pairs in those areas, that problem was resolved. However, I now had distorted sections where the weaving changed back to the wool weft and tabby. You can see solid stitchery across the back where such segments would not steam flat!

Even with all the time and trauma involved, the aba is one of my favorite pieces and I do feel absolutely royal when I wear it. It was an additional coup to have Jack Lenor Larsen designate it as an award winner in a fiber exhibition.

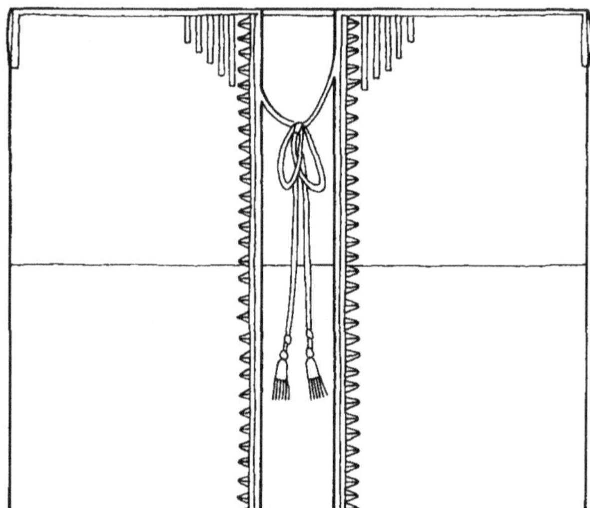

PHOTO: ROGER SCHREIBER

Szur Jacket

The publication, *The Hungarian Szur,* from the Royal Ontario Museum has been in my library for years. I liked the cut of the garments which were all constructed of rectangles and squares, and the richness of the surface embellishment. It was a long time before I learned how to duplicate the melton-like fabric traditionally used for these pieces . . . in fact, I originally thought it was felt. So I learned to make felt. What I made was so stiff it could stand alone and I also questioned its durability as a garment surface. I then learned that szurs were made from felted fabric and further experimentation was then required to obtain the appropriate weight and hand of the material.

I wove the cloth, fulled it to the necessary thickness and size, and then cut out the units for the jacket. Although the cut edges do not ravel (one of the reasons historically that cloth was fulled), I used a knotted buttonhole stitch as an edge finish. The surface detail is thick wool yarn couched into place. I didn't know how to evenly place the yarn until I happened to read a book on beading. The author stated that designs could be accurately transferred by first drawing the design on tissue paper, machine stitching the lines through the paper onto the fabric, then removing the paper and having the necessary guides for the handwork. I didn't like seeing the rows of machine stitching on the inside of the jacket, so after the couching was completed, I covered the machine work with tiny chain stitches using pearl cotton. It evolved that the szur jacket can be worn forwards, backwards or inside out! Most versatile.

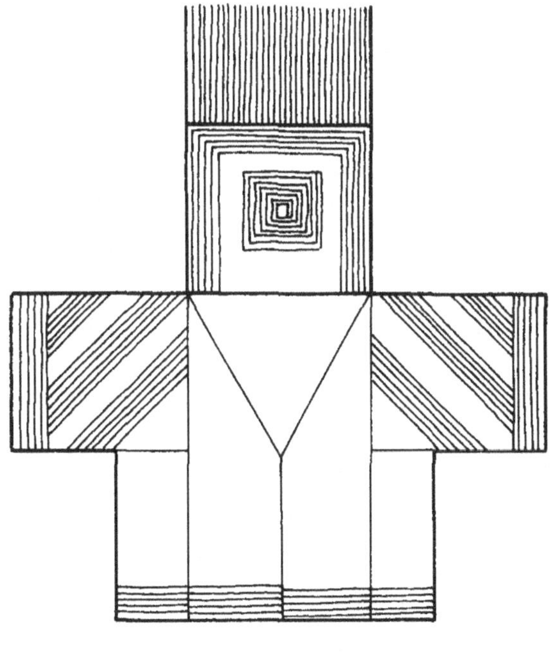

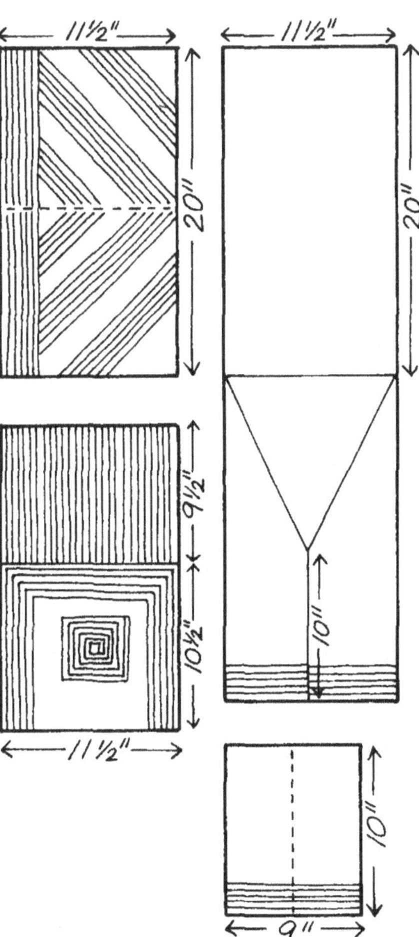
11½"
20"
11½"
20"
9½"
10½"
10"
11½"
10"
9"

Purple Plum

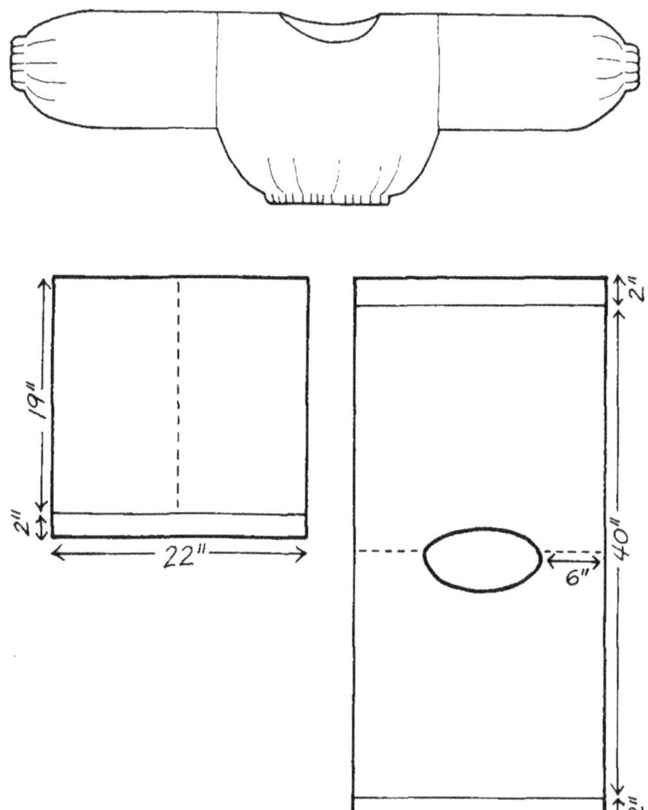

Purple Plum was created directly from the yarn shelf. I was tired of looking at those particular yarns and yet there wasn't enough of any one type for a warp, thus I mixed them together, including the bias cotton strips. I had "discovered" that I could wear tops that ended at the waist and that gathers can create fit both in the bodice and sleeves . . . and that is how the shape of Purple Plum evolved. It is a very comfortable garment but I made the mistake of using rayon chenille in part of the random warp and with the stretch and pulling involved in putting the top on, those yarns have stretched and snapped. I keep removing them and I must admit that the fabric now looks as though I did some type of clever skipped-dent sleying.

This combination of three rectangles has limitless potential for a variety of very wearable garments.

Capote

The concept of a Hudson Bay blanket being carefully cut and divided to make a snug wrap-around coat appeals to my practical side. During the 1800's, the French Canadian trappers used the trade blanket for this purpose. By planning, the blanket stripes accented the sleeves, hood and lower portion of the coat and the blanket fringe was used to help the rain run off the garment rather than soak into the fabric. With the front sections wider than the back portion, adequate overlap as protection in cold or inclement weather was provided.

When I designed my piece, I felt the color should be dark in feeling. I seemed to keep seeing red Hudson Bay blankets somewhere in my past. I used all the odd amounts of the deep wine yarns in my supply and created a mixed warp. The "stripes" were woven using handspun mohair, silk and wool, and brought to the surface with soumak and loops.

The slits for the sleeves were done on the loom. The warp was left unwoven in those areas that would feature fringe. The capote was lined to give added warmth and to feel more comfortable in wearing. A historic coat that is totally practical today.

(Warp layout on page 153.)

Country Kimono

The kimono is one of the most practical, comfortable and attractive garments made from rectangles and squares. Having collected and worn kimonos for years, the time had come to weave my own. The shape of the country kimono appeals to me most because it was worn by the peasants of Japan as they spent their days working in the fields.

I had been doing sett samples using rayon chenille and liked the feel and drapability of the warp-faced fabric. I found that a fine weft simply held the crowded warps together but would disappear into the weaving. I was concerned about having enough fiber for the sleeves, so I tied on a second warp for those pieces. By planning the warp layout and using two shuttles in certain areas, almost all edges were selvedges, so assembling the garment was very easy.

(Warp layout on page 153.)

Two-Drink Dress

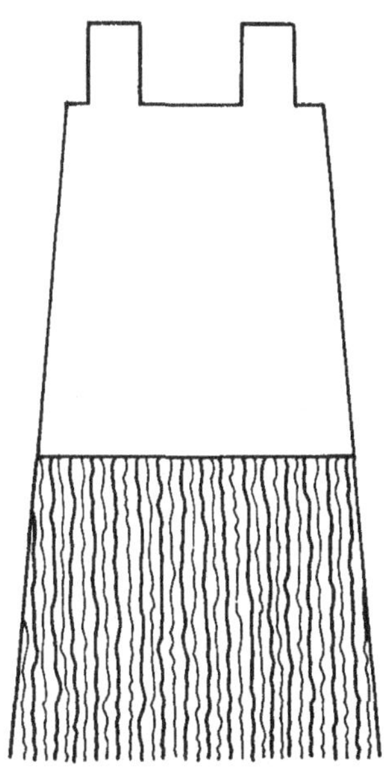

Where can I begin the saga of the "two-drink dress"? It started with an important art event in Seattle that Jack and I were to attend . . . one where I would know no one. The dress began to develop and apparently was reflecting some facet of my personality that had been buried and was ready to emerge.

The yarn was from Uruguay and I combined it with mohair to insure there was enough for the dress. The A-line shape was from a Mexican dress that fit me well. The wrapped warps (done on the loom) showed off the handspun yarn, was a technique I enjoyed doing, and gave the "pizazz" I wanted. All went well until the night of the event. As we were dressing to leave for the big city, I realized that I wasn't ready to be that "me" yet. I told Jack, "I can't do it." He answered, "Have two drinks, you can do anything." I did—it worked! The dress went to the party. I had a wonderful time and met fascinating people in all areas of the arts. I also learned how much clothing communicates. As one friend I met that night told me later, "I felt anyone crazy enough to either weave that or wear it was worth knowing." I was visually saying something about who I was and that allowed those who responded to that message to come up to me and initiate a conversation. The dress has been to many events since that night . . . I *always* have a grand time. It does too.

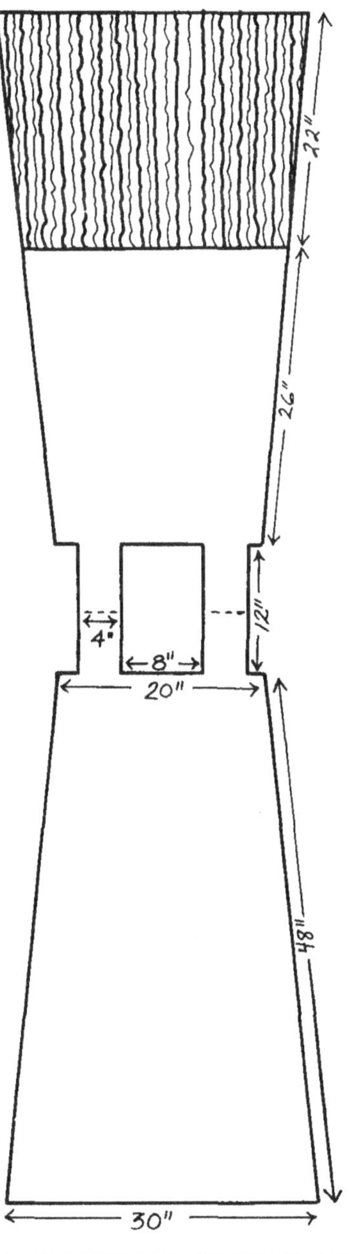

"Remember our heritage is our power; we can know ourselves and our capacities by seeing that other women have been strong. To reclaim our past and insist that it become a part of our human history is the task that lies before us. For the future requires that women, as well as men, shape the world destiny."

Judy Chicago

"Nothing living should ever be treated with contempt.
Whatever it is that lives, a man, a tree or a bird,
should be touched gently, because the time is short."
Elizabeth Goudge
from *Green Dolphin Country*

Chapter 6
The Pattern

When creating loom-shaped clothing, it is essential to have a pattern, so you know what shape and size to weave the garment pieces. A pattern can be made by using:
— A favorite garment from your wardrobe.
— An ethnic garment.
— Someone else's garment that fits you.
— Commercial patterns.
— Patterns from clothing books.
— A drawing of a garment.

If you are working from a drawing, you need to draft a pattern. This is a straightforward process whereby you take a sketch of the garment, draw your figure with body measurements, and pattern your design onto that figure. You then cut the garment pieces in muslin or other fabric to those dimensions, tape the units together and try the garment on for fit. Adjustments are made by retaping or recutting the pieces until the cloth pattern fits and hangs to your satisfaction.

Ease must be considered in pattern drafting, and involves the amount of space between you and the garment. The standard ease in commercial patterns is 3″-5″ for the bust and 2″-10″ for the hips. It is common for coats and outer garments to have 10″ of ease to allow for free movement when worn over other clothing. The amount of ease will be affected by the weight of the fabric, the use of linings, and what is worn under the garment. You have to determine how much ease is comfortable for you.

In drafting patterns, it is helpful to use cloth in the patterning process that is similar in weight to the final woven fabric. Old tablecloths, bedspreads or sale fabrics are possible sources for pattern material. Duck and denim are good when patterning heavier garments such as coats or jackets. When the final cloth pattern is worked out, draw all design elements onto the cloth: embellishment seams, stripes, pockets and so forth. Indicate how you plan to finish all edges, identify each piece and which is the right side of the fabric. This pattern represents the finished garment, and take-up, hems, fringe, or shrinkage are not computed until the warp layout is made.

You will need your body measurements in order to draft a pattern. Have someone measure you so that numbers are accurate, and record these on the following chart.

Body Measurement

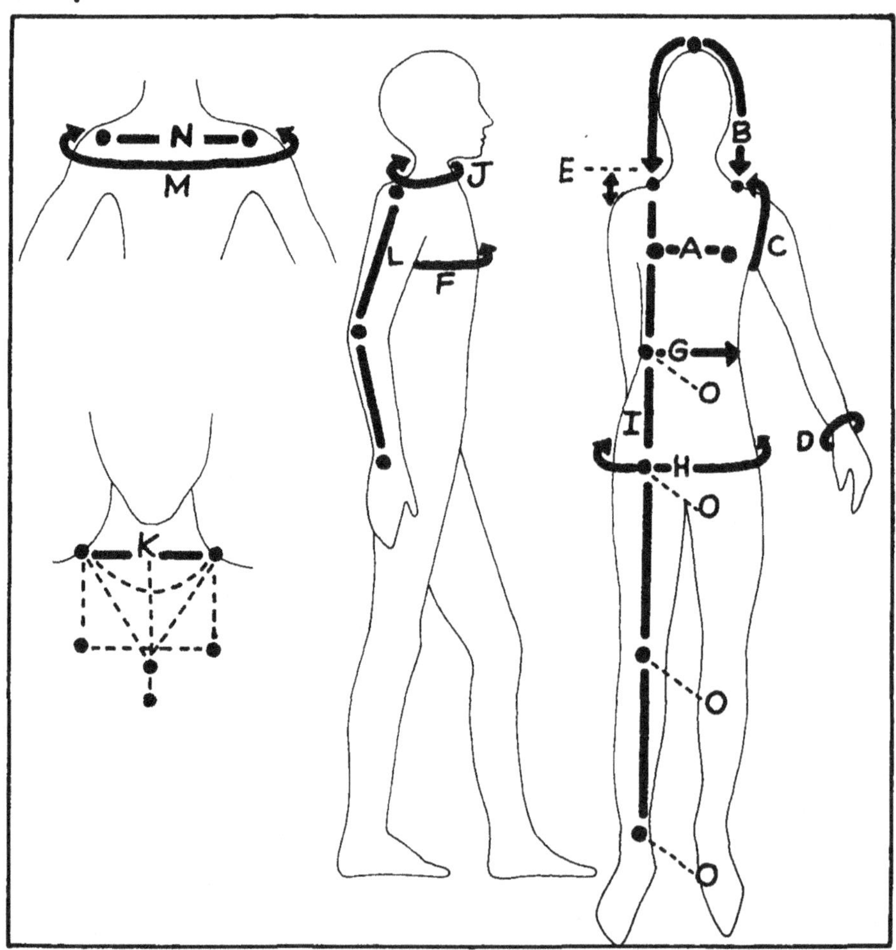

Measurement Chart

______A. Bust point width—point to point on the bust.

______B. Hood depth—measure from base of neck over top of head to base of neck.

______C. Armhole—keep tape loose around arm at armhole so easy movement is possible.

______D. Wrist—keep tape loose enough for the hand to pass through.

______E. Shoulder slope—use ruler held parallel to floor at base of neck; measure space between ruler and edge of shoulder where the arm drops.

______F. Bust—measure at fullest width.

______G. Waist—measure at natural waistline.

______H. Hips—measure at fullest width.

______I. Hips—measure how far down from the shoulder the fullest width is found.

______J. Neck—measure circumference of neck close to the base of the neck.

______K. Neck openings—measure down from shoulder and mark on diagram.

______L. Wing span—measure from wrist of bent arm to neck vertebra (bone at base of neck) to wrist of other arm.

______M. Shoulder girth—measure 2″ down from the shoulder around body.

______N. Back width—measure width between shoulder crests (where shoulder and arm break).

______O. Garment length—measure from shoulder over bust to desired length and from shoulder down back to desired length.

Shoulder to waist.	______Front	______Back
Shoulder to hip length.	______Front	______Back
Shoulder to knee length.	______Front	______Back
Shoulder to ankle length.	______Front	______Back

The first step in pattern drafting is to draw the garment shape folded and unfolded.

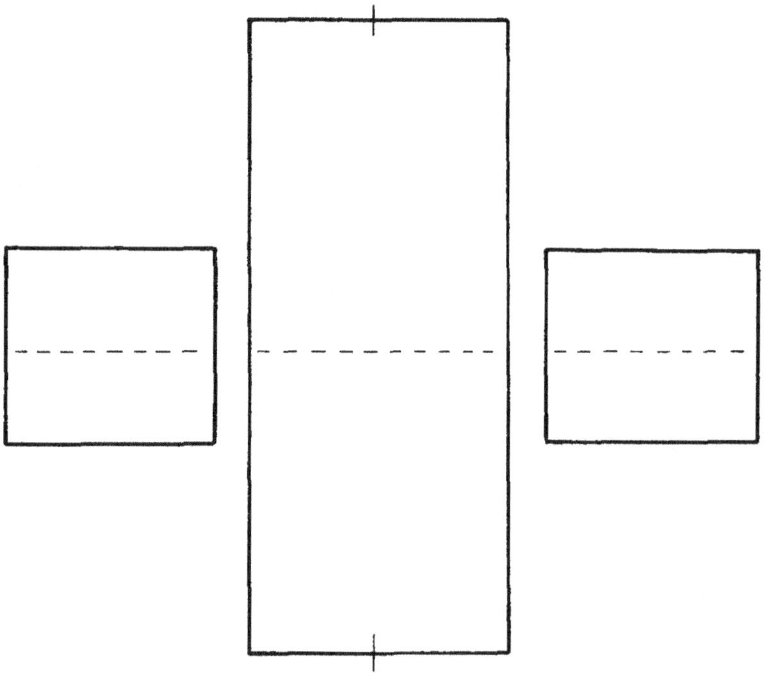

For any garment that ends above the fullest width of the hips, determine the size of the pattern pieces using the following formulas:

Garment Width:
(bust measurement [F] + ease) ÷ 2 = width

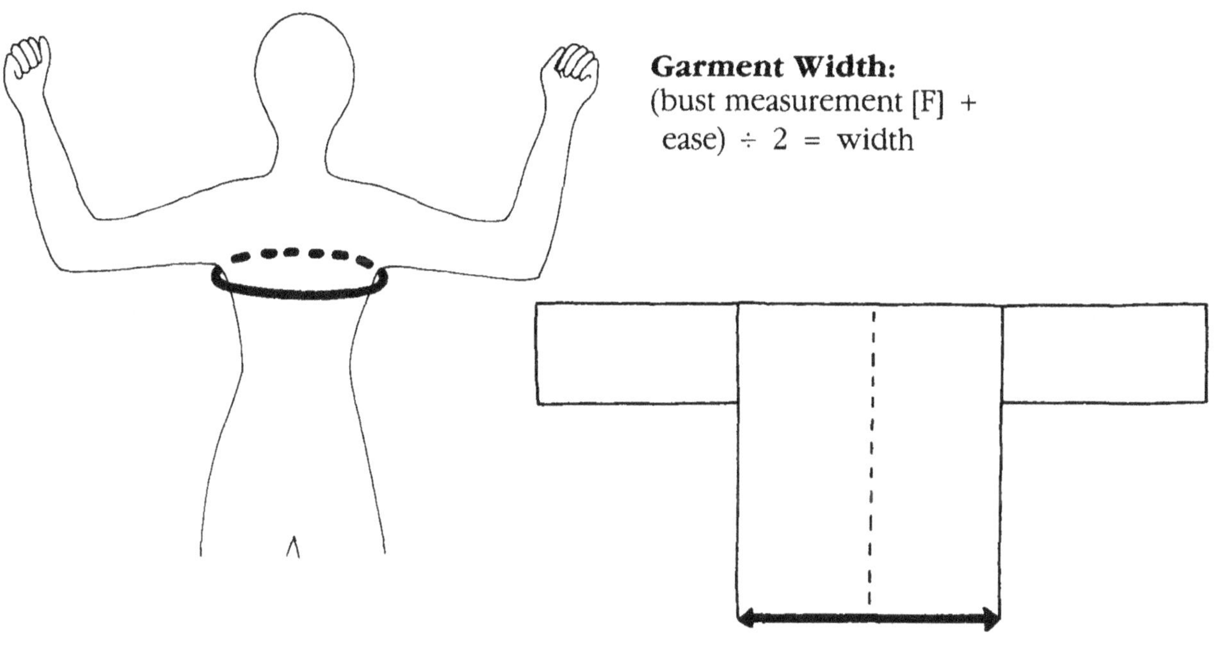

Garment Length: desired length of garment from shoulder (O) × 2 = length of pattern piece

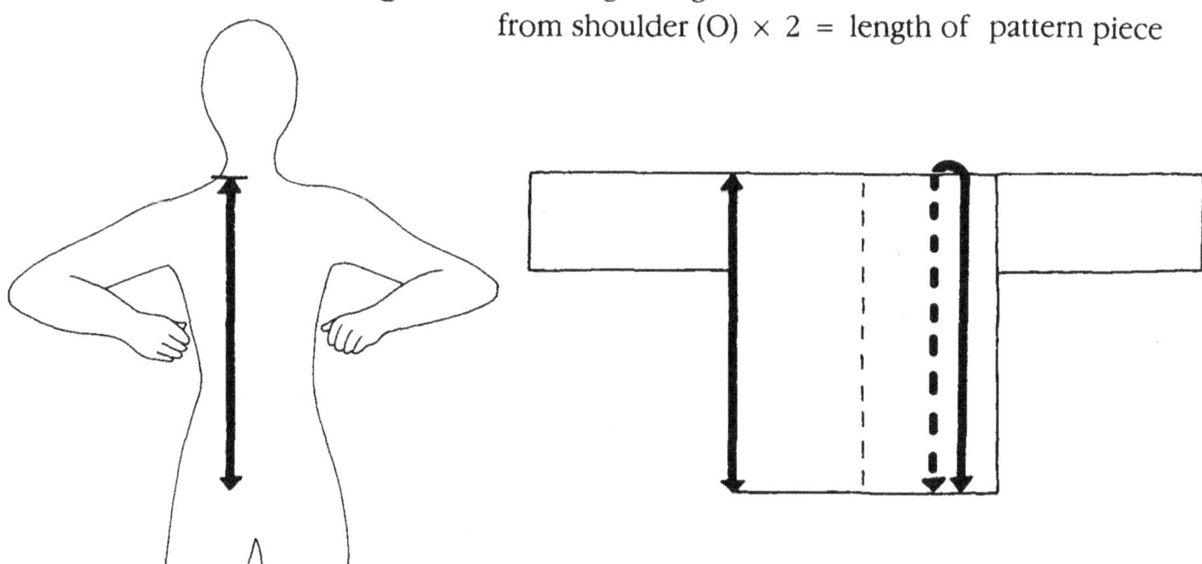

Sleeve Length: (wing span [L] – width of garment) ÷ 2 = sleeve length

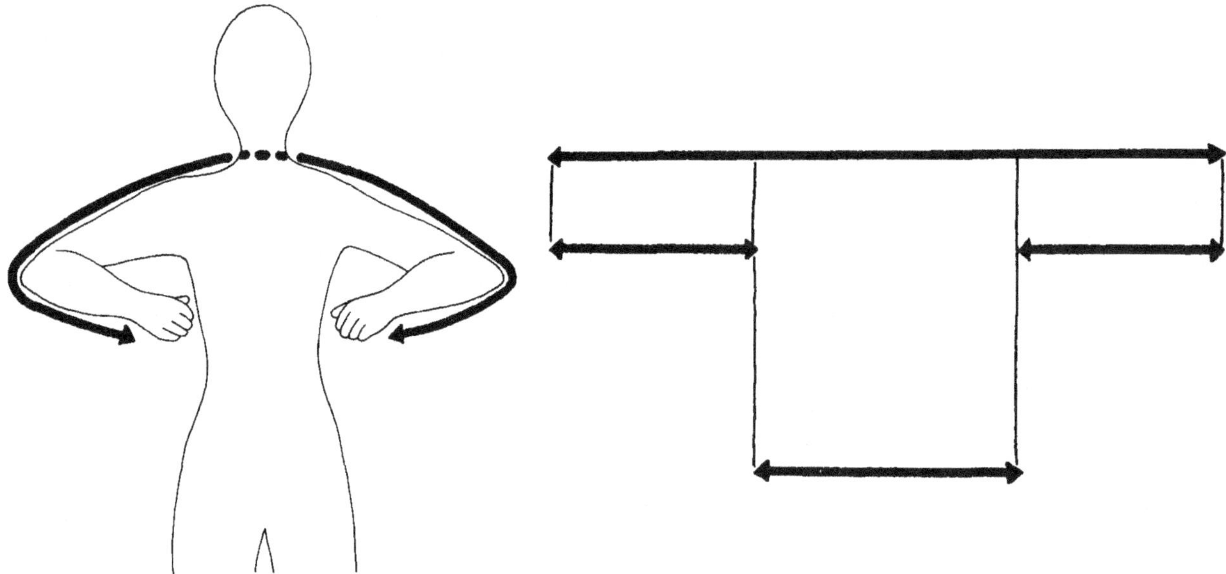

Width of Sleeve: circumference of armhole (C) = width of sleeve

If you want a narrower sleeve use some type of gusset or leave the underarm open (see Chapter 3).

Transfer all these figures to the drawing of the unfolded garment shape. Cut the pieces from cloth and add a neckline of your choice, as described on pages 82-83. Tape the pieces together using wide masking tape, and try on. Continue to adjust and try on until the garment fits to your satisfaction. If the garment fits well in the bust and shoulder area but seems snug around the hips, consider venting, shortening the length or adding side inserts.

For a garment that extends below the fullest part of the hips, pattern draft with the preceding formulas when determining the length of the garment. To compute the width, compare the shoulder girth (do not add ease) to the hip measurement (add some ease to the hip), then use the larger of the two figures.

$$\frac{\text{shoulder girth (M)} \ \text{or} \ \text{hip measurement (H)}}{2} + \text{hip ease} = \text{width of garment}$$

If the hip measurement is considerably larger than the shoulder girth, the garment may hang too far over the shoulder. If that is the case, use the shoulder girth ÷ 2 for the garment width and add fullness in the hip area with side inserts, gores, etc.

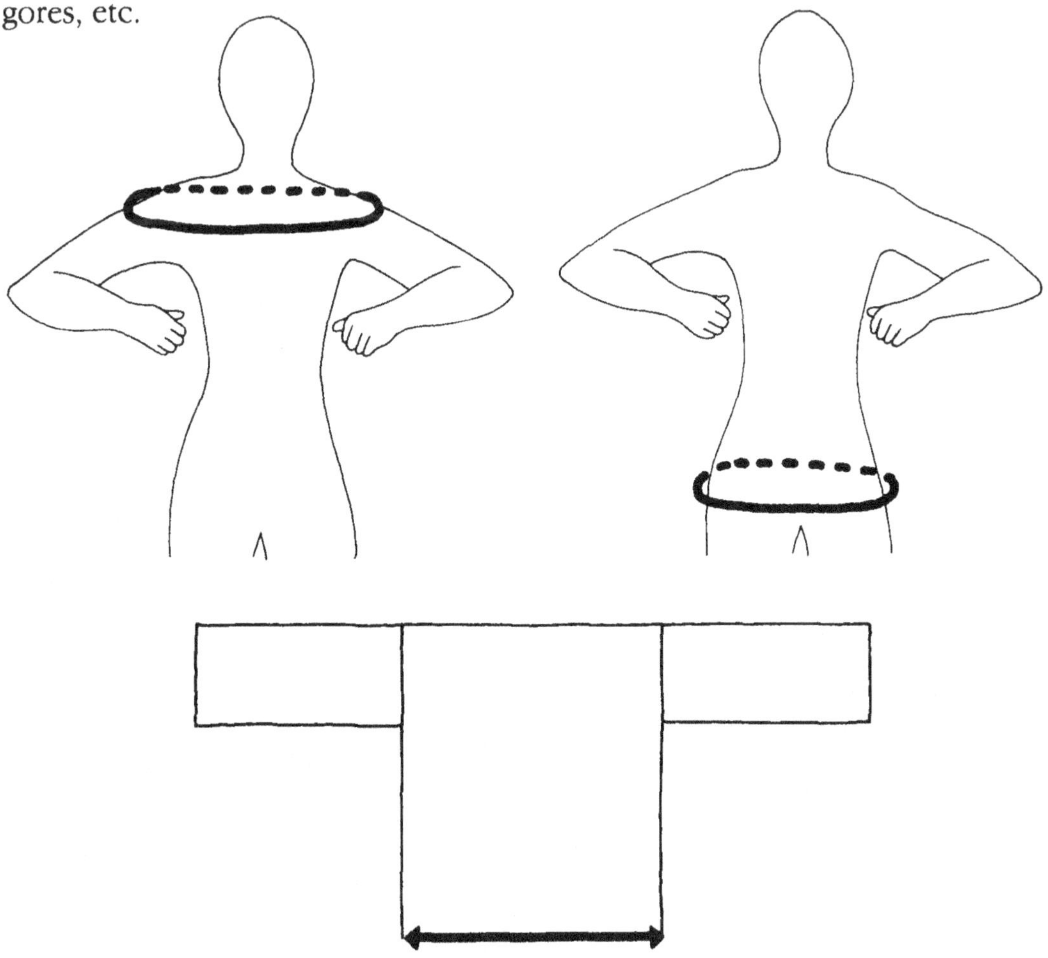

If the garment is to have a narrow center with side panels, the side panel join should be at or near the bust point. A large busted figure should have the joining line 1″-1½″from the bust point.

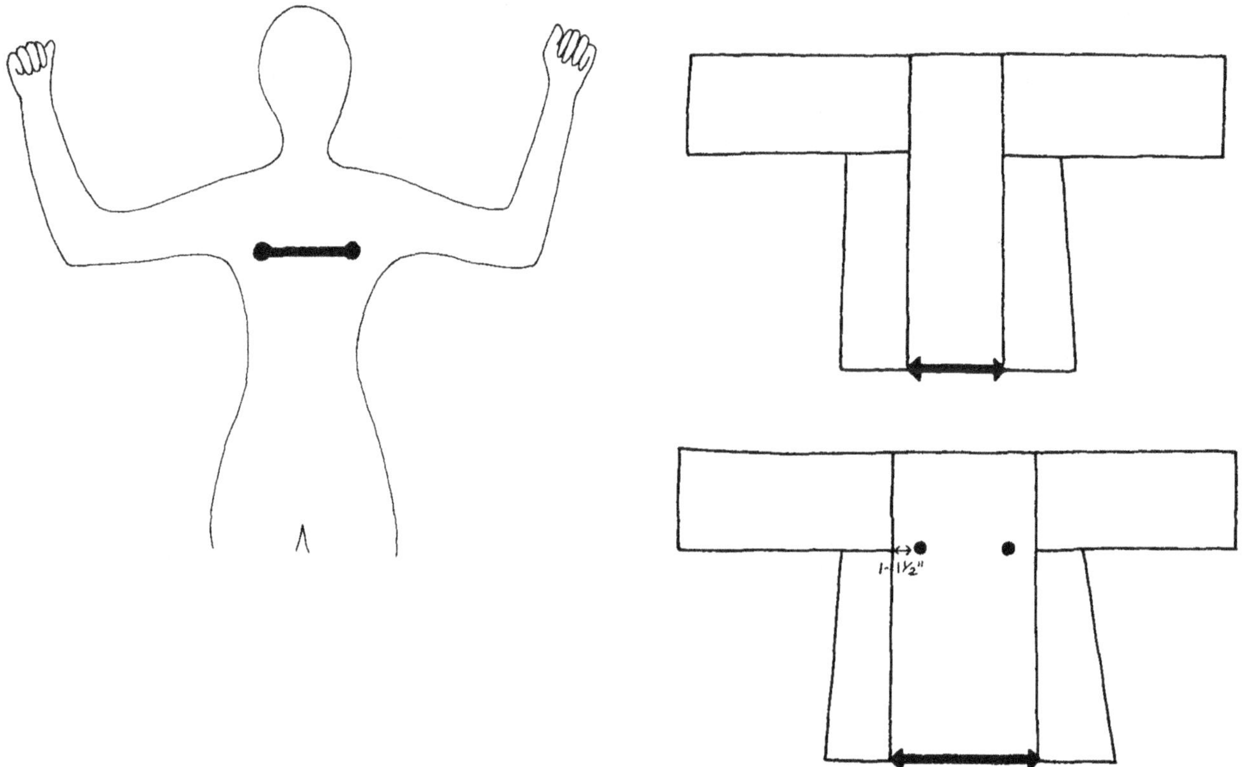

When curved areas are part of the garment design, these lines can be shaped on the loom using a cartoon that is attached under the warp rather than cut from the woven fabric.

To make the cartoon, draw the area to be shaped onto a sturdy but pliable piece of material, such as pellon, using a heavy felt pen. The pellon should be several inches wider than the area to be shaped and about 20″ longer. If the fabric is to be fulled, the cartoon will have to be enlarged to allow for the calculated percentage of shrinkage. Position and center the cartoon *under* the warp, pinning one end near the weaving line and securing the other under a flat stick (such as a lease stick) that is taped to the side of the shuttle race. When weaving, frequently repin the cartoon close to the weaving line to ensure accurate shaping. As the fabric is wound around the cloth beam, the pellon will easily move forward from under the flat stick, but do not let the cartoon wind onto the cloth beam with the fabric. Weave in filler yarn in the unwoven areas so that equal tension is maintained. When shaping an area where two shuttles are involved, as in a neck opening, it is easier to weave with the shuttles coming towards and away from each other rather than with each shuttle going in the same direction.

When the garment is off the loom, the unwoven warp ends can be cut and woven back into the material; or use one of the other weft protectors discussed in Chapter 4.

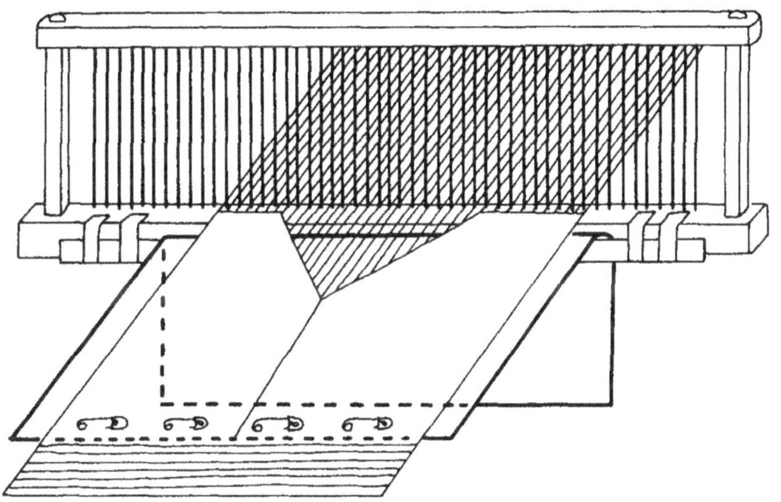

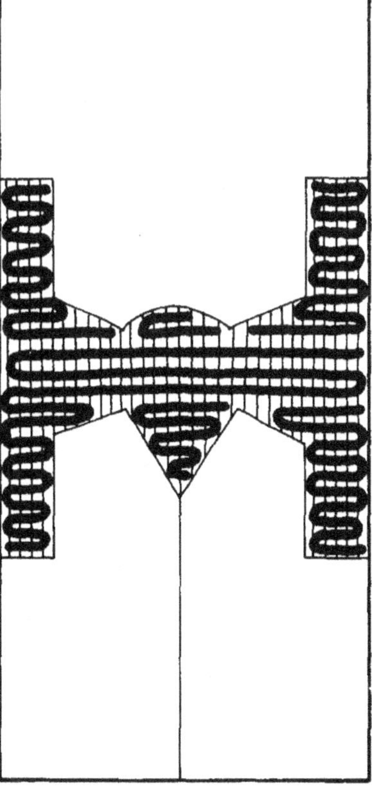

"Too many handweavers are generalists. Trying one course after another, they are jacks of all weaves, masters of none. I feel that specialization is as important for the avocational weaver or the new one as it is to the professionals. I suggest that after a certain point, craftsman should specialize in some aspect or another, say in one material, format or technique, or one combination of colors. I learned this from a student of mine who was both a mother and fully employed, with only a limited time for weaving. She worked in simple double cloths of black and white linen. She soon became so expert in this as to have probed deeper than anyone else."

Jack Lenor Larsen

"Most cloth, when it comes from the loom, is about as ready for consumption as an unbaked cake."

Jack Lenor Larsen

Chapter 7
The Fabric Finishing

The finishing of handwoven material has been a concern of weavers for thousands of years and is still a critical and integral part of the cloth-making process. Historically, early weavers washed and finished their material in streams or in the sea and spread the fabric on the grass or over bushes to dry. In Wales and the Outer Hebrides, the fabric was trodden in tubs and dried across beams in the houses. This finishing was done not only to remove the oils remaining after spinning and weaving, but to add body and stability to the fabric. Goods were often taken to local craftsmen who specialized in finishing. One of these was William Wigham. Carol Thilenius has written: "His method of fulling wool was not universally accepted. He favored beating it with a hammer in a trough filled with water, manure and clay: others said hot and cold baths would do the same if one soaking was in a vat of urine. The object either way was to come up with a dense non-raveling weave that permitted edges to be finished raw, without hemming. Such edges were prized."

Fulling is a part of the finishing process that consists of the opening of threads until they touch and fill in the spaces between warp and weft intersections. Moisture, heat and friction work together to develop the softness, body and hand (feel) of fabric. Heavy fulling causes the fabric to shrink and thicken, obscuring the structure and producing a felt-like surface. Heavily fulled wool is not true felt, which is made by the matting of wool fibers and does not have a woven substructure. The amount of shrinkage can be controlled during the finishing process to transform cloth into the type of fabric desired.

Because wool fiber is the most susceptible to this shrinkage action, fulling is often thought of solely in relation to woolen or worsted cloth. Fulling was traditionally done, however, with linen and cotton; and all natural fibers can benefit from it. Gordon notes that even cloth made of synthetic fibers will show some results from the fulling action.

Finishing and fulling should not be confused with simple washing to clean cloth. The fabric is usually cleaned during the fulling process, but the most important factor is the amount of thickening and shrinkage of fibers. Once fulled, the fabric can be gently washed as needed for cleaning purposes with no further fulling taking place.

The first step in fabric finishing, regardless of fiber content, is making samples. I recommend a sample at least 8″ wide and one yard long that is later cut into four 8″ × 9″ pieces. These are usually sufficient for experimentation with various finishing techniques. The purpose of sampling is to check the percentage of shrinkage, color-fastness, and whether or not seersucker is created due to fibers shrinking at different rates.

I set aside one of the four pieces for steaming only (sample A). If this is my final choice of finishing, the finished garment would be maintained with drycleaning. I code the remaining samples with small safety pins and lay sample B (one pin) onto a piece of paper and trace the size of the sample and record my choice of finishing. I repeat this with sample C (two pins) and sample D (three pins), with each one traced onto a separate paper noting the type of fulling and drying to be used. Each sample is processed accordingly with a load of laundry. After it is dry and pressed I draw the final size within the original measurements. Each sample is later tagged as to warp, ends per inch, weft, picks per inch, weave structure, method of finishing and percentage of shrinkage. This gives me the necessary information to select the type of finishing I want for the garment and is a future reference for that yarn. I have saved hours, dollars and tears by taking the time to weave and process these samples.

Before finishing, the weft must be secured to prevent raveling. Any of the edge finishes such as machine-stitching, handstitching, knotting or hemstitching may be used. The fabric should be examined and any flaws such as knots, weaving errors or hanging wefts corrected.

The type of fulling selected is determined by the fiber content, the use to which the cloth will be put, the desired appearance and the "hand" that is appropriate for the garment.

Wool

Wool is the fiber that fulls most readily because the surface of the fiber is made up of overlapping scales. The microscopic "shingles" on the surface of the wool relax and open up with moisture and temperature change. The agitation of washing causes the individual fibers to tangle together to form a denser fabric. This fulling process can be continued, but it is impossible to reverse it.

The amount of shrinkage will vary according to the heat of the water, the amount of agitation, the drying method, the amount of twist in the yarn, the quality of the raw fiber, how loosely woven or knitted the fabric is, and how the fabric or yarn may have been treated commercially.

The reasons for fulling wool are several. Wool yarn that comes on cones is often flattened out and once skeined off, steamed or soaked, it blooms and swells to a fluffy softness. Also, on the loom, warp and wefts are under tension and remain in place rigidly. Washing the fabric allows the threads to relax, curve around each other and to drape more readily. Fulling fabric also makes it look and feel softer.

There are three factors involved in fulling wool:

1. *Moisture.* The wetting of the wool fiber causes the scales to swell (for total wetting, wool has to be in water at least 30 minutes). There should be ample water for the amount of fabric being finished. A completely dissolved washing agent can be added to the water as a lubricant. Alderman recommends a mild liquid detergent, as used in dishwashing, which has a neutral pH that does not harm wool, is easily dissolved and rinses out readily even in hard water.
2. *Heat.* The level of heat affects the amount of fulling and shrinkage. Warm water of 90° to 120° will cause less fulling than using very hot water or shocking the wool with a hot/cold combination.
3. *Friction.* Friction is the rubbing of one fiber against another, and can be achieved by tromping the fabric with the feet in the bathtub, hand kneading like bread in water, or using part or all of the washing machine cycles. The

more agitation, the greater the amount of fulling and shrinkage. If you choose to use the washing machine, you will have to experiment to determine the degree of agitation of the various cycles of your machine. Remember that the water coming into the machine also produces agitation, so if you remove the fabric between the wash and rinse cycles, you have different results than if you left the cloth in the tub straight through the entire cycle. If you are fulling a considerable length of fabric, stop the machine frequently and shift the material so that it is agitated evenly. Avoid lengthy spinning during the final cycle, because this can add permanent wrinkles. One minute or less in the final spin is sufficient to remove most of the water. Shake the fabric after it comes from the water to remove any remaining wrinkles.

To dry the cloth:

1. Lay the fabric out smooth on a flat surface.
2. Roll the fabric with towels on a tube, smoothing the wrinkles and keeping the grain straight. Hemstitching or machine stitching works well as a weft protector with this method, as any knot can cause deformation of the fabric as it is rolled. Unwind the material several hours later, dry the towels in the dryer and rewind. Repeat this the next day and until the wool is thoroughly dry. Once dry, the fabric can be wound on the tube for storage.

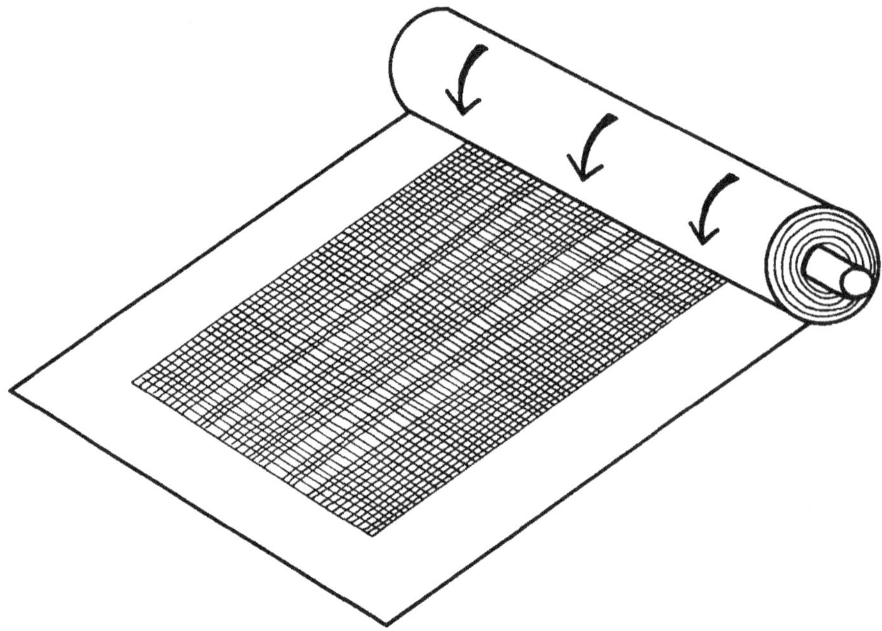

3. Lengths of fabric can be hung to dry. They can be placed on lines warp-wise or in folds pinned at the selvedges. The cloth should be advanced several times so that it dries evenly and without wrinkles.
4. A dryer can be used, but remember that this also causes fulling. Start with short periods and low temperatures and check the fabric frequently.

When the cloth is nearly dry, it can be pressed professionally or by hand. If hand pressing, start at one end and press the fabric, then repeat from the other end. Watch the temperature of the iron and use a press cloth to avoid scorching and shine. Pressing helps to stabilize the material as well as smooth it. Do not let any fabric dry wrinkled.

Younie describes the London-shrinkage method, which is a 200 year old process for yarn relaxation that produces minimum fulling. Roll the fabric between dampened wool blankets or sheets and allow it to relax for 24 to 36 hours. After this time, the fabric will be slightly fulled and should be almost dry. It should be very smooth at this stage, and may need no pressing. If the fulling or shrinkage is not sufficient, the blankets should be dampened again and process repeated.

Felted wool fabric can be created by treating woven wool fabric with hot water, extreme temperature change and considerable agitation. The fabric will shrink in length and width and will get thicker and softer, and the surface fibers of the yarn will felt together. This process obliterates the weave structure; the fabric can be cut without raveling and results in beautiful, heavy fabric such as that used in German loden coats, Balkan native costumes and Hudson Bay and Pendleton blankets.

Felted wool fabric can be obtained by putting loosely-woven or knitted 100% wool fabric into the washing machine. The more open the weave the more fulling will take place. Experiment with samples for the results can be highly variable depending on the fiber quality, the fabric structure, and method of fulling. The fabric can be made to shrink up to 30%-40% in either direction.

The more space the wool yarns have to move around during washing, the more easily they will felt. The fabric can be dried in the dryer, which may cause more shrinkage, or can be dried flat and then steam pressed. The selvedge edges of the fabric may be rippled, depending on how much shrinkage has occurred. If they will not press out, Snover recommends dampening the selvedges, placing weighted boards on top of them, and letting them air-dry.

A felted fabric suitable for a coat or jacket can be achieved by using an untreated 7/2 wool in a 2/2 twill structure set at 8 e.p.i. and woven with 8 w.p.i. Fabric woven this way and fulled in the washing machine using the full normal cycle, warm water and soap will shrink some 20% in width and length and transform a sacklike material into a soft, spongy, lightweight fabric. Lay the material flat to dry or roll it on a tube and then steam press.

Many fibers, if not pre-treated against shrinkage, can be heavily fulled, although some wool blends will not shrink uniformly. Experiment with mohairs, handspuns and novelties using different setts and weave structures to discover the range of cloth transformations that can be achieved.

Heavily fulled garment pieces can be put together by crocheting the edges and then joining these with crochet or lacing. Edges can also be joined using such decorative stitches as fagoting or blanket stitch. Whatever method you use, do not work too close to the cut fabric edge (in ½″ or so) so that no raveling will occur.

You can develop your own favorite ways to finish wool fabric through samples and experimentation.

Cotton

There are several methods for fulling and cleaning cotton. Most cotton fabric can be machine-washed with regular or heavy-duty laundry detergent and dried in a dryer. The problem is that the heat of the water and the dryer causes continuing shrinkage. To avoid this, wash and full handwoven cotton in the gentlest cycle of the washing machine or handwash using cold water and soap and then lay the fabric flat to dry. If you use the washing machine, remove the fabric after one minute or so into the final spin-dry cycle so that wrinkles will not be permanently set.

Lengths of fabric can be soaked in a tub of water overnight and rolled in towels on a tube to dry. Reroll several times, as with wool, and iron when almost dry. Re-roll smoothly after ironing or hang the ironed length to complete drying. Cotton fabric can withstand higher ironing temperatures than synthetics, but be careful not to scorch light-colored fabric. Use a steam iron and always press while damp so that wrinkles do not dry into the material. Cotton mildews, so do not store it until completely dry.

Linen

Washing benefits linen even more than wool or cotton. Off the loom, linen is wiry and stiff, but it becomes more lustrous and softer with each washing and ironing though shrinkage will occur.

Linen fabric is machine washable in hot water with regular detergent and can be tumbled dry or line dried. For tumble-drying, use a medium setting, since high heat may cause additional shrinkage. If ironing is necessary, use a medium to high setting with steam. The fabric must be pressed before it is dry and then ironed dry to avoid mildew.

To hasten the softening of linen that comes with repeated washing and ironing, wash and rinse the fabric in hot water. Blot the material in towels and then roll in a towel, place in a plastic bag and put into the freezer. After it is frozen, partially thaw it, and iron until the material is dry.

Silk

The care of silk is similar to the care of wool, but there are no universal rules for the finishing of handwoven silks because there are so many variables in fiber and yarn type, weave structure, and desired result.

Silk, as it comes from the loom, may be very stiff and in need of a period of breaking in. Cheryl Kolander notes that just wearing or using the silk will soften it, but to speed up this process, the fabric can be washed or simply ironed to remove the stiffness. Washing helps to remove reed marks and returns the loft that may have been pressed out while the yarns were wound on the warp beams and bobbins.

Kolander's book suggests that the washing machine can be used to finish silk, but only after sampling to see how the silk is affected. Use the delicate or wool cycle which uses cool or warm water and has a short agitation period. The silk should be enclosed in a case (like a pillow case with the open end basted or tied) so the silk is not pulled out of shape. Do not allow the silk to go through the spin-dry cycle for this tends to crumple fine silks and crush in wrinkles. With heavy, lofty fabrics it may flatten the texture.

To handwash silk, it is best to use lukewarm rather than cold water. The soap must be chosen carefully since alkalis damage silk. Ivory Flakes or Snow work well, but the soap must be thoroughly dissolved first in a little hot water with cold water added to make a lukewarm bath. Squeeze the suds gently through the material but do not wring silk fabric. A little acid in the next to last rinse will neutralize any trace of alkali left from washing. Add about 1 tablespoon of pure white vinegar per quart of water in the next to last rinse.

Be certain that any colored silk is wash fast before you begin to wash.

If you choose to not wash silk, a light ironing may be enough to soften the stiffness that newly woven silk often has. A steam iron, held above but not touching the cloth, is very good for shrinking the cloth without disturbing its surface. A light ironing with a dry press cloth may be enough to give that finished look, or try pressing with a damp cloth to get the desired effect. When ironing silk, use the silk setting (between rayon and wool) and if ironing directly on the fabric produces a shine, iron on the wrong side or use a pressing cloth.

Some weavers prefer to have a professional cleaner finish the silk.

Silk fabric can be drip-dried, and excess water can first be removed by rolling the fabric in a towel or spinning it briefly in a washing machine. Dry silk in the shade or inside but not in the direct sun.

Many silk fibers can be machine dried using the delicate setting, which does not overheat the silk. Enclose the silk in a case or dry individually,. Tumble-drying leaves fabric soft and fluffy and might make ironing unnecessary.

Tracking

"Tracking" is an effect that may occur in handwoven fabrics when they are washed. This occurs mostly with singles yarns woven in plain weave because the twist in the yarn partially collapses in the cloth and forms diagonal ridges. The direction of these ridges if fairly random, making the surface of the cloth appear crepe-like. Alderman notes that tracking occurs most often with single yarns of fine or medium weight.

If you like the effect, do nothing about it. Simply wash the cloth and smooth it with your hands as it dries. A light steam pressing will not remove tracking.

If you do not want the textured effect tracking gives, steam press the fabric well before washing it. The steam seems to shrink and set the fabric so that the pressing after washing is not so difficult. When the fabric has been washed, begin to press it while it is moderately wet, not just barely damp. Pressing out the texture tracking adds is hard work and involves pulling the wet fabric taut and pressing it so that it is dry and smooth. Once the whole fabric has been smoothed out, it is not as difficult to press the next time it is washed. The fabric may be dry cleaned after the first washing.

"We all live under the same sky,
But we do not all share the same horizons
Always remember to use what talents you possess . . .
For the woods would be very silent
If the only birds that sang there
Were those that sang best."

Author unknown

"I was a fantastic student until ten, and then my mind began to wander."

Grace Paley
American writer

Chapter 8
The Warp Layout

Planning the warp layout means determining the most logical and practical way to weave the various pieces for a garment. Some questions to consider are:

1. Is it better to weave two narrow units using two shuttles or rewarp the loom for the reduced width?
2. Is it more practical to weave the widest width first and then drop side warps for the weaving of narrower pieces, or should separate warps be made?
3. What happens to the selvedge stripes or stripes in the warp if the pieces are woven one direction and then turned when assembling the garment?
4. Is there a right and wrong side to the fabric, and will that affect the direction pieces are woven?

The warp direction is usually vertical on the body and vertical on the sleeves, but in balanced weaves and a number of other structures, these pieces can be woven in the most economical direction. However, a weft faced weave will bend easiest the direction of the warp and a warp-faced weave bends more readily the direction of the weft, so fabrics of this type might have to be laid out and woven in a specific way.

If rya knots of yarn or unspun fleece are part of the design, it will be easier and faster weaving if the pile can be knotted toward you rather than away from you. The use of knots can affect the direction pieces are woven and whether the back or front of a garment is woven first.

In order to determine the warp layout, I draw all design elements onto my final muslin pattern, including stripes, width of decorative joins, pockets, selvedge stripes, rya knots and any other surface details. I write on the muslin, with marker, what each piece is and its right side, which edges meet and how I plan to secure the weft at the beginning and ending of each woven unit, i.e., "weave a 2″ hem", "leave 6″ for fringe", or "leave 4″ for darning in warps". I mark the shoulder line in relation to the neckline and note how I plan to finish the unwoven warps in the neck opening.

After all information is recorded on the muslin, I untape the garment pieces and lay them on the floor to determine the best layout for weaving. Once I've decided this, I draw a diagram of the layout recording the placement of each piece, the dimensions of each unit, the areas for weft finishes, neckline size and the amount to weave up to the neckline and from the back of the neck to back hemline. I then add to these figures the percentage of shrinkage as indicated by my fulling sample plus the amount of draw-in and shrinkage in the width. I don't add shrinkage to the neckline opening unless heavy fulling is being done. Once all final figures are computed, I cross out all numbers but those I am actually weaving to help prevent errors.

To compute the amount of warp and weft needed for a garment, add together loom waste, woven lengths, hems, unwoven areas left for fringe or darning in and a percentage of take-up (I use a generous 10%). A formula for figuring the amount of needed warp:

$$\frac{\text{e.p.i. (ends per inch)} \times \text{width (in inches)} \times \text{total length (yards)}}{\text{y.p.p. (yards per pound of warp yarn)}}$$

Example:

$$\frac{10 \text{ e.p.i.} \times 20'' \text{ wide} \times 5 \text{ yards long}}{\text{500 yards per pound in warp yarn being used}} = 2\#\text{ yarn needed for warp}$$

If the warp and the weft are the same, buying as much weft as warp will provide a generous quantity. For closer figuring, use the above formula but when adding up the figures for total length do not include loom waste or any unwoven areas.

In a warp-faced weave, buy a fourth as much weft as computed for warp and for weft-faced weaving, purchase five times as much weft as figured for warp. These are general and very broad estimates, but they give a basis for determining amounts needed.

Garment Layouts

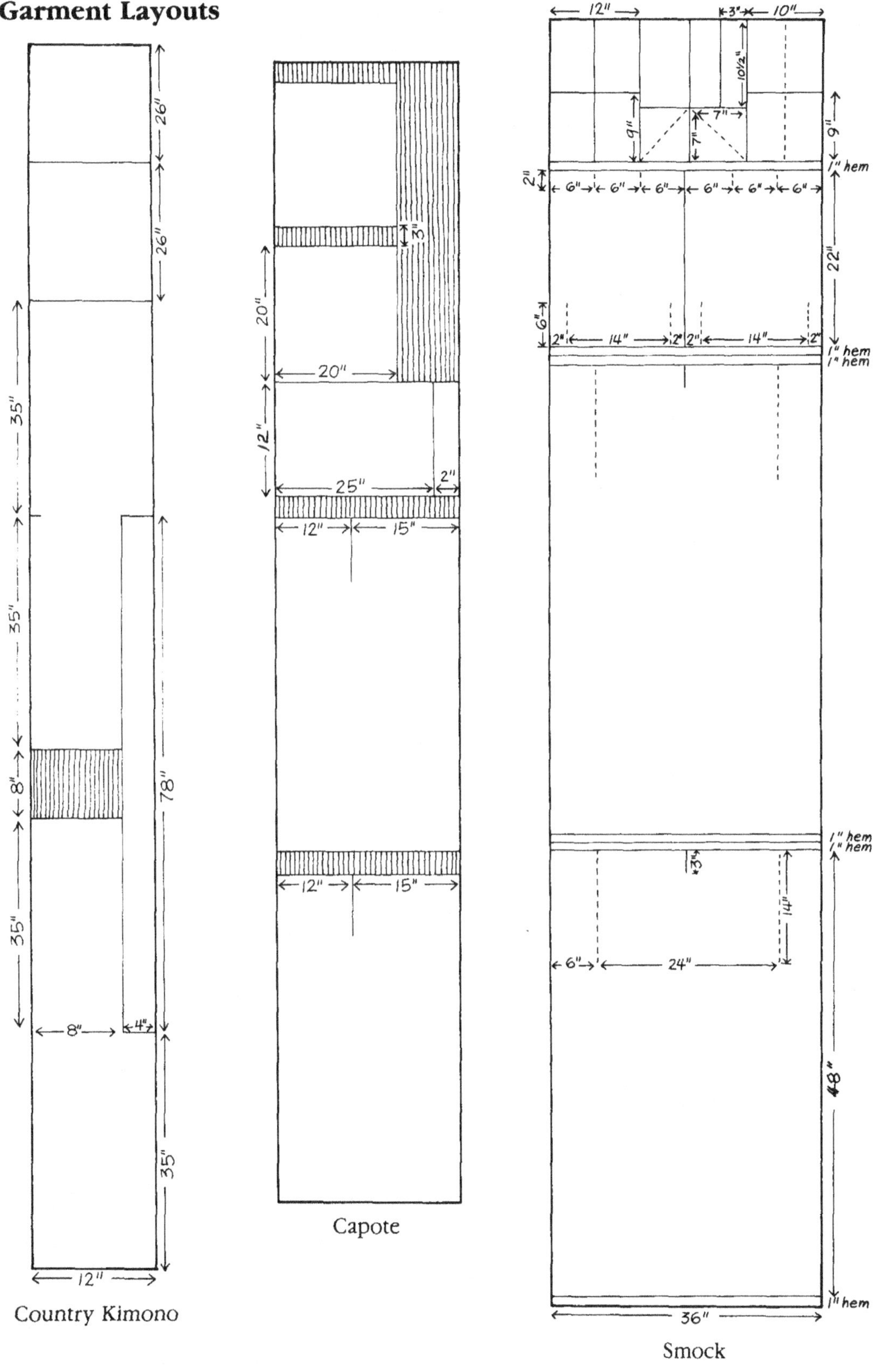

Country Kimono

Capote

Smock

The final layout becomes the guide for weaving the garment pieces with all measurements made with the loom off tension. Here's a review of the steps involved in planning and weaving a loom-shaped garment:

1. Plan the type of garment to weave.
2. Determine the fit . . . sleeves, hips, bust.
3. Choose the yarns for warp and weft, determining the color, sett, fabric weight.
4. Plan the ornamentation and type of joins and edge finishes.
5. Make a pattern.
6. Determine how you will finish the fabric.
7. Make a detailed warp layout.
8. Record what you are doing.
9. Weave the garment.
10. Secure the wefts (darning in, machine stitch, etc.).
11. Full and/or steam the pieces.
12. Assemble the pieces.
13. Put in lining (if being used).
14. Steam garment.

"First, be patient and understanding with yourself.
All learning takes time, patience, commitment and lots of practice.
If you fall down when trying to skate backwards, well, that's part of the learning process.
Do not overload yourself with work. Do only as much as you realistically can.
There is a lot of information for you to remember and you should not expect yourself to keep track of it all.
The tendency for many people is to stop talking about ideas and projects and to put books and notes away. Talk about your "food habit" (or weaving habit). Talk to yourself in positive terms."

Julie Waltz
Food Habit Management

Chapter 9
Records

It is essential to record what you have woven for two important reasons: for your own reference and for sharing with other weavers. You may think that you will not want the information again or that you will never forget the place where you purchased the yarn and the sett used, but invariably you will need those facts. Records can also be a visual review of what you have woven over the years.

Records allow you to share information with other weavers. If someone likes the fabric you have woven and you can provide the yarn type, sett and finish, that information saves them time and money. Whether it is sharing garment patterns or methods of fulling, the more information that is exchanged, the more everyone benefits. There is "nothing new under the sun"; it is what you do with the concept that is unique. Every garment that I have created owes its origin to another time and another people, and I feel an obligation to share that heritage. Each time you give, your ultimate return will be ten times greater. If someone is concerned about being "copied", which is virtually impossible anyway, they should never teach, sell or wear their garments. Records allow the sharing of information which can form links in a chain that connect weavers everywhere.

Weaving books usually have sample record sheets, but you may want to develop your own to meet your particular needs. The following kinds of information might be included on a record:

1. Warp.
   a. Types and color.
   b. Amount used, cost, place of purchase.
   c. Sett.
   d. % of take-up.
   e. Threading order.
   f. Sleying order.
2. Weft.
   a. Type and color.
   b. Amount used, cost and place of purchase.
   c. Treadling order.
   d. Number of shots per inch.

You might want to include the date woven, problems encountered, methods of fulling and percentage of shrinkage, warp layout, sketch or photograph of the garment, fabric swatch and samples of warp and weft.

Disciplining yourself to complete the record may be the most difficult part of this step. Once you have designed a record sheet, photocopy several dozen copies and keep them in a convenient place along with a pen, graph paper, glue and any other items you may need. Record information on your work sheet as you plan and weave the garment, keeping track of the amount of material used, sales slips, method of finishing and so forth. Complete the record sheet before you start the next project and this information will not get misplaced. Remember to weave extra for a sample and add a photograph when convenient. The records can be placed in protector sheets and then kept together in a notebook for easy reference.

Profit Sharing

"When two merchants exchange their products
each one gives up part of his possessions.
But when students exchange knowledge,
each keeps his own and acquires the other's.
Can there be a better bargain than this?"

Author Unknown

WEAVING RECORD: anita luvera mayer

Title/description of project ____________________

Date ____________

	WARP	**WEFT**
Yarn type	____________	____________
	____________	____________
Size	____________	____________
Color	____________	____________

Warp: Reed size ____________ Ends per inch ________

Sleying order ____________________

Total yardage ____________________

Total weight ____________________

Length: Off loom ____________ Finished ____________

Weft: Total yardage ________ Wefts per inch ______

Total weight ____________________

Width: on loom ____ off loom ____ finished ____

Draft name ____________________

Finishing method ____________________

____

____

Cost of project: ____________ Selling cost: ______ ______
wholesale retail

Comments: ____________________

____

When I am an old woman I shall wear purple
With a red hat, which doesn't go, and doesn't suit me,
And I shall spend my pension on brandy and summer gloves
And satin sandals, and say we've no money for butter.
And I shall sit down on the pavement when I'm tired
And gobble up samples in shops and press alarm bells
And run my stick along the public railings
And make up for the sobriety of my youth.
I shall go out in my slippers in the rain,
And pick the flowers in other people's gardens
And learn to spit.
You can wear terrible shirts and grow more fat
And eat three pounds of sausages at a go
Or only bread and pickles for a week
And hoard pens and pencils and beermats and things in boxes.
But meanwhile we must stay respectable
And must not shame the children; they mind more,
Even than we do, being noticeable
We will keep dry with sensible clothes and spend
According to good value, and do what's best
To bring the best for us and for our children
But maybe I ought to practice a little now?
So people who know me are not too shocked and surprised
When suddenly I am old, and start to wear purple.

Jenny Joseph

Appendix

All pattern dimensions are the *finished* sizes of garments and were designed to fit a size 14-16 with a height of 5′8″. Always make a muslin pattern to assure correct fit and appropriate length.

Hungarian Szur, *page 107.*
Source: Hungary.
Warp: Harrisville 2-ply wool, 8 e.p.i., twill threading.
Weft: Harrisville 2-ply wool, 8 w.p.i., woven twill.
Comments: Heavily fulled in the washing machine using the normal cycle and warm water. Rolled in towels to dry. Crocheted roundlets and braid over joins with wool stitchery as embellishment.

Smock, *page 109.*
Source: England.
Warp: 22/2 cotton-linen blend and 5/2 pearl cotton, 20 e.p.i., threaded 1, 2, 1, 2, 1 and 3, 4, 3, 4, 3.
Weft: 22/2 cotton-linen blend, 20 w.p.i., weave structure of tabby.
Comments: In weaving the areas to be smocked on the front, back and sleeves (indicated by fine lines on the pattern), a second weft was used every ½″ to serve as a drawstring for the smocking. The drawstring was the same weight as the weft but a different color. Tabby was treadled with the regular weft, 1-2 treadled followed by one shot of the second weft, ½″ of tabby with the regular weft, 1-2 treadled and the second weft returned to the right selvedge and cut off, leaving a 4″ tail for pulling. This procedure was continued for the length of the smocked sections. After gathering and smocking, the drawstrings were carefully removed.

To determine smock size:

a. The finished garment width is determined by taking the bust measurement and adding desired ease. Divide this total in half to find the finished width of the front and back pieces. *Example:*
38″ (bust) + 6″ (ease) = 44″ ÷ 2 = 22″

b. Subtract the two box widths (box size optional) from the woven fabric width. Fabric is traditionally woven 36″ wide. *Example:* 36″ − 12″ (boxes) = 24″.

c. Gather up this amount so that when it is added to the two box widths the total equals the needed finished width. *Example:* Draw 24″ up to 10″ + 12″ (boxes) = 22″ (finished garment width). The back would be done in the same manner.

Silk Aba, *page 111.*
Source: Middle East.
Warp: 10/2 pearl cotton, 15 e.p.i., twill threading.
Weft: fine cultivated and tussah silk, weft-faced, plain weave.
Comments: Shoulder detail made by wrapping the herringbone stitch with buttonhole stitches. Gusset area is a braid edging stitch. Stitchery in silk satin stitch.

Akba jacket, *page 112.*
Source: Southeast Asia.
Warp: 22/2 cottolin, 22 e.p.i., twill threading.
Weft: 22/2 cottolin, 22 w.p.i., plain weave.
Comments: Size 3/2 pearl cotton used for the stitchery embellishment.

Culottes, *page 113.*
Source: Middle East.
Warp: 5/2 polyester pearl, 8/2 cotton, 30 e.p.i. and 45 e.p.i., twill threading.
Weft: 8/2 cotton, twill treadling.
Comments: The sett and the beat produced a warp-faced fabric. To assemble the two rectangles join a to a, b to b, and c to c on each leg. Pleat in the extra waistline width at the front and turn down a casing for the elastic at the waist.

Shepherd's Coat, *page 114.*
Source: Portugal.
Comments: Fine silk used for the warp with handspun silk used for the weft. Unspun mohair laid-in for the surface texture with rows of tabby between. All fibers natural dyed with madder.

Sweetie Pie, *page 116.*
Source: Greece.
Warp: Harrisville 2-ply wool, 8 e.p.i., twill threading.
Weft: Harrisville 2-ply wool, unspun mohair, 8 w.p.i., twill treadling.
Comments: Heavily fulled in the washing machine using the normal cycle and warm water. Dried flat. The shrinkage in both length and width was 20%. The surface texture was created with unspun mohair tied in rya knots. The side widths and the waistband are crocheted. The edging braid was made by crocheting a chain and handsewing it into place.

Nimsha, *page 117.*
Source: Northern India.
Warp: Harrisville 2-ply wool, 8 e.p.i., twill threading.
Weft: Harrisville 2-ply wool, 8 w.p.i., plain weave.
Comments: Heavily fulled in the washing machine using the normal cycle and warm water. A cloth was sandwiched between the folded length of cloth and the edges basted while the fabric was fulled. Dried flat. Rya knots made with unspun mohair. Crocheted cuffs used to narrow the full sleeve.

Batikari, *page 118.*
Source: Northern Ghana.
Warp: Tussah noil, 12 e.p.i., threaded twill.
Weft: Tussah noil, 12 w.p.i., plain weave.
Comments: The silk gores were crocheted to a pattern shape and then handsewn into place. The edges of all the strips were crocheted and then laced together for joining. All the silk was natural dyed with logwood.

Grey Sky, *page 121.*
Source: Sudan.
Warp: Silk boucle, 10 e.p.i., threaded to twill.
Weft: Silk boucle, 10 w.p.i., plain weave.
Comments: The top can be worn sleeveless or with long sleeves or short tapestry sleeves. Each set of sleeves buttons onto the blouse. Elastic in a casing creates fit at the waist and at the wrist.

Aba, *page 122.*
Source: Middle East.
Warp: Harrisville single wool, 15 e.p.i., twill threading.
Weft: Harrisville single wool, 15 w.p.i., plain weave.
Comments: Fine silk used in tapestry areas. Treadled pairs of warps in those areas so that the silk could completely cover the warp. Stitchery embellishments around the neck and down the front.

Szur Jacket, *page 124.*
Source: Albania.
Warp: Harrisville 2-ply wool, 8 e.p.i., twill threading.
Weft: Harrisville 2-ply wool, 8 w.p.i., twill treadling.
Comments: Heavily fulled in the normal cycle of the washing machine using warm water. Dried flat. The width and length shrank about 20%. The embellishment created by couching in place heavy yarn.

Purple Plum, *page 126.*
Source: Ukraine.
Warp: Mixed warp of silk, cotton and rayon; twill threading.
Weft: Cotton and bias rags, plain weave.
Comments: Elastic in a casing creates the fit at the waistline and the wrists.

Two-Drink Dress, *page 129.*
Source: Ancient Asia.
Warp: Handspun wool and mohair alternated, 6 e.p.i., twill threading.
Weft: Handspun wool, 6 w.p.i., plain weave.
Comments: The fabric was lightly brushed during the weaving to create a surface nap. Warps were wrapped while the garment was on the loom. The knotted buttonhole stitch was used on all edges and laced together for the joins.

Bibliography

Adams, Donald J. *Naked We Came.* New York: Holt, Rinehart and Winston of Canada Ltd., 1967.

Alderman, Sharon D. "Finishing Handwoven Fabrics." *Shuttle, Spindle and Dyepot.* (Winter 1977) Issue 33, pp. 13-15.

Baizerman, Suzanne and Karen Searle. *Finishes in the Ethnic Tradition.* Minnesota: Dos Tejedoras, 1978.

Beard, Betty J. *Fashions From the Loom.* Colorado: Interweave Press, 1980.

Bennett, Suri and Eileen O'Connor. "Second Skin: The Coat." Unpublished workshop report, 1983.

Broby-Johansen, R. *Body and Clothes.* New York: Reinhold Book Corp., 1968.

Brown, Rachel. *The Weaving, Spinning and Dyeing Book.* New York: Alfred A. Knopf, 1978.

Burnham, Dorothy K. *Cut My Cote.* Toronto: Royal Ontario Museum, 1973.

Chaudiere, Joyeanna with Clare Kapitan. "Second Skin: The Coat." Unpublished workshop report, 1983.

Collingwood, Peter. *The Techniques of Rug Weaving.* New York: Watson-Guptill Publications, 1968.

Cram, Martha. "Second Skin: The Coat." Unpublished workshop report, 1983.

Dickey, Enola. "Modern Interpretations of Ethnic Garments." *Shuttle, Spindle and Dyepot.* (Spring 1978) Issue 34, pp. 28-30.

Erickson, Lois with Diane Erickson. *Ethnic Costumes.* New York: Van Nostrand Reinhold, 1979.

Finishing Handwoven Fabrics. New Hampshire: Harrisville Designs, Inc., 1981.

Fisher, Margaret. *Palm Leaf Patterns.* San Francisco: Panjandrum Press, 1977.

Goday, Dale with Molly Cochran. *Your Guide to Dressing Thin.* New York: Simon and Schuster, 1981.

Geary, Kay. *A Course in Textile Design for the Weaver.* Robin and Russ, 1956.

Gordon, Beverly. *The Final Steps.* Colorado: Interweave Press, 1982.

Hamre, Ida with Hanne Meedom. *Making Simple Clothes.* London: A and C Black Stdl, 1980.

Karaz, Mariska. *Adventures in Stitches.* Funk and Wagnalls, 1949.

Kent, Kate P. *Introducing West African Cloth.* Colorado: Denver Museum of Natural History, 1971.

Kolander, Cheryl. *A Silk Weaver's Notebook.* Myrtle Creek, Oregon, 1979.

Plummer, Karen with Murph Shapley. "Second Skin: The Coat." Unpublished workshop report, 1983.

Reed, Kathy with Inge Buley. "Second Skin: The Coat." Unpublished workshop report, 1983.

Redding, Debbie. "It's Good To Be All Wet, Sometimes." *Handwoven.* May 1981, pp. 22-23.

Snover, Susan. *Sew-News, Inc.* August/September 1983, pp. 30-31.

Sullivan, Jean. Seattle Weavers' Guild Garment Study Group. Unpublished report, 1977.

Thilenius, Carol. "Finishing Handwoven Materials." *Interweave.* Spring, 1977, pp. 18-20, 30.

Tilke, Max. *Costume Patterns and Design.* New York: Hastings House, 1974.

-----. *National Costumes.* New York: Hastings House, 1978.

Wilson, Jean. *Joinings, Edges and Trims.* New York: Van Nostrand Reinhold Co., 1983.

-----. *Weave With Style.* Seattle: Madrona Publishers, 1979.

Wilson, Jean with Jan Burhen. *Weaving You Can Wear.* New York: Van Nostrand Reinhold Co., 1973.

Younie, Christine. *The Finishing of Handwoven Woollen Fabrics.* Quebec: 1981.

Index